LEE TRUNDLE

LEE TRUNDLE

MORE THAN JUST TRICKS

LEE TRUNDLE
WITH
CHRIS WATHAN

EDINBURGH AND LONDON

First published in Great Britain in 2010 by
MAINSTREAM PUBLISHING COMPANY
(EDINBURGH) LTD
7 Albany Street
Edinburgh EH1 3UG

ISBN 9781845966744

A catalogue record for this book is available
from the British Library

Typeset in Erhardt and Optima

Printed in Great Britain by
CPI Mackays Chatham ME5 8TD

1 3 5 7 9 10 8 6 4 2

For Brooke
For Emilie

Acknowledgements

WHEN YOU MENTION to others that you're writing your autobiography and they get excited, I think it suggests it's something worth doing.

I always liked the idea of doing a book but it's only recently I felt it was the right time, that I'd done enough on the pitch to do a book justice.

Hopefully that's proven the case, but I'm glad to have been given this opportunity and that's why my first thank you is to Chris Wathan, who has done so much in making this happen. Thanks for all the time and effort you put in, the research and the ringing around on my behalf – it's been a pleasure working with you and I'm sure this book will be the first of many for you . . . and for me (ha ha!).

To Neil Sang, my mate and my agent, thanks for supporting me in my career and in life, you've been a massive help over the years and you've always been there for me.

To Brian Flynn for having the confidence in my ability and taking the chance on me and letting me play with freedom. You brought the best out of me and without you I wouldn't have this story to tell. Thanks for everything, Gaffer.

To all my family and friends for supporting me through the good and bad times, for the nights in and the nights out. There's too many of you to mention but thanks for being there when I needed you.

To me dad – I know you weren't there for the start but you've made up for it over the years and thanks for supporting me in my non-league and pro career, for following me home and away.

To Pat, thanks for everything – a great man, thanks for making my mum happy.

But my special thank yous have to be to the four girls in my life.

To Mum, thanks for all the cold mornings standing in the rain watching me, for all the games you took me to, the sacrifices you made to make me happy while going without yourself. I hope I've made you proud – the hard work you put in paid off. Thanks for the way you are with Brooke, I know it's hard with me away but I'm so glad you are there for her like you were for me. I love you with all my heart.

To Nan, thanks for always being there for me, for looking after me, for always standing up for me, for the money you'd give me on a Sunday night out after I'd spent my own on a Friday and Saturday! I love you.

To Brooke, it was you who made me change my ways and make it in this game – it wouldn't have happened if it hadn't been for you. I'm so proud of you and I love watching you play, just as I loved you watching me. Everything I do is for you – I love you so much.

And to Charlotte, for being there when I needed you, for always making me smile when I was down – you have been so good for me since I met you. I'm so glad to have you in my life and I love you so much.

Finally, thanks to everyone for helping me in the making of this book, from publishers to photographers to all my former clubs.

Hopefully my story doesn't end with this book, that there's a few more tales yet, but I'm proud of what is in these pages and I hope you enjoy reading them.

Lee Trundle
June 2010

Contents

Introduction

I ALWAYS REMEMBER Brian Flynn, the Swansea City manager at the time, telling us his views on his new signing.

'The way Lee Trundle plays is like a Scud,' said Flynn at the press conference to unveil him. 'When he gets the ball, you know something's coming – and there's nothing you can do about it.'

Only no one knew what was coming. No one at that press conference in July 2003 could have foreseen the impact one player was going to have on a club, on a city even. But then I doubt many would have predicted that a basement division striker, only just out of non-league, would pretty soon be the biggest thing outside the Premier League, charming his way right through the game with a flick of the ball and a flash of a smile. It seems far-fetched just writing that down, but that's why Lee's tale is a fascinating one, and one that deserves telling.

Hopefully I've helped him do it justice, even if trying to describe some of his goals or outrageous pieces of skill and showboating is as hard now as it was reporting it at the time.

And it's not been easy trying to put into print those disarming cheeky grins and winks, along with the arrogance about his undoubted ability.

But ultimately, this is Lee's story, as told by Lee. It is his own experiences and his own thoughts in his own words – and in the way he said them.

That's why my first thanks are to him for relenting to my suggestions to start this project and embracing it with his usual enthusiasm. Not many would have been willing to be as honest about themselves as Lee has been here.

Thanks to Lee's friends and family for their support – especially Charlotte, who was banished from the room on so many occasions!

Thanks also to all those who helped us in putting the book together from all Lee's clubs, from Burscough to Bristol City, with particular mentions to Stan Strickland, John Newman, Rob Urwin, Dave Pover, Geraint Parry, Andy Gilpin and Jonathan Wilsher, while thanks also go to David Price for his patience and his eye for error.

There is a big thank you needed for Huw, Gareth and Matthew at Huw Evans Picture Agency and for Les Evans in Wrexham regarding the illustrations.

Thanks to everyone at Mainstream for their faith in our ideas and also to my colleagues at Media Wales, especially Delme Parfitt and Simon Roberts for their advice and support and Angus Morrison for the late lend of his expertise.

I must also take this opportunity to thank all those who have helped put me in this fortunate position of being able to do something I love for a living – you know who you are. Chiefly, Mam and Dad – Richie and Ann – I hope I can continue to do you proud.

But lastly, special thanks must be reserved to my wife Jen, without whose support – even while we got used to life with a newborn baby – none of this would have been possible.

Chris Wathan
June 2010

Foreword

THERE ARE CERTAIN players – most players – who unless they do everything right, cannot perform. Lee Trundle is the opposite.

Trunds has so much quality, so much ability, that all he needs to do is feel happy. To me, he is special.

You could tell he wasn't your typical player the first day he arrived at Swansea City. It was pre-season and we were at the university for a fitness test – a bleep test. It was the first time I'd met him, and it's something I will always remember as he arrived in a white shirt, dyed blond hair, sunbed tan all over – but you sensed straight away he brought an aura with him.

It was clear he was different.

We went to Holland for a pre-season tour and I remember looking at him in those first few games and seeing how selfish he would be in the final third. We had been a team who had had to work really hard as a unit to stay in the Football League the year before, and for a new player to come into a side and play with that kind of arrogance he needed to be very special.

Trunds was. By just being who he was he earned the respect of the dressing-room; the way he was as a person earned him that role on the pitch. When it came to the lads in the team, he would have time for everyone right the way through the squad; he cared for each of us and wanted to understand us.

We had given him a licence to win games and because of that he could push boundaries on the pitch. There was an allowance to use that flair, that special touch, to be the star – and it made him untouchable.

It also meant he could get away with murder – he would have his say on the ball and then ten others would win it back for him. That shows you how he was as a character in our dressing-room, because you do not get that freedom unless you earn it, but Lee had respect from the quality he had as a player and as a human being.

There was the arrogance on the pitch, but off it he was part of the city. The kids who watched him meant everything to him and he loved the chemistry he had with the people of Swansea, the ones he felt he was representing. To me, he just genetically fitted Swansea City Football Club, the same way Alan Curtis had before him. The resemblance is clear, that he could do something on the pitch no one else could, was loved by everyone and could, in turn, make anyone feel special by just being around him. He was the flair player that everyone wanted to see. He was the star of this passage of the club's history – a Premiership player in a lower league side.

He was someone for people to be proud of and, just as he earned the licence from the dressing-room, he earned one from the fans – and he used it cleverly. He was able to have a happy balance of being the best player on the pitch and not necessarily being the ultimate professional.

What mattered was that he was happy, because that was when he was at his best – and happy meant spending time with and speaking to fans, socialising, having a drink, enjoying himself.

Not many can get away with it in the modern game, but Trunds could because of his gift. I remember once calling him the last of the playboys – and it is a real compliment because there is a culture behind that term in football, a select type of player. You can only be that type of player if the talent is there. Players like Mágico González, Paul Gascoigne even, players who are so extremely gifted and so good on the pitch they can get away with not being perfect off it, whether it's the nights out, the diet, the right amount of sleep, whatever. Lee Trundle is the same; he is special.

That's why he has a story to tell. Not just of his career but of his life and of the full picture that is more than just football – more than just tricks.

He is someone I have the utmost respect for as a human being first and foremost, while as his teammate and as his captain we shared great emotions on the pitch and in the dressing-room.

Whatever my role, I always enjoyed seeing Trunds be himself on the pitch; my only regret was that I didn't manage him as a player for longer at Swansea.

I never had a problem with him wanting to go to a higher level, and at the stage of his career that he was at it was something I understood. He deserved his chance. With him leaving one week before the start of the new season, I cannot say I was happy with the timing because I knew I couldn't replace him. Even though we had already signed another striker in Jason Scotland, I didn't even try. Instead, I changed the whole way we played, and that's the biggest compliment I think I could ever give him. For me, Lee Trundle is irreplaceable.

Roberto Martinez
June 2010

CHAPTER ONE

August

Saturday, 8 August 2009

IT'S SATURDAY. I don't want it to be. But it's Saturday.

The day I'm supposed to come alive, and yet today is dead for me. The first day of the season, the weekend where everyone is supposed to be excited about the next nine months – but I'm not part of it. Not part of the excitement, not part of the buzz, not part of the hope that flies around football on this day like no other, not part of the team.

Not even part of the squad. We're away to Preston, but I'm back in Bristol, lying in bed and lying to meself.

I've known this has been coming. All summer I've known I'd wake up on the first morning like this. All that time to brace meself and kid meself about this being a good thing.

I'm still being paid more money than I'd ever dreamed of as a kid, still kicking a football around during the week for a living. I'm not tied to this place on a Saturday; I can drive up to Liverpool and see me daughter, Brooke.

I might do that. Do what I want and forget this whole mess for the day.

There'll be times when I'll still have to be there, when I'll have to put the club suit on. Put the club tie on. Put a smile on.

But I'm not going to be putting a Bristol City shirt on again. And certainly not today, the opening day of the season.

Not part of the team, not even part of the manager's plans.

As much as I try to put a spin on it, I know that's never a good thing.

But, worryingly, I'm not as bothered about it as perhaps I should be.

And that's what's bothering me. I've been ground down to a point where I don't care like I should. I feel frustration, bitterness – but not the disappointment and the determination to put it right. I've not felt like this for years, not since before Rhyl and Wrexham and getting out of non-league, not since before Brooke was born. But this is worse. Back then, I just wasn't bothered about taking football seriously, about doing the right things and all that.

But at least I was playing. When it came to a Saturday I was out there, like I'd always been.

I won't be watching it today. I've not watched any of the build-up, nothing. I'll just keep kidding meself. Just keep telling meself that I'm the one who's got the last laugh, still picking up me money.

But I'm not laughing. In fact, I've struggled to smile when it's come to football recently.

It's probably shown in me training. Gary Johnson used to talk about me being enthusiastic, but if you're not enjoying yourself, how can anyone have enthusiasm?

I've not stopped trying. Everything he's asked me to do I've done – the running, the sessions on my own when everyone else was away playing friendlies; I did it. I wasn't doing it for him, I was getting meself fit so if I could find a way out, then I'd be raring to go for it, to seize my chance.

I'm not going to get a chance under him, so it's about finding a new opportunity elsewhere.

I'll be all right. You don't turn into a bad footballer overnight, do you? I'm not sure even the gaffer thinks that. He thought enough of me to pay £1 million for me two years ago.

But we've gone too far to turn back now.

It started a while back – I'd had words with him at the end of last season, so this whole thing hasn't been exactly a bolt out of the blue.

I'd been out training with the rest of the squad and it just so happened that David Noble, Gavin Williams and me all had hats on. Johnson was always one for sly comments, and this time was no different. 'No wonder you three don't score headers with fucking hats on.'

The other two took theirs off. I never did.

'You, get over there.' He'd stopped the session.

'What for?'

'For not listening to me when I tell you to do something. I said take the hat off.' Stupid really, but I wasn't in the mood for this any more.

'You never said that. You just said no wonder we didn't score headers.'

He was hardly going to let this drop now, but neither was I.

'You just want to do your own fucking thing all the time,' he said.

'Oh just shut up, you fucking prick.'

And that was that. Something as pointless and petty as that and I'm doing running sessions on me own. I got on with it – the fitness coaches probably enjoyed getting their hands on me anyway – and I got meself back involved.

But when it came to the end of the season and going in to see him one-to-one, we both put our cards on the table and told each other we'd try to sort out the one thing we both wanted: me out of Ashton Gate.

I'd not been playing anywhere near as much as I'd have liked, as I need to if you want to get the best out of me. I need confidence to play like I can, to get going with the style that makes me different as a striker. And it's been dragged out of me. I'd gone from forty games in me first season and that run to Wembley where we got so close to the Premier League I could touch it, down to just four starts last year. When we'd talked before the summer, we'd both known that stat wasn't going to get any better this time around. The best thing for everyone was to see if I could get out.

But apart from a couple of sniffs from League One – Huddersfield and Charlton were thinking about it I'm told – I'm still here.

And that's why I've woken up in me place in Bristol rather than in a hotel somewhere in Lancashire with the rest of the squad. Charlotte's here – and thank God for that. The reason I've even lasted this long is because of her. Don't get me wrong, I've not been thinking of jacking it all in or anything like that. I'm not stupid, I know I've been given a good living from football and I'm not going to throw all that away. I'm not that arrogant. But there have been times when you just think 'I've had enough,' and Charlotte's been there just to help me forget and put it into perspective. If I'd been on me own, I'm not sure how I would have dealt with all this. I would have gone mad.

It sounds a bit extreme, a bit over the top. After all, a footballer being frozen out of the team isn't exactly headline news. But it's the first time I've gone through this. I didn't turn pro until I was 24, and every step I've made since then has been a forward one. I've been good for managers wherever I've gone, so all this is a new experience.

Before me and Charlotte met last year, the only way of putting it all out of me head was to get back to Liverpool whenever I could. But since we got together, she's been me escape – and will be again today. She knows as well as I do that missing out today is not all down to the manager. I didn't exactly help meself in the summer. I knew I wasn't going to be involved whatever I did, so what was the point of killing meself in me time off? If I'd come back thinner, fitter, stronger than I'd ever been I'm not sure it would have made a difference.

I needed to enjoy meself so I did, with the plan to use pre-season to sharpen up. I knew I was going to come back carrying a bit of extra weight, but I'm talking about a couple of pounds, something like that. My body fat was up, but so is everyone's when it comes to these tests after a couple of weeks off.

Doing the sessions, I beat a few lads, but Johnson came over and told me I wasn't fit enough. But why just me? I'd beaten others, one being John Akinde, the big centre-forward.

'But look at his body compared to yours,' he said.

'So? Just because he's got a six-pack, does that mean he's fitter than me?' I argued, knowing there was no point.

And there wasn't.

He left me behind from the pre-season tour with the words: 'I'm not giving you another holiday when you've come back unfit after your first.'

I was on me own. It wasn't even a case of training with the youth, it was me doing fitness work and that was that. Michael McIndoe was there for a few days, another who'd fallen out with Johnson and wanted to leave. When others had a day off, I was in running – whatever was needed.

This wasn't justified. We both knew I didn't have a future, but this was a punishment outweighing the crime. Only it wasn't a punishment, or so he was trying to tell me. I was still fitter than others, if that was his problem.

So why was I on me own? I had no issue with the extra running – I would have happily caught up. But being singled out? It just seemed like a way of wearing me down and making sure I wanted to get away.

He needn't have worried.

The most I got in pre-season in terms of football was 45 minutes against Hereford. When Ajax came to Ashton Gate for a friendly, I wasn't even in a squad of 22. Kev Reeves was at the game, having just been given the job as chief scout at Wigan under Roberto Martinez.

Reevesy was always someone you could rely on to make you smile, and someone I owed a lot to after his time as coach at Wrexham and Swansea. He asked me why I wasn't playing and I told him about having blisters – which was true – but with a look in my eye that gave away the actual truth. He cracked a joke about me pace – or lack of it – and left for his seat with the message to keep my chin up. But it was hard.

I sat in the stands that night, looking out at the pitch where I'd celebrated with thousands after scoring the goal that took Bristol City to Wembley and put me to within 90 minutes of me dream of playing in the Premier.

I've always believed I could get to the top. I've never taken the easiest ways of getting there, I'll give you that, but I've always believed. Now I'm awake wondering how to spend a Saturday and wondering when the call is going to come to get me playing again. If the call is going to come.

I'm not done. I'm 32 – 33 in October – and I can still cut it at this level. I can see that in training up against other lads. I'm probably fitter than I ever was when I was making all the headlines with Swansea. If I'm getting on a bit – in football terms at least – I've not lost any pace, because it's not as if pace has ever been me strong point. Being different, being confident, has always been me strength – so as much as I need to go and find a new club, I can't go just anywhere. I need to go somewhere where I can get the chance to show me strength, where I can start enjoying football again.

I don't want to be bitter, I don't want to have to try and con meself that getting paid is all that matters, because it's not.

Yes, the money is a big part of why anyone wants to be a footballer, the lifestyle and all that. But it's not why you start. You start for the love of the game, the love of the crowd. The love of being loved.

CHAPTER TWO

Huyton Born, Huyton Red

I'VE ALWAYS LIKED attention. I've always loved being the middle of it.

It's just always been part of me make-up, never embarrassed to have all eyes on me whatever it was. If me mum took me to the pantomime in town and they'd ask someone to get up on stage, I'd be the first one. Things like that didn't bother me like it would some, it was the opposite. I remember me mum and me nan getting me to enter singing competitions on the radio because I'd never be too shy for things like that. I even won tickets to see Michael Jackson once for his big gig at Aintree – I sang 'The Way You Make Me Feel' to get into the final before I won it with a bit of Rick Astley.

I was happy to be in the centre of things and more often than not I was. Perhaps it's not surprising considering I didn't have any brothers or sisters – it was just me with me mum and me nan at ours on Ashbury Road, the street where I grew up in Huyton, just outside Liverpool.

But to say I'm an only child doesn't really tell the full story, because it was never only me. I had cousins all living close by – Stacey and Sean, Tasha and Ryan, Anthony and Paul Trundle – all growing up together. You had us at No. 10, me aunty at No. 21 and me uncle at No. 23 – a Trundle triangle. But then the whole street was like a big family. We all knew each other; the front doors were always open. Everyone had each other's back.

Don't get me wrong, Huyton's a rough place – and a lot rougher now – but you don't see it that way when you're in the middle of it. To you, it's just life. It was normal to be in school and for someone to come rushing up saying there's going to be a show on down the field – and everyone would go over to see someone from the estate racing around in a robbed car. We'd all be watching and cheering, waiting for the police to turn up so we could see the chase afterwards. No one thought anything of it because people did what they had to – to get by and get on.

Take those Michael Jackson tickets – sold in the local pub for £70, which meant me mum could go and buy me new clothes. Or you'd know when the catalogue van had been robbed because all the kids would be out on the street the next day all wearing the same make trackies, just in different colours. Whoever did that made a killing down our way one week.

Me mum never worked, apart from the odd part-time job, and neither did me nan, so we just lived off whatever benefits we could get – but I never wanted for anything. You'd have to wait to save up for things now and again, like if me trainies got ripped from playing and that, but I was looked after well. It was probably hard for me mum, especially because there weren't many single parents around on our estate. But she wasn't naïve; she could be feisty and looked after herself as much as she was protective of me. If I got in a fight on the street, she'd be round the other lad's house arguing for me.

I didn't have too many boundaries, probably because I was too much trouble if I got told no. The thing was we were as strong-minded as each other, and she'd be hard on me too. I didn't get away with anything over the top and I wasn't spoilt. But then I always knew I could win her round soon after if I'd been naughty, flashing a smile or coming up with something to make her laugh.

And she made sure I never missed out because I didn't have me dad around. As often as she could treat me, we'd walk down the main road, called Princess Drive, to catch the No. 13 bus. It took about 20 minutes to reach our stop by the Belmont Pub and then a short walk up to Anfield and Liverpool FC. I'm not sure she even knew the rules, let alone who the players were and how the team were doing in the League, she just knew that I enjoyed it. Who wouldn't?

This was Liverpool. Football is part of the city, part of the psyche even. It's just in your blood, no matter who you are or what age you are. I'm not sure many other cities would treat FA Cup day as if there was a royal wedding on. Back in 1986, when Liverpool played Everton in the final, we had a big street party before and after the game. Everyone had dressed their windows ready for the day with crêpe paper, ribbons and whatever we had to hand – the bottom window in red for me and me mum and the top in Everton blue for me nan. You'd put up posters and the souvenir specials you'd get from that week's *Liverpool Echo*. The road would be shut off – you didn't ask for permission from the police, you just did it – and everyone would bring their kitchen tables out into the street, giant pasting tables too, all full of sandwiches, cakes and drinks. When the match was done – Liverpool won 3–1 – everyone was back out in the middle of the road, all there celebrating together.

Everyone was involved – just like everyone would be glued to the telly when they'd show a league game, all the kids rushing out into the street at half-time to pretend to be Kenny Dalglish, making sure you were back in time for the second half. No one wanted to miss a kick, especially when there wasn't the wall-to-wall coverage then like you have now. You watched whatever you could.

I remember one of the older lads on the street being allowed a sleepover party especially to watch Liverpool play Independiente of Argentina in the 1984 Intercontinental Cup out in Japan. I would have only been about eight at the time, so I was begging me mum to let me go and begging the lad – Brian Jacobs – to let me stay. In the end, and after all that, I couldn't keep me eyes open as we waited for the kick-off dead early in the morning and missed the match. To make matters worse, I pissed the couch as I slept. And Liverpool lost.

But going to see the big games and the big names in the flesh was something else. We'd always go early to stand on the Kop – you had to go early or you just wouldn't be able to see. But the walk up the stairs and out onto the terrace was always me favourite part, this massive pitch just opening up before you and letting you dream of being out there, playing in front of all those people.

The players were gods – players like Dalglish, Jan Molby, Paul Walsh, John Wark, Alan Hansen, Ian Rush: a great side. Every week I'd wait behind to catch a glimpse of them coming out after the game. I'd get every autograph I could, and those few seconds stood next to them meant everything to me and the hundreds of others just like me. It was nothing to them, the stars, but everything to us.

Dalglish was my real hero; he was a genius with the ball and didn't know how to score a simple goal. He was someone who used to make you want to go to the football just to watch him – isn't that what it's all about?

I remember once me mum taking me to a meet-and-greet session at a shop in town because Kenny was going to be there. We set off dead early to make sure we were near the front of the queue, and as it happened we ended up being first into the shop. I had a quick chat with him as I posed for a photo – the *Merseymart* free sheet was there taking pictures – and remember going home feeling like I'd met the king. Which I had. The next Saturday Liverpool were at home and as usual I'd made me way round to the players' entrance after the final whistle, trying to push me way through all the other kids. I'd got to the side and I managed to shout over, ''Ey, Kenny, do you know when that picture is going in the paper?'

He turned to face me and said, 'Oh, all right, Lee. I think it should be in soon.'

With that, everyone was saying 'move out of the way, let the lad through' as though Kenny Dalglish knew me. Something as simple as remembering a name and it made me year, bragging to anyone we met on the way home. It's one of the reasons I swore if I ever made it I'd do the same, because what may be only a couple of minutes for a footballer is something that can last a lifetime with others.

It's been the case with me. Dalglish is still a hero of mine and only the other day I was made up when I managed to get a big canvas of him in his playing days signed 'Good Luck for the season, Kenny Dalglish'. Although I'm not sure he remembered me from the picture in the *Merseymart*.

But it just shows what a big impression such a small thing can make, and it's something I've never forgotten going into football and seeing young lads queue up for autographs. Plus, I remember how I used to take an instant dislike to any of the players who didn't stop for autographs – like Bruce Grobbelaar, he used to walk straight through carrying a box of some sort or pretending to be in a rush, so I had a downer on him.

I would go with me mum to every home game we could, more often than not on the Kop where it was the cheapest, but for a special occasion we'd get tickets for the Kemlyn Road end. You couldn't ask for a better introduction to the game than me mum had given me, although I was mad on football before we ever first got on that No. 13 bus. I loved going with her, but as time went on I was desperate to go with the older lads, to be at the back of the Kop with them. I can remember sitting in the Kemlyn once, waving over to them on the Kop on our left. I was still young, but these lads had taken me under their wing a little bit, this cheeky kid who could make them laugh. They were happy for me to go with them, so Peter Morley from across the road had to come over to ours and ask me mum if it was OK. She took a bit of persuading, but the next week off I went, the lads perching me on one of the bars at the back of the stand to make sure I could see.

But if I loved the thrill of going to watch the footy, it was nothing compared to playing. And I played everywhere.

Ask around me estate and anyone would tell you the same – I wouldn't be seen without a ball. The neighbours would be commenting on it to me mum all the time, about how it was attached to me foot. It sounds like something out of the 1950s, but that's what I did. Even when I got to about 13 and started getting interested in girls, I'd still be bringing a tatty old ball with me, knocking it around on me way, keeping it up, dribbling along, trying to juggle. It wasn't a bad way to impress them either.

It all seemed to click for me with the ball – I guess it would do if you played that often. I wouldn't call it practising, because that sounds like it was work. I wasn't going out onto the street thinking, 'I've got to work at this or that if I want to make it'. Every kid wants to be a footballer, but you start for the love of the game.

So I'd be out on the road with the older lads knocking it around, lads four or five years older than me, which meant I had to handle meself against the bigger challenges or learn to see the tackles coming. It was the same at the youth club; there'd be no ref, you called the fouls, so you had to come up with ways of avoiding the two-footed lunges or get a kick. You learned fast.

It wasn't just me; so many kids around the estate would have the tricks and the skills just from spending so much time with a ball. There'd be a load of us, lads I still call me mates to this day - David Green, Joey Dooley, Kevin Fisher and Phil Dears - all out playing until all hours. If there was no match on, you'd be out there on your own until you were called in, showing off what you could do to whoever was passing and then boasting about who could pull off the best bits of skill.

It doesn't surprise me that so many lads out of Huyton made it as professionals. I don't mean Liverpool as a city, but just around us. In recent years, you've had the likes of Steven Gerrard, who was from the Bluebell, the next estate down, and David Nugent, who went on to play for England. There was Joey Barton, who I remember as a kid coming to watch me play when I was in a pub side with his old man. If you want to go back further, Alan Stubbs, Terry McDermott, Peter Reid – they've all came out of the borough of Knowsley. And I reckon there would've been even more if different lads had been lucky enough to get the right breaks or if they'd listened to the right advice.

I'd play anywhere, down Jubilee Park or at St Dominic's Youth Club at the end of the road, but the majority of times it would just be on our road, on Ashbury. Ashbury Road was this big horseshoe, two rows of council houses facing each other all the way around with gardens too small to play in. Everything was on the street, the lamp post just outside mine acting as one of the posts.

Other estates or other streets would come over and play at ours, or we'd go to their place for an 'away' game – matches that would last all evening and mini-tournaments between each other that would go on forever.

It was all that mattered to me. School was somewhere you went for a laugh, nothing else. St Dominic's Catholic School was just round the back of mine, close enough so I could jump over the fence at five to nine, race up the path and be in class on time.

I was always in trouble but never for anything serious, more for being the joker – surprise, surprise. You know the type of stuff – messing about in class, getting caught and then starting off again the moment the teacher turned around. I was never a bad lad, I'd never go on the rob or anything like that. Some would do it for a laugh, but I was always too scared more than anything. I remember once there being a fair down Newsham Park, about 20 minutes away from ours. Me and two other lads – Tony Lokko and Tony Corrie – were on those grab machines, the ones with the Smartie tubes with the fivers wrapped around them and you had to control the claws with a joystick to win it. It was ten pence a go, but we were down to our bus fare and had already blown all the money we'd been given to buy our lunch. We decided to go for it and put our fares together, risking the long walk home. Of course, we didn't win and we were about to start the journey back – but on the way out we were going to pass a stall selling toffee apples. As we came closer, we could see there was a tray on the side of the stall full of fresh ones just cooling. We'd been there all day and were starving by now, so the plan was to race past, grab one and rush straight out through the gates. I wanted to go first to make sure I was away before the others, so I did, watching as they followed behind. We'd got away with it – even though one of the lads had dropped theirs on the floor in the rush – but I was so nervous that every time a car passed I'd be jumping behind walls or bushes thinking it was the police and that I was going to get nicked for taking a toffee apple. It was enough to put me off. But it didn't put everyone off around us – that was the area we were in; it was a fact of life.

The local pub was the Eagle and Child on Liverpool Road in Page Moss. It's not there now; it's been knocked down and a McDonald's has gone up in its place. But in its day it was quite a place – I think the *Liverpool Echo* called it one of the roughest pubs in Liverpool. Some of the things you used to hear about or read about happening there were just crazy. There were shops like a KwikSave the other side of the road, and they were forever getting stuff robbed because someone had run out of money in the Eagle and wanted another drink.

I remember one story in the paper saying how this lad had held up the off-licence across the way, walked out with the money and just gone straight into the Eagle for a drink before the armed police turned up.

We also had St Dominic's Parish Club at the end of the road. You had to be members there and no kids were allowed, so me uncles and me mum would always go to the Eagle instead. Then, when I was old enough, I started playing for their junior sides, me first proper games.

Our junior school wasn't really geared up for football like some of the others in the area, so getting a game at the weekend was a huge thing for me. I got me first boots around the same time, a pair of Kenny Dalglish Puma Silvers – beautiful black leather with the leaping puma logo in silver on the side. I thought I was something special in those, and I loved them. There was something different about playing football in proper boots and kit – and there was nothing better than the sound of studs on the pavement as you walked to the game on the weekend or just for a kickaround on Jubilee or the Doms field, already changed and ready to imagine you were King Kenny.

I started off with the Eagle when I was eleven and carried on for about four or five years with the same team just going through each season, winning the leagues and cups and hardly getting beat. I can remember the first taste of success, beating a side called the Boundary in extra time and heading back to theirs for the celebration, spraying around the fake champagne and drinking out of the cup – being the centre of attention.

And I was always a striker. It's hard to visualise certain games, like I can't remember my first official game with boots and the kit and all the business – but I can remember scoring goals. Tons of them. It was something that came naturally, a bit like the tricks.

I played up front alongside a lad called John Murphy, who was absolutely massive for his age. He was six foot before anyone knew it, so I guess I got used to playing alongside a big lad early on. But he was a good player in his own right; he went to Liverpool for a bit if I remember and ended up with Chester and got his League chance there. Got a few goals too, something like a hundred spread across four clubs.

There was John and a few others, but I was one of the ones standing out, and it was clear to me and everyone else I had ability even at that age, although no one needed any encouragement to want to be a top player. Everyone dreams like that when they're young, and I didn't think I had more of a chance than anyone else.

Perhaps others did. I can remember a fella who used to drink in the Eagle called Tommy Marsden who took a couple of us to Bolton Wanderers to train a few times. But one of the problems round by us was that not everyone had cars, so we'd only get to go when Tommy could borrow one for the day. With all that trouble for every different session it kind of petered out without anything coming of it.

There were open trials for Everton at one point too. The manager of the Eagle, a man called Mick Duffy, took me along to one of those days where you played a couple of games against other lads who'd been invited by their school or their clubs – but nothing came of that either. Although it's not as if I was heartbroken; all I was bothered about was getting the chance for an extra game or an extra kickaround.

I'd play for the Eagle, play on a Saturday for a side called Huyton Labour with lads older than me, play for the school side – secondary school by this point – play at the youth club and play in the street. There was nothing else for me.

School was just a chance to catch up with me mates or impress the girls, so it was no surprise I didn't get much in terms of qualifications. A B in Art was about the best of the lot – Art was the only other thing I was good at. I went to sixth form but that didn't last because they got fed up with me not taking it seriously enough, and I was chucked out. Not that I was bothered, nor was I the only one. Me mum couldn't give me hassle because, one, I would charm my way out of it and, two, there wasn't much going for you on our estate anyway.

When you come from a background where no one's worked then you don't know anything else, so why should I have been concerned that I didn't have the right grades or that I didn't know what I was going to do with me life? There were probably a handful of kids in the school who thought they needed good results to get the job they were after, but, as daft as it looks now, they were the ones who got made fun of, who had the piss taken out of them. Most of us were there because we had to be, because it was a laugh. Besides, I thought by this point I had a chance of making it if I wanted to.

I'd started playing for St Dominic's, the local amateur side, in the Liverpool County Combination. They played close to ours at Ashbury and, as much as we all wanted to play for Liverpool or Everton growing up, playing for the Doms was a big thing for me. I'd go and watch them as a kid, standing on the toilet lid in our bathroom and peering out of the window to check for cars in the car park as a sign that they were home that day. And although it was hardly the top level, you were on that pitch, with a clubhouse, playing in front of a little crowd and getting the recognition that went with it.

We played in a local cup final, quite a big deal at the time, and I came on as sub when we were behind in extra time. I got the equaliser, and we ended up winning on penalties. The Doms club was really strict, being a parish club – there were no kids allowed, full stop, not even on Christmas Day. But this was proof that football changed things, that if you could do the business on the pitch, doors opened for you. How else could you explain me being allowed in the clubhouse and having a pint as everyone made a fuss of me?

Of course I'd started drinking by then; I probably started at around 14 like the rest of the lads on the estate. You'd finish school on a Friday and a few of you would get together, wait outside the offy or the supermarket until someone would go in for you and buy you a couple of cans of lager. It was the super-strength stuff and it'd go down like tar, but you weren't doing it to savour the flavour, were you? It was about being with your mates and getting drunk.

It was part of life growing up. Me late uncle Tony's wife Jackie used to tell a story about the first time she met him, that after a night at the Eagle he said he had to stop in the shop to pick up a couple of cans of Guinness and a packet of crisps for me. She came to the house expecting me to be Tony's brother or something, but there I was, hardly out of junior school, watching *Match of the Day* and thanking me uncle for the beers.

It went from drinking on the streets to whatever pubs you could get served in; by the time we were 15 it was the local nightclub. I'd tell me mum in the week I wanted to get me own dinner, so I'd save the money I was given for the chippy and put it aside for the end of the week. I'd end up with about £15 and we'd all go to a place called the Coconut Grove – the Cokie – and have a few cans that would last you the night, walking the half-hour journey home because you never had enough for a taxi. It was brilliant, it was something to look forward to and another chance for me to be in the centre of things, whether it was with me mates or the girls.

It probably all came at the wrong time for me. I still loved football as much as I ever did, but what was the harm in going out and having a good time? I'd only played football to enjoy it, so as long as that was still the case I was fine. Besides, I was still on course as far as I was concerned, because by the time I was 16 I'd been spotted and selected to play for a Knowsley Borough side.

Every year the council arranged for a side to go out to America and play in this tournament called the Dallas Cup. Lads from Kirkby, Roby, Prescot and all the local areas were called up for trials before they picked a squad.

I'd made it into the side, and we began playing a few games as warm-ups before the tournament started. We'd played against Tranmere and Everton youth sides locally before they then arranged for us to go up to Scotland and play Stirling Albion on a Friday night. The game was on AstroTurf under floodlights and we won 3–1, me getting one and a lad called Davie Rowe getting the others. I was buzzing, I was man of the match, I'd loved the step up in standard and here I was, really feeling something special.

We were staying the night, with training scheduled for the following day, but there was no posh hotel or anything like that. We were staying in a sports hall gym and had all been told to bring sleeping bags with us for the trip. Going back to this draughty hall was a bit of a comedown after the high of playing, so the fella running the side, Gerry Smith, got us all together and said, 'Lads, youse're allowed to go out for a couple of drinks, but we want you all back by 12 midnight at the latest.'

It was just what I wanted to hear. We didn't waste any time getting our gear on and heading off out the door to find the nearest pub. It didn't take long for us to start getting a bit tipsy and loving the banter of all being out together, teenage lads from Knowsley all up for a laugh.

We'd already had a girl come over to hand out fliers for the nightclub upstairs, and I was in no mood to go back just yet. So we didn't. I stopped the rest of the lads in the hallway and did me best to coax the others to join me.

'Look, if we all stay out he can't sack us all,' I told them. 'He won't risk messing the team up after we've won.'

And that was that, we all headed upstairs and stayed there until three in the morning.

'Youse have let me down, I'm not putting up with this, I'm not managing you lot.'

All we could hear was Gerry ranting as we tried to drunkenly sneak into our sleeping bags, trying to hold back the laughter as we said our sorrys for losing track of time.

By the time the stragglers came in and caught the worst end of his swearing, none of us could hold it together, all rolling about laughing – by the end even he saw the funny side of it. Not exactly a good lesson learned, in the grand scheme of things, but it had been a laugh.

That was the thing, we all trained the next day as well as we'd ever done – we were all pains in the arse, but we were good kids deep down, with smiles on our faces. Coming from our area, from our backgrounds, going away like that was a big thing. We never went on trips. I never had a summer holiday going abroad or anything like that – you couldn't afford to do it. We had to save up £150 to go to the tournament in the US, but the council stumped up the rest because we were representing the borough. Not that it was in our heads like that; this was us getting to go away together and having a laugh.

But the tournament was a big deal. There were local teams like ours, but they also had a 'super-league' running, so there were teams like AC Milan and São Paulo – and little old Knowsley Borough.

One day we were outside the hotel where the Milan side were staying and a couple of the lads noticed they were looking down to where we were. One of the lads threw me the ball and told me to show them what I could do. Like I needed asking. I started messing around and there were claps from the Milan boys before they called for us to come up.

There they were in their top gear, all their tracksuits and kit in the famous red and black of Milan, while we were in Fruit of the Loom sweaters with Knowsley Borough embroidered into it. Not that it stopped us from swapping whatever we could, eyeing up their best stuff and not giving these poor Italian lads much of a say. They couldn't have had much left by the time we left.

When it came to the football we wouldn't have come close to teams like that, but we did ourselves proud reaching the quarter-finals. I'd managed to finish top scorer for our side, and it was a real eye-opener coming up against these different styles of play.

But for me the best thing was the buzz of feeling like a proper footballer – all in posh and specially made gear, flying out to another country, being made to feel as though you were someone, the fuss made of the games, the people watching – all the attention.

I loved all that. There was an official tournament photographer who you could pay to go to your game and get pictures of you playing. They were my first action photos, and I was made up taking them home to show me nan and to put in her scrapbook – one she still keeps today.

And I'm not ashamed to say I like all that side of the game. When I was really young, I would plug in the ghetto-blaster in the kitchen, stretching the lead as far as I could to the edge of the back door, and put on a tape of 'The Way It Is' by Bruce Hornsby – the theme music from *Grandstand* at the time. I'd throw the ball off the back wall, volley it back and scream, 'That's it, yes, Trundle has scored . . .' with the music blaring in the background, picturing meself on the screen playing in the First Division, being a hero.

When they used to show a montage of someone's goals I would dream up mine and play it through in me head. Who wouldn't want all that? Who wouldn't want the adulation?

Everyone wants to be a footballer, not just because of the big games and all that but because of the status. Everyone loves the local football team – especially in Liverpool – and they see the life that goes with it. Any lad in the city would say the same, because it's a way out. No one round our way thought of life as being tough, but you knew you would have it made if you could get your chance in football. And that always seemed more likely than getting a great job.

Yet I'd say all this and dream all this and not do a lot about it when the chances did come. I didn't even see them as chances. Now, of course, it's clear I had more back then than many others would be lucky to get in a lifetime.

I was 16 when a fella named Tony Kelly set me up with Bolton. He was from our way and was a fan favourite of theirs, a very good midfielder who was voted as one of their top players a few years back, and I think he is still involved with the club now as a fans' liaison officer or something. Back then, Bolton were in the old Third Division, but they had a good side and after watching us play for the Doms Tony had arranged for me and another lad called Steve Moran to go down.

It meant catching a bus to Bolton, which for me was a real pain, and then heading for the ground. Incredibly, I saw that as a chore, that I had to get up first thing in the morning and catch a bus to somewhere I didn't know. I should have been thinking it was a big chance for me, but I would be messing around more than anything until it came to playing in the games. That's the only time I took it seriously. Everything else, all the running and the drills, was boring to me. I just wanted to play.

One day we got off the bus and just didn't fancy it, so we ended up going off to find a McDonald's in the town centre and then going into HMV and listening to the latest singles with the headphones on. I was wasting time rather than taking me chance.

When we got to the club, we hid behind cars until the bus left for the training ground, hoping we'd get away with it for the day. But when we went into the office complaining the bus from Huyton was late, we were told to go and do laps.

David Lee was out there doing training on his own – I can remember running behind him just incredulous at the size of this professional footballer's calves – but after a couple of laps me and Steve went off into the stands, splashing the rainwater from the barriers onto our shirts to make wet patches to try and look like we'd been sweating.

The problem was I wanted the whole football experience without putting in the work for it – I couldn't see why just playing wasn't enough, especially at that age. I couldn't see why they wanted me to do all the running and the drills when I could just show what I could do with a ball in a game. It wasn't as if they weren't prepared to give lads like me a go, take a bit of a gamble if you like; Gary Martindale was a couple of years older than us but went from St Dominic's to Bolton.

But I just didn't have the desire to go the extra yard. Perhaps half the problem was that we'd see some of the lads who'd made it and see that they got by with having a drink and a laugh at the same time. Tony was the same. He was at Wigan in the mid '90s, and I remember laughing when he used to tell me about him going into training after a good session the night before and how this young Spanish lad just didn't know what was going on. Of course, Roberto Martinez has never bothered with drink.

It wasn't so much the drink for me. I would never want to go out and play after having a skinful like one of me mates had done when he got signed on a YTS by Tranmere – going out and playing after a good few pints in the day. I could never do that. It was just about the nights out and meeting up with the lads.

Some coaches tried to have words with me, and the lads who used to set these chances up for me must have been tearing their hair out, but it would all go in one ear and out the other. I'd stand and listen to what they had to say, nod, and then run off without giving any of it a second thought.

I had a mate called Tony Blythe who was a decent player at the time.

His dad, Brian, ran the Doms and would be on top of Tony all the time. He wouldn't be allowed out, and we all used to feel sorry for him and say his old man was being harsh – even me nan would say how the poor lad couldn't go anywhere. Looking back, his dad could see he had talent and was doing what he thought was best to try and make the most of it. It might've worked – Tony spent a year or two with Peterborough but then broke his leg.

Being surrounded by women, they didn't understand what was going on, that these chances were coming and I wasn't taking them. Having a man around might have made a difference, he might have been able to grab hold of me and ask what the hell I was doing. I'm not sure I would have listened, because of the person I was, but I had no one to try for me.

Me granddad – me mum's dad – had come over to Liverpool from Ireland for work but died when I was a few months old, and me dad wasn't even around at that point. He and me mum had been nothing serious; they'd been seeing each other, she'd got pregnant and they'd split up.

He never tried getting in touch. I never bothered trying to get in touch with him either – it wasn't as if me mum had banned us from seeing each other or anything like that. And it didn't upset me, didn't make me angry even. It's not as if he was there one minute and gone the next, leaving us in the lurch. I grew up without him and that was that. It's only since I became a dad meself that I wonder how on earth anyone could not want to see their child. How could you not want to see them grow?

Me mum would do the best she could. She'd be brilliant taking me to football when I was small, watching every week from the sidelines. But it was hard looking around seeing all the other dads. You could see them having a word in their boys' ear, ''Ey, lad, you should have given it inside there,' or whatever. How was me mum going to be able to do that?

We first met when I was 16, me and me dad. Knowsley United, a local side in the Unibond League, used to have a pound-a-pint night on a Thursday at their clubhouse, about five minutes from mine.

Me dad, Gerry Preston, worked on the door. He wasn't a big lad, but the Prestons were quite a big family – five brothers and six sisters. They were well known in the Huyton area and sometimes a reputation was all you needed. He could handle himself at the same time, but I knew who he was, just as everyone knew he was me dad.

That night I was in the club and one of the lads I was with must have mentioned it to him, so he told them to ask me to come over and see him. I wasn't nervous, because it didn't mean anything to me. He was me father but he was a stranger at the same time – I wasn't about to start calling him Dad. We started talking football. His brother, me Uncle Mick, had watched me playing for Huyton Labour down Jubilee and seen me scoring a fair few goals. Dad ran a side called the Dovecot and said he'd heard I was a good footballer and why didn't I go over and play a few games?

So I did. 'Why not?' I thought – it was another chance for a game and something different. I played for them in midweek and met me cousin, Frankie Preston. Me and Frankie got close pretty quickly, and from the moment we met he looked after me, making sure I always had enough money for a drink after a game, never letting me go without and just generally being there for me.

I would get close to me dad too. Eventually. To be fair to him, he made the effort to put things right, and we now speak once a week on the phone. I also get on with his two sons and daughter, me half-brothers and -sister. He's come to watch me a lot in recent years, and I know he's said he missed out – but that was the decision he made.

Who knows, if he had been around perhaps I wouldn't have been as strong-minded as I was. Perhaps I would have been more of the YTS type – more prepared to take being told and to follow the rules rather than do it me own way.

But, back then, I was going me own way, and – in me own mind at least – it was doing me fine. I was still progressing. I was playing for Liverpool County in the FA County Youth Cup, travelling away to play different sides and still scoring goals.

And then came Liverpool Football Club.

CHAPTER THREE

September

IT'S THAT SOUND again.

Even better than that, it's that feeling again.

I bounce through the gap in the fence and onto the small road that separates the training pitches from the gym car park in Llandarcy, heading in out of the rain.

Me studs clatter on the concrete just as they did on Ashbury – only there's 20-or-so pairs of boots making the same rhythmic noise.

It's music to me ears and my smile shows it. I'm part of something again. And have been for the past week or so.

I'd always kept in touch with Huw Jenkins, the Swansea City chairman. We'd had a good relationship all the way through me time at Swansea and even after the rigmarole of me leaving for Bristol, we'd still stayed close. I'd call him when the lads were doing well or send the manager, Roberto Martinez, a text after a good result, not to mention staying friendly with a lot of the lads like Alan Tate and Garry Monk.

Huw knew me situation under Gary Johnson, and he would've known I was desperate for any chance of getting away from Bristol and coming back to the club where I'd enjoyed life so much. I would have begged him if I'd had the chance – and I wouldn't have been ashamed. There'd been talk before of something happening, more paper talk than anything, but this time I knew there was a chance.

The club was still down in the dumps a little after Roberto had left for Wigan and the Premier League in the summer, taking with him Jason Scotland, the top goalscorer. He'd been the man who'd filled me boots after I'd left for Ashton Gate, and I'd already joked with a couple of journalists after bumping into them that I should be the one to fill his.

Only I wasn't joking.

And when the call came, a few days before the end of the transfer window, the adrenalin ripped through me. Only a loan deal until January, but someone was opening the door for me and I couldn't wait to walk through it.

I had trouble getting the words out to tell Charlotte – me mind racing all over the place, throwing clothes, kit, whatever I could think of into me bag as fast as I could. If she hadn't known any better she must have thought I was going on the run from someone, that me life depended on getting away. Not quite, but close – me footballing life did. Or certainly I felt it did.

My smile must have been as wide as the Severn when I crossed the bridge, the 'Welcome to Wales' sign like a welcome home banner. I wasn't just getting me football chance back, I was getting it at a place where I'd got the same buzz for the game as I had down the Doms field, a buzz that'd been missing for months and months.

Charlotte understood. I think I talked to her about Swansea more than I spoke about meself. When we'd got together a year earlier, she wasn't given long to twig it was part of who I was. In fact, I think it was about two dates. Monday it was the pictures, Tuesday it was the Swansea–Cardiff derby at the Liberty Stadium. If ever a night had rammed home what I was missing it was then. The place was pumping, the first South Wales derby in years and it was everything I'd imagined it would be. Only I was a fan rather than a player.

I hadn't really wanted to leave the club in the first place, but I'd made me choice. I said at the time it was all about playing at a higher level, and that was true. Still is. But money was a factor, just as it would be for anyone, just as it is in everyone's life – just on different scales. I was desperate for the club to turn around back then and say they'd match Bristol's offer – but I knew they couldn't, just as they knew I couldn't turn down the chance of setting meself up for life and making sure I could give Brooke everything she'd want.

I'd made my bed in Bristol and I'd been lying in it for two years. Now I was home.

Even signing the contract had been a thrill, pulling up outside the reception doors on that Thursday and walking in. The smiles had said it all – on the staff and on me. I signed the paperwork with Jackie Rockey, the club secretary, as if it were my first ever contract.

My first questions? Where's the fixture list and when are we playing Cardiff? But that would wait.

I'd gone back downstairs looking for Sue Eames, the club's kit lady who had been so good to me when I'd first come down to South Wales from Liverpool, one of the first people to meet me. Just as then, she handed over me gear. I looked down at the black and red collection of T-shirts and trackies and saw a white No. 19. It didn't take me long to convince myself that it all added up to No. 10, the number I had worn for the Eagle, the number I'd made me own first time around in Swansea and not even taken off me car registration plate since.

The message came over to go and see me new manager, Paulo Sousa. A Champions League winner as a player, he'd been captaining Juventus when I'd been down Jubilee and had won the instant respect of the Swans lads when he'd replaced Roberto.

His English was fluent, if a little broken, but we were speaking football. He told me he'd watched all the clips of me, that he knew the type of player I was, how he saw me playing in this position and that position. He told me he thought I could play anywhere in the central corridor – at No. 9 or No. 10. My new squad number was looking better already.

He'd given me his ideas, now it was time for mine as he asked me what I thought I could bring to his squad.

'I'll get you goals and I'll create chances for others,' I told him, before making sure he knew I could be a good character to have around the place, to lift team morale, lift the fans' morale if I could. The old confidence was already flowing. I think it was what he wanted to hear.

What I wanted to hear was that crowd again, from the middle of the pitch and not from the stands. All I could think about as I buzzed around the training pitch was running out at the Liberty again. But that was nothing new. That had been on me mind from the moment I'd left. Not always at the front, the noise of the fans in me imagination not always as loud, sometimes simply a passing thought – but always there.

There were no guarantees given when I signed the three-month loan deal, Bristol happy to agree to keep paying the majority of my wages to get me away from Ashton Gate.

But there was every chance I was going to get a game against Watford on the Saturday. As was Craig Beattie, the Scottish striker who'd signed on the same day as me and become the club's record signing after a £500,000 move from West Brom. The fee could have risen to £800,000 – double Swansea's previous record – so it was a big deal in more ways than one. We'd already met at Morgans, the five-star hotel in the city centre where we were both being put up for the time being.

And when we met after the joint press conference on the Friday we got on fine, despite the fact so many of the questions were being directed at me, a loan signing. I think he had got the whole scene with me coming back, and it might well have suited him. The back pages of the Welsh newspapers that morning had already been about my 'homecoming' and there'd even been a crowd at the training ground earlier on. It was great stuff for the press, good copy as they'd call it. But it was new for Charlotte. She'd had a taste of it from the times I'd brought her to Swansea for the day, the way people had been with me, the way I'd interacted with fans. Footballers get attention, and I'd been popular with a lot of the Bristol supporters, but it was different here.

If that was new, so must I have been on that Saturday morning. Charlotte had seen so much of me moping and going through the motions on the morning of a game. She was now seeing the other extreme. It's not often you get asked to autograph someone's back so they can get it tattooed later.

The walk from the car park to the reception entrance at the Liberty takes a few minutes, but it's not a walk separated from the fans, which suited me. Every step and every smile gave me an extra shot of confidence, an extra inch to me height, one less pound on my shoulders that I'd felt for the last year or so.

This was what I had needed. You always find new belief in yourself from joining a new club when you've been out of the picture. This was an old belief restored.

I wasn't blind. I'm still not. I knew not every fan saw my coming back as a positive, forward step – but that has happened to a lot better players than me. If it happened to Robbie Fowler when he went back to Liverpool for a second spell, I was hardly going to get away with it. But I just hoped the majority of fans would welcome me back. When you leave a club, the more people like you as a player, the more they hurt when you leave and let them down. Coming back after walking away wasn't going to just wash that feeling away in some.

But I've always worked for recognition, and this was no different. The Watford game was no different. It was about me being on the pitch, not in the papers – but at least I could get on the pitch.

As I headed towards the main doors, one half of me was rushing to get in and get out there, the other desperately trying to hold back. To savour the moments, to take in all the warmth from a match day that I'd lost for the last year, to keep a lid on the nervous energy threatening to bubble over with every handshake and 'welcome back' that dotted the walk to and through the reception.

I was conscious of keeping it in for another reason. When the double doors that led to the tunnel areas at the Liberty closed, I turned to the left and entered the home dressing-room and remembered I was the new boy, not the old hero. OK, I wasn't quiet – I don't think I could ever be accused of that. But I wasn't the life and soul like I would be normally, not like I was the last time I was inside those walls. I knew I needed to earn the respect of my teammates all over again. Being back was important to me, but not to these lads. In that first game it was me club, but not me team. Not yet, anyway.

But at least I had a Swansea crest on me chest again. I'd been back with Bristol City, on the bench the previous April, and there had been a few jeers. There was even a chant of 'Trundle what's the score . . .' when Monks had put Swansea one up. I told meself at the time that had been down to Roberto's reaction in the game at Ashton Gate. The fans had been amazing, singing my name as I warmed up for Bristol, but Roberto had told them it wasn't on, that I wasn't a Swansea player and that was to be remembered.

This time none of that mattered, there was no confusion. I was in a Swans shirt.

There was a buzz around the place; the papers had talked of me putting a few extra on the gate. The manager hadn't enjoyed the easiest of starts – there was a big injury list and then there'd been three red cards and three suspensions to deal with after a Carling Cup game with Scunthorpe. The side had had its first League win of the season the previous week at Coventry, but a lot of supporters were suffering from the comedown from the previous year under Roberto, where it had been flair football all the way. Paulo had wanted to keep the same style but probably needed a bit of time to make his mark, and things needed a boost. If my signing was partly because of that, I wasn't complaining.

Beatts got the start, I was named as sub, but things hadn't gone to plan – Watford going ahead when Danny Graham was played in from a quick free-kick. Four minutes later, twenty minutes to go, the nod came.

'And coming off is No. 7 . . .' – Leon Britton trotted over to the touchline, me old teammate, me new teammate – '. . . for No. 19 Lee Trundle.'

I sprinted on, the noise making me nerve endings dance with excitement. The first couple of touches were neat enough, straightforward and settling. Then a pass through to Beattie; the shot saved.

'I'll create chances for others . . .' just like I'd told Paulo.

A chance a minute from time, Beattie knocking a ball to the back post and I headed it wide. Unmarked too. I'd tried to be too clever, tried to glance it as I saw the keeper come, and it went wide. I'd tried too hard.

'I'll get you goals . . .'

Tatey was the one who did the business with an injury-time header, a great lad and a player known for a lot of things, but goals were not one of them.

He's still crowing about it now as we finish training, ten days after.

I have a dig back, taking the piss out of the size of his neck and how he should be getting more headers. 'I'll catch him up soon enough,' I told the press after the game.

I better had. The session is over, there's no game tomorrow, Saturday. The international break has given time for the squad to recover; the 11 players that missed the Watford game, that helped spark the need for my signing, are coming back.

First impressions don't last long, and despite all the past, these are very much first impressions I'm making. I am trying to hide it with the old smile, but there are nerves, perhaps more now than ever before. How can you have nerves when you have nothing to lose?

The clock is already ticking for me – three months to play for me future, to be kept on, to get another loan agreed and then, who knows? At a club where I want to be, in a place where I want to stay, where I want to settle.

It feels like it's all on the line in every training session. We get handed our schedules for the following week. I'm on trial all over again – only this time I know what's at stake.

CHAPTER FOUR

Non-leagues and Nightclubs

I GUESS I thought I'd made it already.

It was only a trial, a few weeks with the club, but for me it was all done and dusted – I was a footballer. More than that, I was a footballer with Liverpool FC.

I just don't think I really got the 'trial' part of things – I didn't see it as a big chance, as this amazing opportunity. I didn't see it as a few weeks to set up the rest of me life. Christ, I couldn't see past the next weekend, let alone what this was going to mean for me future.

I was around 18 at the time, an age where most pros in the game now are all already well established in the youth systems at this club or that. Even lads in the lower divisions have all come through the ranks somewhere, many at the top clubs. Take Steven Gerrard. He's a few years younger than me but had been with Liverpool for years when I went for my extended trial at the start of the 1995 season. Everyone knew he was well thought of at the club, making a bit of a name for himself. I was knocking a ball around Jubilee when Steven passed by and said he'd heard I was going to Melwood in a few weeks. 'Sound,' he said – and it was, for me. He's a huge star of the club now, but he wasn't training with the seniors then – players like John Barnes, Ian Rush, Robbie Fowler, Stan Collymore, Steve McManaman, Jamie Redknapp, players I was suddenly thrown in with. There were no nerves – getting invited was getting told 'you're good enough' in my mind. And as far as any girls I'd meet on a Saturday night were concerned, I was already playing for Liverpool reserves anyway – along with half the other lads in the nightclub when it came to chat-up lines.

Being so relaxed about the whole thing actually probably did me the world of good to start with. The confidence I'd got from just being there meant I was determined to pull out the tricks and show what I could do in front of all these stars – the 'Spice Boys' I think the media ended up calling them. Neil Ruddock called me 'Le Tiss': probably a throwaway comment for him, but being compared to Matt Le Tissier and what he could do with the ball gave me the boost I needed to carry on letting my skills do the talking.

I wasn't exactly busting a gut running around, trying to impress, trying to look keen – I was more concerned with what I could do with the ball. That was what made me different and it was that that I thought they wanted to see.

I must have done OK; I remember Redknapp asking how long I'd signed for. When I replied I hadn't, he said he would be snapping me up if he was the manager. But then I don't think there was ever a doubt about me ability – it was about how I applied meself. Or didn't. Even then, even when I should have been thinking about making a breakthrough, I was still happier making me mates laugh, making anyone laugh – that whole centre-of-attention thing.

Like when I was asked to play for the reserves against Barrow during the trial. We'd been beaten, but I thought I'd done OK, so I wasn't paying much attention as Sammy Lee, the reserve team coach, went on and on in the middle of the changing-room.

Opposite me, this lad from the north-east called Lee Brydon started trying to catch me eye and pulling daft faces behind Sammy's back. I got involved, and I'm the one who got caught.

'Do you think getting beat by Barrow is funny, son?'

No, but I wasn't going to start getting serious about football all of a sudden. Not even for Liverpool.

It came to the final week of me trial and Knowsley Borough – who I was still playing for – had been entered into a tournament called the

Keele Classic down at the university. They made it to the semi-final, and I travelled down to play on a day off, even though I had a game for Liverpool's reserves against Nottingham Forest the next day. As it happened, I scored two and did enough to impress a scout from Crewe who'd been watching and told me to give him a ring if it didn't work out with Liverpool.

But the idea had been for me to go down, play, and then drive back with another lad the same night, nice and fresh for the Forest game. Only it didn't happen that way. After the win, everyone was celebrating on the campus, all planning to stay the night ahead of the final in two days' time. I was in the middle of it, all the banter, all me mates, and I wasn't going anywhere. No problem, I thought, and I turned to the other lad to tell him we'd stay for a night out and drive back first thing.

Of course, by the time I got back to Ashbury after a night's drinking I had just enough time to get me trackie on before heading to Melwood to be picked up.

It just wasn't sinking in that I was playing for Liverpool reserves – playing with the likes of Jamie Carragher and David Thompson – and what it could mean.

But I just didn't know any different – and probably didn't want to. It was a laugh, and if it was a laugh you were doing nothing wrong. That was how we were brought up, it was how we got by. It wasn't in me head that I shouldn't be doing it.

I loved being with me mates more than anything; I loved the feeling of being with friends, having a good time together. The buzz of winning that game, the high of being around people I liked, was bigger than everything.

A lot of lads wouldn't put themselves in that situation, but I couldn't say no – I didn't want to say no. I hadn't been brought up in a world of boundaries anyway, so I doubt I would have enjoyed being told what to do if they had taken me on.

Although it turned out there was no danger of that.

I got called into the office on the Monday by Sammy. The conversation was pretty simple – I wasn't being kept on and that was that.

But it didn't mean anything. I wasn't gutted. It wasn't the end of the world like it should've been, like it would've been perhaps when I was a young kid.

I'd shown I was a good player, I'd shown I had the ability to share a pitch with some of these professionals, and, besides, now I wasn't lying to girls when I told them I'd played for Liverpool. And soon enough I wouldn't have to fib – I was a footballer, I was getting paid to play football. Not with Crewe though.

I'd phoned the scout who'd seen me at Keele and he arranged for me to go down, getting their big striker Dele Adebola to pick me up on Princess Drive. Dele lived nearby and things started OK with them – I'd scored two playing for their reserves – but one day, for some reason, he couldn't pick me up. Crewe arranged for me to get the train and had someone waiting at the other end to meet me – but I wasn't on it.

Of course I look back now and realise how stupid I was. People don't get many chances in life. I was getting plenty but just wasting them. It was obvious I had ability, so obvious that it might have been part of the problem. But I was blowing it.

Yet in me own bubble I was doing fine.

I'd played in a cup final for Liverpool County at Burscough's ground, Victoria Park, at the end of the previous season and I'd caught the eye, so it didn't take long before I started turning out for Burscough themselves in the North West Counties League, three divisions below the Conference.

One night I'd scored four against a side from Blackpool, two being long-rangers, and came off to a standing ovation about five minutes from the end. Right after the game the Burscough secretary, a man called Stan Strickland, got me into his office.

'Well played again tonight, Lee, some great goals,' Stan said. He'd been the one who'd first got me number after the County FA Cup final and persuaded me to join Burscough.

'Oh, thanks very much,' I replied, just waiting for him to get to what he was after. He got to it soon enough.

'Look, I've just noticed you're not on a contract.'

'No,' I said. I was picking up the standard £15 a game.

'Well, listen,' Stan went on. 'We want you to sign a contract here and we want you to sign it tonight . . . we'll give you £50 a game.'

Bearing in mind I'd never taken a pay packet home yet, that was big money for me, especially just for playing football on a Saturday as I'd always done, just as I'd planned to do if they were paying me or not.

But at the same time I didn't know anything about contracts. The only thing I knew was that they scared me; I didn't know what I was tying meself down to and I didn't like that. I didn't like the commitment. I'd come and gone as I pleased so much I really didn't fancy this idea, even though I could start getting me hands on some good money for it.

I went to see Brian Blythe, the manager of the Doms, and straight away he said not to sign it, trying to explain if a bigger club came in I could go off and join them without having to arrange a transfer fee. It was a compliment that he thought I wouldn't be at Burscough for long, but the thought of £50 had begun to sink in.

I was made up with £15, but £50 . . . I thought I'd made it.

So a couple of days later I signed the contract – and the transfer fee Brian was worried about didn't put Chorley off when they came in for me after no more than ten games.

Chorley's manager, Dave Sutton, paid £7,000 for me – a real bragging figure as far as I was concerned. For me, it underlined the fact I had ability and only cemented me belief that I didn't have to work that hard with it.

I'm not sure anyone believed Dave when he told the papers I'd be a £1 million player one day, but it was all the confidence I needed – even though he hadn't seen a lot of me before signing me. I'd been recommended to him by a fella called Verdy Goodwin, a well-known scout by us who'd spotted Paul Mariner when he was younger. This time he'd spotted me, coming to watch me at different games and then telling Dave he just had to sign this kid at Burscough.

So he did, and I moved to the Unibond, up another league and another step up the ladder, without even having time to realise it.

Straight away I was going to better grounds, getting a nice little crowd at games and having a good standard of football to enjoy.

And I was enjoying it. Chorley were ambitious and wanted success, wanted promotion, and they were happy for me to go out and do my thing up front.

It was working. I never used to pass – it was either score or see it taken off me – but I'd get enough goals so no one could say anything.

I was flying, and I remember Dave coming out and saying in the media that England Under-21s should be looking at me. Just the other day I read a piece saying I was a match for Kevin Keegan and Chris Waddle for skill,

Dave having played against both of them. When you've got a manager who believes in you like that then you're bound to perform for them – and it was showing. I was doing the business and so were the team.

We'd gone on a good little run in the FA Trophy, which gave me a first taste of the spotlight. Me nan had always kept her scrapbook for match reports, and our run to the quarter-final against Gateshead had given her plenty to cut out, especially after I scored late on to help us to a 3–1 win. We were two games from Wembley, although I was more interested in the video of the match I'd been given, making sure everyone in the street had got a good look.

We went out in the semis – Macclesfield beat us over two legs, although that was no shame as they went on to win the Conference under Sammy McIlroy that season.

And the strange thing was, just like when Sammy Lee told me Liverpool wasn't for me, I can't remember being that upset. The kid in me would have died to get there, to play under the old twin towers just like I'd seen Liverpool and Everton do all those years before. I'd never actually been, making do with watching it on the telly because we could have never afforded it, even though I told anyone who listened it was because I wanted me first trip to Wembley to be when I played there.

Actually, that did turn out to be the case – but how was I going to know that at the time? I was still just in the moment, all about the now rather than thinking what I was going to do about tomorrow.

And what was wrong with that? After all, I was getting everything I wanted – I was getting recognition, getting paid and getting me nights out. Nothing was getting in the way of that, it was all too easy for me. So when offers came with the potential to disrupt it, out came the excuses.

Like when Macclesfield invited me down to Moss Rose at the start of the following season. They'd been promoted into the Football League and McIlroy must have thought I was worth a second look after the FA Trophy games. I knew I could compete with the players he had there because I'd shown as much a few months earlier.

And in those first few days of training I was on fire – the tricks were there, the goals were there, he fancied me and I fancied meself. Then, at the end of the session, McIlroy pulled me to one side, telling me that I'd done well but he wanted to work with me on me fitness.

'If we can improve that, it will help you as a player and you'll have a chance,' he said. 'We'll put you on a programme this week, we'll get you running and working on a few things, and we'll see the difference.'

I nodded my OKs to start this programme the following day – and immediately made the decision I wasn't turning up.

If I was going to play football, great – I'd happily head down there. But I couldn't face the effort to travel down for the running, the stamina work, the fitness drills – where was the enjoyment in that? If there was no enjoyment, what was the point? We would only train twice a week with Chorley and then it was basically warm-ups and a game. That was all I wanted.

And a night out with the mates, of course.

I wasn't looking for a career; I was looking for a game of football, for someone to see that I was a good player. Don't get me wrong, I still loved the idea of it. I loved the thought of someone coming up and asking 'What do you do?' and being able to say, 'Me? I'm a footballer' – I just didn't want to put in the work for it; it was as if I was waiting for it to happen by magic.

It didn't stop with Macclesfield. Chorley had played Bolton in a friendly and I murdered a couple of their defenders so they invited me to go back there – but I didn't turn up because a couple on a Sunday afternoon had turned into a session on a Sunday night. On the Monday, I told Bolton the car had broken down.

The chairman at Chorley, a man named Trevor Hemmings, had ties with Preston and had set something up for me there. Even getting there was arranged for me – David Moyes, the assistant manager at the time under Gary Peters, driving to me home in Huyton to pick me up and then take me back afterwards. I did OK there too, scored a few for them in the reserves – but when I was asked to go back a few weeks later, only this time I'd have to make me own way, I didn't want to know.

And I remember Charlton ringing me on a Sunday teatime after being tipped off about me, asking if I could go down for a week and to get on a train to Euston later that night.

'I can't, sorry, I can't leave me nan on her own.'

Which was bollocks of course. We were going out on the lash, and I was more worried about missing out on that.

And all the time in me head I still wanted this idea of me as a pro, as a footballer. God knows how I thought it was going to happen, but for me that was still the idea. I just wasn't making the connection between the fantasy and the reality of these chances. Mates would call me daft, saying that I should be going to these clubs and giving it a go, but I would just brush them off and make a joke out of it.

'Shut up and get the round in.'

When I've told people since about not bothering to turn up here and there or turning down different chances, some have asked whether I was scared, scared of coming face to face with the dream and then realising I wasn't good enough. You couldn't get further from the truth. It's different now – if I had to go on trial somewhere now, then I'd be nervous as anything. But back then, when I did bother to go to places like Macclesfield or Preston I wasn't fazed by what was going on. No, I was too concerned with meself to worry 'what if?'; I'd go down there, take the football seriously, pull out the usual tricks and that was that. If they didn't want me – and want me for who I was – then so what? I'd had a game of footy somewhere a bit different and I could go and catch up with the lads later. That's not a fear of failure. Besides, in me own mind I'd convinced meself I could make it happen if I really wanted. That if I tried, I'd make it. And when I say make it, I didn't mean just playing league football – I meant the top.

Confidence? Arrogance? Both, probably. But at that time that's what I believed – rightly or wrongly. As far as I was concerned, if I wanted to knuckle down then it would all fall into place. It was just that, for the time being, I told meself, I was happy living life as I was – as I wanted. It was nothing deeper than that, I was just doing what I wanted.

Which wasn't a lot by then. I was living with me nan at that point. Me mum had met a man called Pat Williams – who she'd later marry – and they'd been together for four years. He was from Ireland, and so they wanted to go and live there – and take me with them. But at the age I was I didn't want to leave Liverpool and all me mates, and I knew I could visit any time.

I was 20 and in me nan's, although me cousin Tasha from next door more or less lived with us. She was quite a bit younger, still a kid, but she was like a sister and we'd always be messing or fighting. I wouldn't do a lot during the days, probably sleeping more than anything after the previous night. And if I wasn't out I'd stay up watching telly and chatting with me mate Mark Smith from round the corner.

I wasn't signing on, I never did, but I wasn't having to pay me nan any lodgings or stump up for any bills. I had me football money and that was sound, enough for me to save up for the big nights at the weekend. That was the focal point of me week, never mind who we were playing on Saturday. Football was a laugh – Friday, Saturday, Sunday nights were serious stuff.

Fridays especially. The Cokie had been renamed the Venue and they'd introduced one of those all-you-can-drink nights – pay £10 on the door and all the drink free when you got in.

I loved the whole scene – the music, the smart clothes – and I'd be the first out of the lads to try new fashions, spending me footy money on Ralph Lauren shirts and never afraid to put on the mad colours that were popular around then – the bright pinks and oranges. When we'd finish at the club, it was back to some lad's place or some girl's flat by ours for a party afterwards – real all-nighter stuff.

I remember once me uncle Tony letting on that he'd been asked to be a watchman for the Eagle because of the problems they'd have overnight with people on the rob. He liked a drink himself so he told me to come back after me night out and join him. So I did – knocking on the door with about eight others.

'Come on, Tone, it's all right,' I said after he asked what I was playing at bringing all those others with me. And we stayed until the cleaners came to kick us out.

There would always be somewhere to go, and most weeks I'd be opening me nan's front door at eight in the morning with just enough time to get me trackie on before I'd be picked up for an away game. Then, straight after, I'd meet up with me mates in the Farmers in Page Moss and start all over again with lads like Joey Shacklock, a real character who lived for the weekend too, being the life and soul of the party and buying everyone drinks even though he'd spend all his money in those two days to make sure everyone could enjoy themselves.

I wasn't working nine-to-five, but I was still living for the weekend. And I reckon there's not many 20-year-old lads who don't – especially when there'd be girls involved. I'd always enjoyed being around girls and just found it dead easy to talk to them. Just as I would find it easier than other lads to keep a ball up on me knee or pull off different skills, I seemed to find it a lot easier to go up to girls and have a laugh.

It started when I was young, back when I used to hang around with the older lads on Ashbury, girls the same age as them always saying how cute I was – a great early boost for the confidence. I remember going to the senior school disco when I was still in juniors once, the lads reminding me which class to say I was in or which teacher I had for maths if anyone asked. I went in with two of the lads – John Regan from next door and Dean Cullen from another part of Ashbury – and before we knew it I was in with Nicola Barton, the girl everyone fancied in their year, having a slowy on the last dance. Not a bad start. I actually ended up going out with Nicola's sister, Lindsay, when I got to secondary, but I didn't do girlfriends. Girls, yes, loads – just not girlfriends.

At least not until I was 18, when I went out with a girl called Leanne Simpson. She was lovely, but even though she came from a very good amateur boxing family – her brother Gary won the Golden Gloves once – I still didn't treat her right.

Leanne still keeps in touch with me nan and our Tasha, but back then I wasn't any good for her, going with other girls behind her back and not even trying to hide it. She was younger than me, so she didn't come out with us, and when I was out I just loved the attention from other girls. It was that centre-of-attention thing again and probably something to do with me growing up without a dad, needing to have someone make a fuss out of me all the time. Even playing football at the youth club, I'd be desperate to do well in the games because it was winner stays on and the girls would all be watching in the gallery above the pitch. With them up there to impress I wanted to show off – perhaps that's where the whole showboating thing started.

I tried to use football to impress, but I didn't have to rely on it because I didn't have any worries trying to chat a girl up – and it wasn't long before I was getting more than just a slow dance. Like earlier, when me mum would go out for a night I'd be telling her to make sure she enjoyed herself and not to rush back because I had half an eye on the babysitter. I'd be full of confidence in the nightclubs, and by the time I was playing non-league it was half the reason I went out.

It wasn't just the sex but the laughs you had getting it. I remember once me and Tony Blythe went back with two older girls to their place, dancing around the front room to Tom Jones. I was trying me best not to piss meself laughing as Tom belted out of the stereo and I expected Tony to be the same so I tried to catch his eye – only to see him in full swing, looking deep into this lady's eyes and singing every word.

I wasn't afraid to use the 'I play for Liverpool' line if I needed – although I wouldn't always give me real name. Normally I'd say I was Lee Jones, a young striker doing well for Liverpool's ressies at the time – plus having the same first name was handy to stop me mates slipping up if they forgot I was blagging. One night I went back to this older woman's place – she might've been around 28, but it was old to us at the time – and as far as she knew she had brought Lee Jones home. Before we knew it, she'd got her son out of bed, saying, 'Come and have a look who's downstairs, love.'

He came into the front room.

'There you are, lad, who's that?'

'I dunno,' he said, looking a bit confused.

'It's Lee Jones, he plays for Liverpool,' she said as I started to get worried, thinking I was going to get blown up.

'All right, lad, how are you?' I said, trying to look confident.

He turned back to his mum. 'He doesn't look like Lee Jones.'

'Nah, mate,' I said. 'I've just had me haircut last week.'

Somehow I got away with it, and I couldn't resist telling Lee when I first met him a few years later at Wrexham.

'Funny you should say that,' he told me, explaining how he'd been sent a letter to the club from some woman he'd never met saying how she'd had a great night, thanking him for saying hello to her boy and that they'd have to do it again. He saw the funny side.

Back then there would be a tale for the lads after most nights – and it carried on until I met Hayley. The place to go in Liverpool on a night out was a club called the 051 – named after the old dialling code for Merseyside. It was a huge place, but I knew one of the fellas on the door to give me and the lads wristbands for the VIP area. There weren't any actual VIPs in there, but there was this gorgeous-looking blonde. We ended up talking all night and then agreed to go out the following day. Now, Huyton Labour club wasn't the smoothest of places to take a girl for a first date, but me dad was on the door and we always went there on a Sunday because they had karaoke on and you'd be guaranteed a good night with everyone up singing and dancing at the end. Anyway, it must have worked because we started seeing each other properly, and it didn't take the lads long to realise it was serious when I started to bring her out with us.

But while I wasn't chasing skirt, I was still out in a big way. I'd grown up a bit when it came to girls, but I was wild as ever otherwise.

Chorley had a few ex-pros in the side, lads like Neil Sang – who's now me agent – who'd been at Everton and Torquay, and Mark Wright (not that one) who used to play for Huddersfield, and all they could do was laugh at what I was getting up to. A few of the older lads used to call me Georgie Best. I saw it as a compliment but you couldn't ask for more of a back-handed one.

Drinking wasn't the problem, it was just the going out. And even then, I couldn't see it as a problem or an issue – I just enjoyed nights out. Football was something I did for a laugh – whether I was getting paid or not – and it wasn't going to stop me going out with me mates. I didn't love football in the way I did as a kid. I'd stopped supporting Liverpool a while back, and I'd got to a point where I wouldn't even watch a game in the pub. I still loved playing, but even then there were times when I wouldn't turn up for games or for training sessions if it clashed with plans to go out, just making up whatever excuse without a hint of embarrassment or shame.

But I was still doing the business when I was there. I'm not going to say it wasn't affecting me because it must have done, but no one was looking at me performances and saying, 'Hang on, he looks like he's been on the booze all night,' because I was still standing out. I was still scoring goals – and good goals too. I remember one against Witton where I'd gone past three or four men, opening up some space on the edge of the area and looped it into the top corner. I didn't do tap-ins.

There was still all the talk of scouts from different clubs at games. Arsenal and Wimbledon cropped up once or twice. I don't know if there was any real interest in me or what, but there was one game we played against Manchester United's reserves – basically a youth side – where I overheard one of their coaches in the tunnel asking 'Is Trundle playing?'

What a boost. I wasn't thinking that I was suddenly going to get signed up by United, but the fact someone at a club like that knew me name was a sign for me that I was going along just fine.

But of course the drinking was affecting me, just as it would anyone, no matter their age or ability. I wasn't throwing up or suffering with hangovers, but if I was impressing while playing without any kip or after ten pints the night before then what could I have done if I'd stayed in? How much sooner would I have moved up the divisions if I'd just eased off on a Friday?

Still, I was enjoying life at Chorley under Dave. He'd backed my way of playing and looked after me. When I had been on trial at Deepdale, he'd given permission for me to miss a big cup game for Chorley because I was supposed to be playing for Preston's firsts in a Lancashire Cup game against Blackpool. Needless to say he was fuming when I was kept on the bench – as was I.

So when he went it wasn't the same for me at the club. The chairman, Trevor Hemmings, had put a lot of money in – he was the owner of Pontins Holidays – and some of the lads were on as much as £400 to try and make sure we got out of the division. When it was clear that was not going to happen, after we went through a bad patch, Dave was out. One of the older pros, Steve Doyle, came in as caretaker before Brian Griffiths took over. Both had tried to get into me, having a go at me to work harder or for taking the piss by not turning up, which I was, but then I was even more likely not to turn up if someone was having a go at me for it.

Brian Griffiths tried his best to sort me out, arranging to meet me at the Jolly Miller pub, not far from Anfield, and trying to get into me head. He wanted to find out what motivated me, why I was wasting this talent I had. To be fair to him, he was trying to help me, but I didn't want to know and we eventually fell out.

With Dave gone and all that going on I'd had enough of Chorley, and although I was going to have to wait a little for me big break, I knew I could at least play higher up the non-league system. I told the local press that was it, that I wouldn't play for Chorley again, and even though they threatened to hold my registration I couldn't have cared less. They were trying to tell me I wouldn't have been able to get a move if I wasn't playing football, but I knew they were just after a bigger fee for me. I was stubborn, with nothing to lose, so in the end I had my way and Brian Kettle, a Scouser, took a punt on me. He paid Chorley £8,000, and I signed for Stalybridge Celtic in time for the 1997 season.

I enjoyed it at Stalybridge – and not just because I'd stepped up another level and into Conference football. Brian was happy to let me carry on with the things on the pitch that had got me noticed, and he put me up front with a lad called Tony Sullivan. Sully was another Ashbury lad, the two of us in attack together. We hit it off, being from the same background, and we used to get a lift together from Huyton over into Cheshire. A fella named Ronnie Golborne used to take us in, a sound lad who I'd met when I'd been on trial at Liverpool. He was great to me and the free lift was brilliant, but the only problem was Ronnie suffered with a form of Tourette's, although we weren't to know that at the time. It wasn't something I'd come across before, so when you were in the car and he'd have an episode it was quite something. He'd go into a kind of trance, muttering and repeating 'I don't wanna crash, I don't wanna crash' before turning around and saying 'All right, lad, where's you going out tonight, then?' without a second's breath. It didn't exactly fill you with confidence when he came to pick you up, but it was a free lift. I'm just thankful I was off injured when he did crash one night – Ronnie got knocked out and Sully remembered the window going through completely. If I'd been in the back, it could've been worse.

Still, life was good for me there, even if the results weren't so great. Brian Kettle went in the December and they then brought in Mel Sterland and Imre Varadi as manager and assistant, the ex-Sheffield Wednesday and Leeds players.

A lot of people I'd played under had good experience in the game – Dave Sutton had played for Plymouth and Bolton and then managed Rochdale; Brian Kettle had played for Liverpool as a defender, although he was better known for playing a record number of games for their reserves – but these two were a bit more high profile. They'd only left Leeds a few years earlier where they'd won the title, so I had a lot of respect for them and what they had to say.

And they didn't take long saying it. After my first game for them, they called me into the office at Bower Fold and Sterland said, 'Listen, Lee, what do you want to do with yourself? Are you happy playing non-league or do you want to make a go of it as a professional? Because with the ability you've got you shouldn't be playing in these leagues – you've just got to apply yourself in the right way if you want it.'

My replies were right, the words were right – 'Yeah, I want it' – but my actions were the opposite. All it had done was send me on an ego trip having these ex-pros tell me I could make it.

I didn't have the greatest of records at Stalybridge – although I managed ten goals – and the side were relegated out of the Conference that season, but I was still catching the eye. I'd still find it easy to beat a man or show a bit of skill to stand out, and when I managed 15 goals by Christmas the following season, it was enough for Southport to pay £16,000 for me to go back to the Conference. That was a huge fee, double what Stalybridge had paid for me, and the Stalybridge fans weren't happy that I'd gone. I was, although it didn't take long for it all to go sour.

Initially it was great, the buzz of another new club, another new set of fans. We're not talking thousands, but I'd gone from playing fields to a proper stadium in the last few years, dressing-rooms rather than changing in me own house or on the side of the pitch. In some of the non-league grounds, from Burscough up, there was only enough room to get a few players in at a time, but these grounds were like Wembley to me. I remember going to Boston's York Street ground and getting so pumped for the game because they had a good-sized stand on one side and were expecting a crowd of more than 1,000. And although there were only one or two, there were autographs being asked for – and I thrived on all that. I felt like a footballer even though I was still just pretending to be one.

I mean, what footballer doesn't turn up for pre-season?

I didn't – and all because the club weren't prepared to pay me through the summer. If they weren't prepared to do that, I thought, I wasn't prepared to spend me own money travelling to Southport. Yet I was happy enough to turn up on the first day of the season with me bag and me boots, expecting to play. The manager, Paul Futcher, exploded when I walked into the dressing-room, wanting to know where the hell I had been.

'I'm here now aren't I?'

I don't know what wound him up more – the answer, or me shrugging me shoulders as if it were no big deal. I didn't have a leg to stand on, but I was happy to argue back. He was quick to tell me I'd never play for his club again, and I was just as quick to tell him to pay up the rest of my two-and-a-half year contract and I'd go.

This club had paid good money for me, but I couldn't see that as a responsibility on me shoulders to be professional. I wasn't a professional; I wasn't getting paid like one, so I wasn't going to make sacrifices like one. That was me logic, anyway.

I didn't think I owed it to them to work hard just because they'd paid out for me. It was all about me. I was getting more money, a new club to play for, and that's where me concerns ended. But it wasn't about me being arrogant and thinking they couldn't afford to do without me, that I could come and go as I pleased and fuck everyone else. I knew the consequences – I just couldn't have cared less about them. It was pure selfishness.

The thing is, I'd started well at Southport too, getting six goals in twenty-odd games in the league. I'd even played in goal once when our keeper got sent off against Rushden & Diamonds. I'd always fancied meself as a keeper when I was younger, and I'd played in goal for the Eagle when we'd been short, although I let in a fair few that night.

But although I got back in under Futcher, I wasn't doing meself any favours. I'd miss games at the drop of a hat. Me and Hayley went over to Ireland to see me mum for one New Year's Eve and I missed a few games in the process. As I was getting closer to our Frankie, me cousin, I'd go to Everton games with him rather than turn up for Southport. He was a mad Evertonian and he'd have a box or sponsor a game now and then, so I'd have a meal and a drink with mates up at Goodison rather than play meself.

We had training twice a week – on a Tuesday and a Thursday – but I'd regularly miss the second session because I'd rather have a kickaround at the youth club. I was playing football almost every night – youth club was on a Monday and a Thursday and then five-a-side at a place called Strikers in Kirby on a Wednesday with a lad called Vinny Machen, a taxi driver who used to run me all over the place for footy for free.

I'd even go back to me old secondary school for a game. I'd go in and see Mr Mellon, the PE teacher who I looked up to for supporting me in the only thing I'd ever been good at in school, asking if it was all right to join in with the class and help out. Any excuse to be playing with a ball.

I never minded training in non-league – it was usually ball-work so I was always lively – but I'd find an excuse not to go if I fancied a game somewhere else. I didn't drive – I didn't pass me test till I was 25 – so I'd have easy get-outs of not being able to get a lift, that the bus hadn't turned up, whatever I could come up with. They saw right through me anyway.

And I wasn't getting away with it when Mark Wright came in halfway through my second season. Yes, that one.

I'd only managed three sub appearances under him before things came to a head at training one night. We were in the bottom few places in the table when he took over, and he obviously wanted to make a go of the job. It was his first as manager and he'd only been out of the game a couple of years since leaving Liverpool so he was keen to make an impression, but it had not been easy for him. He'd been used to all the best facilities, the best coaching, the right attitudes off the pitch about things like nutrition. Me, on the other hand, I'd still be eating what I wanted, when I wanted, and it was beginning to show with me weight. Not massively, but enough. It's not a great surprise with the booze and the diet I had. I didn't like veg, I'd always been fussy over what I ate, and if I was watching telly at two in the morning and I fancied a pizza, I'd put one in. Like others, Wright had seen the ability I had but was looking for a bit more effort from me. So when we did a weighing session and I came in at 14 stone he told me he wanted me to drop some pounds, do some training on me own, go running.

'I want to get the best out of you,' he said.

'Yeah, OK, sound.'

When we got weighed a couple of weeks later I'd put half a stone on. We started the session, but it didn't last long before his frustration came flooding out.

'We try to get through to you to help you the best we can and some of you are just not taking any notice. Like you, Lee. . .' And he detailed his issues with me in front of the whole squad. I didn't like that. He'd come at me in front of others and embarrassed me. I was taught to fight back in those situations, coming from where I'm from, so I had a go back. I wanted to go for him.

'You're taking the piss,' he told me, spelling out exactly what he thought of me. He was right. Still, that didn't stop me.

'You prick, who do you think you're talking to?'

Who're you talking to? Someone who's played for England in the World

Cup, who lifted the FA Cup for Liverpool and I'm asking who he thinks he's talking to? I don't think even he could believe it.

I was blind to the fact he was actually trying to help me; all I thought was that he was attacking me. I'd never been told what to do, I'd had no boundaries, no rules growing up, and as far as I was concerned some fella I didn't know was questioning me and my life. So I did what I'd done all me life and had a go back – in the middle of the AstroTurf, under the floodlights in front of the entire squad.

He phoned up the next day to try and sort things out, but I'd made up me mind and I told him I wasn't going to play for him.

'Well, I'll hold your registration and you'll rot here,' he said. We blew up again, with him at one point telling me to have the guts to say some of these things to his face. He would have fucking killed me, but our Frankie was keen for us to go down to meet him and get it sorted one way or another. Thankfully, before the situation got any worse, I think Wright realised that he wasn't going to get through to this kid, whatever he said, and that he was wasting his time.

'If that's what you want, you can move if we get the right money.'

I went sooner than that, dropping down a division to play for Bamber Bridge on loan. Without a care in the world too. Looking back, there was every likelihood I'd blown my chance in the Conference with that one row. I hadn't set the world alight at Southport, and it could have easily all come to an end before anything had begun. The offers of trials had dried up, and there didn't seem to be too much of a way out at this point. But I didn't care. Even if he did leave me to rot and I only played Sunday League with me mates, it wouldn't have bothered me. I wanted to be a footballer, but I didn't see it as my career, I didn't see it as me living. It was a game, and as much as I enjoyed it, I enjoyed it the same on a park field as I did in the Conference.

I was still playing on a Sunday anyway, turning out for our Frankie's side, The Quiet Man, in Mosscroft and loving that more than the hassle of playing for Southport.

And Frankie had even sorted me out with a few shifts at a sports shop he owned in Page Moss, so I didn't even need the money from footy that much any more.

But then something changed. Everything changed. I changed.

CHAPTER FIVE

October

THEY SAY NEVER go back – but who wouldn't want to come back here?

'It's stunning, isn't it?'

It's not the first time Charlotte has seen Swansea Bay sweeping across to the Mumbles, but it's the first time she's seen it from inside our new place. It's a flat in the Marina, not far from the place I had when I first came to Swansea, and the huge lounge window frames the Bay beautifully. What a picture to wake up to.

We'd seen a few flats around the place, but you just couldn't top this view. It's perfect. It might only be home for a couple of months, but it definitely feels like home right now.

Charlotte can see that. It's difficult for any player to feel settled when they're only on loan somewhere, but I'm probably like a different person to her right now. I'm settled in meself.

She's come away with me before, when I went to Leeds for a few months not long after we started going out. We'd been serious right from the off and had gone through a lot together since, especially with all that went on at Bristol. I'd never take what was happening out on her, but everyone brings their work home with them from time to time, everyone lets it get to them. She could see that then, she can see a happier me now, and she can see this is somewhere where I want to be. I'm feeling more like me old self, getting involved in the city, the hospital visits, the charity dos, the special guest stuff. I never did any of that at Bristol because it never felt like it was my place to. I don't know why – I did well enough to start off there and had a good enough relationship with the fans too. I guess I just never felt comfortable enough. So when the chances on the field dried up, is there any surprise I wanted away? Is there any surprise I wanted to come back here?

But then, it's not gone exactly how I planned here, how I dreamed it even. There's been just the one start, against Preston – a club I can't seem to keep out of me footballing life – but nothing happened for me, or the rest of the side, that afternoon. And when you're a team that plays only one up front, there's not a lot of room for error – just a place on the bench.

But at least there's been the goals, the ones I need to make sure this place stays home. Important ones too. We were twentieth when Sheffield United came to the Liberty a few weeks ago, the press on our backs and goals in short supply.

I still had to wait for the call from the bench, and when it came it was really flat as I ran onto the field, with everyone rightly more concerned about Ferrie Bodde, who looked like he'd damaged his knee ligaments on his comeback from the very same problem. We were already missing players through injury, so Paulo's instructions had to be to fill in in midfield, to play the link-man to Gorka Pintado up front. It was a lot deeper than I'm used to, but I've never been afraid to go looking for the ball, to go short and drag a marker away. It wasn't the chance I wanted, but it was a chance, and I was determined to make the most of it.

The touch wasn't always there. I was still rusty, which is always going to happen when you've been used to a few minutes here and there for so long.

But then came the one opportunity I needed to show what I could do. Nick Montgomery was too close, too tight to me, and when the pass came from Jordi Lopez I knew I had him. A turn, a trip, a penalty.

Even before I got to me feet I knew I'd scored. I grabbed the ball and headed to the spot, almost daring someone to take it off me. Gorka rushed forward looking like he wanted an argument, but I got a good luck kiss from the six-foot Spaniard instead. I think he wanted to put me at ease, but there were no nerves. When I've missed penalties in the past I've always felt a danger of it happening before I've even begun me run-up, something in me head telling me it's not right.

There was only one thought running through me head here.

'Here's me first goal, here's me first goal.'

In a few seconds, I knew that roar was going to be for me, the one I'd missed so much. The moment I'd played over and over in me head when I wanted a way out, when I wanted to come back, it was coming.

And there it was –14,000 people that could have been 40,000 for all I knew or cared, all screaming for me. I was home.

Of course, in me dreams me first goal was when I'd beat three men and curled one in from the edge of the area, but putting it in the bottom corner from twelve yards was fine by me. For now.

It hadn't been a pretty game; you could feel the tension from the fans on the pitch, but even with two men sent off we got the win, the first home win of the season, and all of a sudden things were looking up.

And then there was another, against Queens Park Rangers, from open play too, which made it sweeter. It still wasn't the most spectacular, but it's about getting up-and-running first for me now, getting the belief back. And every score helps, every time me name is read out over the Tannoy is another step closer to it – if I'm given the chance. The QPR one might have come from the bench too, but if I can prove my worth as an impact player when we need to press on, so be it.

This time it was a cross from Nathan Dyer that left me with only the keeper to beat. I had time, almost too much time, and the thoughts started.

'Keep it low, just enough power . . .'

I side-footed the cross and the ball rolled home. It seems simple, but it's a lot easier when it's instinctive. You just do it without thinking because it feels right.

And all this feels right, standing with Charlotte looking out over the Bay with the boxes and bags to be unpacked behind us.

She seems happy too. Swansea is a lovely city to live in and it's still close enough for her to pop home to Weston in Somerset when she needs to. It's a new place for us to explore as a couple, things and places I've been wanting to show her for a long time.

I'm seeing them in a different way now; I'm different from the lad who left here. A 100 per cent different, and although I might have been 30 when I joined Bristol, I've still grown up since then. It's not about the nights out any more – I went out for a meal the night of the Sheffield United goal – it's about keeping hold of this view.

I'll come home and watch a game on the telly now like I haven't done since I was a kid – taking it in, learning even now. The diet, the fitness, the drinking, it's all changed massively because the realisation gets to everyone in the end – if you want to stay where you are, whether playing or coaching or whatever, then you have to change. But it's not a chore, not when you look out and see what the rewards are; it's enjoyment, it's what I do it all for.

From not wanting to get up in the morning to not wanting the days to end, I'm enjoying life again. Of course I still have frustrations, frustrations because I'm not involved as much as I'd like, frustrated that I know it won't be long before I'm worrying about whether I'm going to be kept on past Christmas and that all this will be taken away from us before we know it. Right now, I couldn't think of anything worse. But I'm not kicking up a fuss – not yet anyway – because I'm just glad to be back, glad to be able to watch the sun set from where me and Charlotte sit.

But just give me a chance. I've always taken them.

CHAPTER SIX

Growing Up, Moving Up

'I'VE GOT SOMETHING to tell you.'

Hayley would stay over with me at me nan's almost every night. We were just like any young couple – she'd come over after finishing work at the hairdressers in town and we'd go out, go to the pictures, watch a video, whatever. Me nan never minded, she liked a full house anyway, and it suited us both fine. One night Hayley came into the little front bedroom and, looking right at me, told me I was going to be a dad.

Now, different people take being told they're going to be a parent in different ways at different parts of their life, but for me there was only genuine excitement. And for Hayley too.

It wasn't as if we'd only been going out five minutes; we'd been together a few years and we loved each other. I was 23 at the time, so I wasn't too young to think about kids, and it wasn't getting in the way of my career – I didn't have one. There was just no fear about the whole thing. I hadn't been scared about anything before, so I guess I wasn't going to start over something that I could only feel good about, feel excited about.

It did mean I had to start thinking about getting me own place, and it wasn't long before I'd left Ashbury for a nice little brand new two-bed in Knotty Ash, just outside Page Moss, ready for when the baby came. With it, though, came bills to pay – something new for me to get me head around. Our Frankie helped me out as much as he could when I needed a bit of extra cash to go with me money from footy. Preston Sports was the name of his shop, and I would turn up when he needed a hand, getting the different trainers for the customers from out the back or just helping out when it got busy in there. But, to be honest, I would normally just hang around talking, and he was pretty much paying me for nothing. It didn't stop him giving me a few hours with another company he had, a sign company – you know, the ones in a box with a light behind them. From wanting me own name in lights to putting up someone else's.

I was still contracted to Southport at the time, so me football career wasn't going anywhere fast – but none of that mattered on 7 May 2000. I was the first to hold Brooke – it had been a long labour so Hayley was still quite out of it – and all I could do was stare, just watch her as she breathed. I didn't think I'd be emotional, I'm not sure if anyone does, but it just comes from nowhere – and the more I looked and looked at my baby girl the more I cried. We both brought her home soon after and it really didn't take long for it all to sink in, what now lay in front of us. When you're in the hospital, there's nurses to lean on, doctors on call, people to reassure that what you're doing is right, pointing you in the right direction. Back in Knotty Ash, there was just me, Hayley and Brooke and we had to figure it out, we had to sort it. I'm not saying I suddenly changed the way I was thinking there and then, but there was a growing realisation that it wasn't just about me any more, like it had been for all of me life. I could get by the way I was just fine, but Brooke needed someone to provide for her and that someone had to be me. The selfishness had to stop because I'd found someone more important than me.

I needed to earn more, to provide more, and the only way I'd known up to that point was football. I'd earned OK money out of it so far, so what could I do if I put the effort in? I might not enjoy it, but it was a better career than anything else I could think of. I can remember the conversation clear as day as me and Phil Dears, me best mate, walked back from the Doms.

'That's it, Philly, I'm going to give it a go. I'm going to give it two years and see what I can make of it. I owe it to meself and to Brooke.'

Philly admitted I'd be stupid if I didn't. But then, most of me mates had been saying it for a while – I just hadn't wanted to listen. It didn't just dawn on me out of nowhere that I still had a chance of doing something with me career. It had always been there. It was just this time I couldn't ignore it.

And even then, it wasn't a case of not being able to forgive meself if I didn't start taking these opportunities seriously – I just knew Brooke being here meant I didn't have any other choice but to grow up and get on with it.

It only started off with little changes, a bit of training in the day, going off on a little run around the estate, things I should have been doing anyway. But it was amazing how quickly that extra bit of fitness showed in just helping me get around the pitch more, getting involved in games more.

I was still on loan at Bamber Bridge when we happened to play against Colwyn Bay – one of the Welsh clubs playing in the English system – and Pete Parry was one of those in the crowd that saw me score four in a 5–1 win. Brian Kettle, me old manager at Stalybridge, was now at Rhyl in the Welsh Premier and had told Pete – the club director – to go and have a look at me. Not long after, it was all agreed – I'd join Rhyl for the new season. It was a fresh start for me in a new league, and with Pete looking after me during the summer I was in a different frame of mind than before. There were new grounds to play at, the chance to play in Europe and the Champions League if we did well – which is a pull for any player – plus I was actually getting paid more there than in the Conference.

But the idea was to keep moving, to show that I could move up by getting fit and giving meself a chance rather than waiting for others to hand it to me. I eased off on the nights out and, although I didn't suddenly start enjoying running, I had found a motivation. More than anything, because it wasn't about me, I couldn't stop and give up halfway through a session because I didn't fancy it. Someone else was involved, so I had to keep going and push past the pain.

The good thing was, though, Rhyl had given me the green-light to go out and play as I'd wanted. Brian obviously knew me from Stalybridge so knew what I was capable of and wanted to encourage it, but Mickey Thomas was also involved as a director of football and that was a big boost for me. Mickey was a great player, someone I'd watched as a kid, and his goal for Wrexham to knock Arsenal out of the FA Cup had been something special. He was a flair player, and that was a sway for me joining Rhyl in the first place – I thought that if he was involved with the club that would mean they would let me be me on the pitch.

I wasn't wrong. We were playing a pre-season game, Mickey had turned up a bit late and the game was already going. Soon enough I could hear him shouting from the side of the pitch, 'C'mon Lee, show us a few of these tricks then.'

That was the type of encouragement I needed, the type of approval I was after – he'd rather see a bit of skill and be entertained than worry about winning some pre-season friendly. He was a man after me own heart and it helped me open up as a player, made me happier to try more things. He wasn't there all the time, but when he was he made sure we'd have a chat about the game and just have a laugh together. But he'd be the same with everyone – such a bubbly character who could make anyone feel welcome, special.

And it was showing. The extra fitness was only adding to me confidence, because I could carry on with the type of game I wanted to play for longer, able to make that extra run to get on the end of a ball. And the goals came because of it. It started off with two against Manchester City reserves in pre-season, and they just kept coming. I still wasn't the tap-in type – I never have been. In fact, my record in the non-leagues suffered because I'd try something too over-the-top, like going back to beat a man after already going round him once. I'd cut that out by now, but me goals were still a bit different, because I'd always try something different. I think it's because I'd enjoyed watching those type of goals more growing up that I'd deliberately get meself into a position to score a similar type. I wouldn't run across the six-yard box like Ian Rush or Gary Lineker, I'd pull meself out of the close-range area to work the space better. It wasn't about making it harder, it was about making it better.

I'd take any goal then, just as I would now, but look at how Matt Le Tissier used to play – he'd never slide in at the near post because he didn't have to; he was able to put it in from where he liked, and he still scored more than 150 goals at the highest level. I don't know whether it's also to do with neither of us liking too much running in a game and wanting the ball to our feet more, but it worked for us. Gazza was another one – someone who would look for the spectacular just because he could, because he wanted to. I remember watching a video on him when I was in school called *The Real Me* that showed him growing up, talking to family and other people who knew him as a kid about what he was like, and it struck a chord. He played on the pitch the same way he played on the schoolground, the same way he played on the street. He was still a winner, he still wanted every game as badly as the last – but he never took it too seriously, always messing around having a joke. Even now I see meself as a similar character, wanting to make people laugh, being loud, wanting to entertain and draw the attention, and I take that onto the football field with me. That's half of the reason behind the tricks. It's not just because I can pull them off, but because I want to, because it adds something to the game. In fact, it was at Rhyl I first pulled off the shoulder roll in a game. It was only the second game of the season, and we were playing a side called Rhayader. I was near the touchline when the ball came over in the air and I managed to catch the ball on me neck and let it roll down to me left foot as I turned, dummying past a defender before running through on goal.

There weren't any Sky cameras at Belle Vue to capture moments like that, but there was Welsh telly that used to screen highlights of every game and show all the goals after the results came in on a Saturday. You could pick it up in Liverpool if your aerial was right, so I used to get me nan to tape it every week. I couldn't understand a word, but I could see me name and me goals, and that's all I wanted. I felt like I was getting somewhere, I had something to work towards.

And it was showing with me record in front of goal. There was a couple that stood out – scoring a long-ranger in the derby against Bangor and then scoring three and setting up three in a 6–1 win at Port Talbot. Not long after Christmas, I'd managed 15 goals in 17 starts.

But while everything was going right for me in one sense, it was falling apart between me and Hayley at home. We'd been arguing for some time, pretty much all the way through the pregnancy and then carrying on well after. There always seemed to be tension around the place, and not just because of the baby and all that went with caring for a newborn. Before it had been easy to blame things on the hormones, like when she'd accuse me of going off with other girls. I remember once being picked up by one of the lads to go and play five-a-side, coming back sweating in me footy kit an hour later and Hayley screaming that I'd been with someone else. I probably didn't help matters by still going out with the lads at a time she was feeling insecure about herself, but it wasn't all down to me.

And after Brooke came it was just a case of us growing apart – as much as we didn't want to. We'd had enough of each other, and we couldn't go on living together much longer.

So we didn't. We agreed to split and Hayley moved back into her mum's with Brooke. It killed me not being able to be around the baby every day – especially since I grew up without me dad. Growing up, I'd always said that I'd never leave me kid, that I'd always be with the mum no matter how bad it got. But it's not until you're actually in the situation that you realise it's just not right. If we'd tried to stay together it would have affected Brooke even worse than it has, because you just can't live like that.

It was tough, especially that first night when everything that had happened sank in, but Brooke was still my drive. Even now I dread to think what would have happened to me if she hadn't come along. If she hadn't been born, I don't know where I'd be now. It was only when she came that I had a reason to really go for it in football. I probably would have been sitting in a pub telling anyone who'd listen how I could have made it. And what makes that stranger than anything is that when I went out I used to hate those times when people would say, ''Ey, him over there, he was a good player, he could have played League football, he could have gone to the top.' I would just think that he couldn't have been a good player, otherwise he would have gone to the top. I hated people who made excuses as to why they never made it. I couldn't see that for so long I was the same.

But me chance to make sure I wouldn't be sitting in the pub was coming – not that I knew it at the time. When Wrexham came to Belle Vue for a friendly in January, I just saw it as a game where I might be able to impress a few people. I hadn't built it up in me mind to be the biggest game of me life, to change everything, but it was.

What I didn't know was that Brian Flynn, the Wrexham manager, had wanted to take me on trial but, in return, Rhyl wanted this match to get a few quid through the door. Walking out onto the pitch I still thought it was a great opportunity for me, even if I didn't realise it was already set up to be exactly that. All that was in me head was that I was up against pros with people watching, that I could prove a few things, that I was as good as them. How it would have affected me if I'd known Flynny's eyes were already on me, I don't know. Whether it would have made me nervous, I'm not sure.

But I did know this was an opening for me, and 'don't blow it, don't blow it' was running through me mind as we went out.

I didn't. The first was from way out when I'd worked some space for meself and chipped the keeper. I'd taken someone on outside the box and put it in the bottom corner for the second, and the third came when I'd turned my marker twice inside the area and slotted it home. All inside 20 minutes.

The game finished 4–1, and I was already thinking, 'I've given meself a chance here' before Joey Jones caught me as I was walking off the pitch.

'Great finishes, lad.'

He didn't give away a lot, but Joey was a coach under Brian at Wrexham – and a Liverpool legend – and I knew something could be on from that moment.

But the first call wasn't from Wrexham, it was from Tranmere. Stan Boardman, the comedian, of all people, had been in the stands watching, and he'd got on the phone to John Aldridge, the Tranmere manager, telling him he should take a look at me. Still, when Wrexham got in touch and asked me to go in on the Monday, I knew where I wanted to go. It wasn't just about the fact they had shown an interest in me first by arranging the game but having played against them they would have known me – they'd seen me first-hand and knew exactly what I could do. Plus, they knew the type of player I was and wouldn't have been expecting anything different when I turned up on that first Monday. That was important because to me this wasn't a week's trial, this wasn't me cleaning boots and catching buses like it had been before. This was what I'd wanted. It was an opportunity served up for me, an invite to just go there and perform. If I'd made a different choice there and then, things could have worked out very differently – life could've taken a very different direction. One bad week's training and then who knows? Without really appreciating it I'd made a massive decision, and made it fairly easily.

But I knew I hadn't got there yet. Not this time. I'd made that mistake before and hadn't been bothered about it. This time even I realised this could be the last chance. By then I'd figured out that people in football talk, and the way I had acted in the past would have got around. Sometimes I've wondered if clubs have ever stopped coming in for me because of the way I was and the reputation I earned when I was in non-league. I don't know what the answer is; what I do know is that back then I was a massive gamble. It's a risk for any League manager to take on a player from non-league – I was an even bigger risk. I was too unpredictable and had never given a manager everything I had. Going to Wrexham was different – I'd woken up and knew any hopes of a career could rest on how I did there.

That was on me mind as I walked into the club's Colliers Park training ground on the Monday. But I also knew I deserved the chance. The week before, I'd played against these pros who were now getting changed alongside me – and scored a hat-trick too. I wasn't a no one, even though I hadn't had a sniff of League experience, and I sensed that little bit of respect which helped me come out of me shell from the start.

Darren Ferguson was a big help in that, making sure I was OK as I travelled in each day from Huyton. A lot of people immediately think of his dad, Sir Alex, when you mention his name, but he was a good player, a good midfielder in his own right and an important part of the good team Wrexham had at the time. There was Carlos Edwards, the Trinidad international who played in the 2006 World Cup and later signed for Sunderland and Ipswich, Brian Carey, Kevin Russell, Craig Faulconbridge – it was a good set-up. Training had gone well, and I was told to play for the reserves on the Tuesday against Blackpool at the Racecourse. Two goals later I'd done it, I knew I'd done it, and I waited for the call.

It came on the Wednesday. Neil Sang, me mate from Chorley, had become me agent. I remember thinking it was a huge deal when he signed me up before I was at Southport, sat in me nan's living room signing the contract. It was another thing to tell the lads about, bragging about having an agent, but Neil was good for me. He'd dropped out of the pro game and he knew he wasn't going to find a way back, but he was a good people-person, a good character I could trust, and the agent thing suited him down to the ground. And he was the one who told me I'd made it – a two-and-a-half-year deal. I was a professional footballer. Wrexham had agreed to pay Rhyl £45,000 up front with a few more add-ons, and I was on £500 a week. The funny thing was, I can remember being in non-league thinking if I could get me hands on £500 it would do me, it would be enough to get what I wanted, the clothes, the bills, the nights out – all nice and comfortable.

I signed the contract in Flynny's office at Colliers, not without asking straight away what day we got paid. I couldn't wait to get me hands on the money – not forgetting the £5,000 signing-on fee.

I was buzzing, on such a high, and I didn't want to come down. It was all happening so quickly – a non-leaguer on Sunday, a trialist on Monday, a reserve by Tuesday, a footballer on the Wednesday.

It wasn't slowing. On the Friday, I was named in the first-team squad to play Colchester. When Saturday came, I was on the bench.

I remember being at me nan's the night before, not thinking about going out on a Friday but about seeing that first proper shirt hung up for me and finding out what number I'd been given. In non-league you didn't get squad numbers, but I'd always try and use No. 10. I used to have it printed on the shirts I wore for kickarounds. I'd wear other players' names too, like Gazza's. Gascoigne was No. 8, what was Trundle going to be? When I was dreaming of making it, I used to think a real sign would be when you saw a kid with your name printed on their shirt. Walking through Liverpool, everywhere you went there was Owen or Fowler or whoever – what a feeling that must be, to know you've not only made it as a pro but really made it as a player. That's what I wanted.

I walked through the small players' entrance and turned to the left to the home dressing-room. Even this was all a thrill for me. I'd played at a League ground before when I was at Preston, but this was different because I belonged here, felt I had a right to lap it all up. It wasn't pretending any more, it was real.

I didn't get long, but I got long enough to make me debut – 17 February 2001, Wrexham v. Colchester United. In fact, there were only five or so minutes left when I got the nod, the fourth official taking ages to put the No. 28 up. It felt like forever, but all of a sudden it was happening, the moment I'd waited for, and yet it didn't feel any different from any other game I'd been involved in. Brian Carey, the captain, came over to wish me luck and tell me to do what I'd been doing in training and not be afraid. I wasn't. I just wanted to get on the ball and show what I could do. Not long in, I managed a nice bit of skill on the touchline near the Kop behind the goal, pretending to cross but dummying and going past the defender, having a shot and seeing it go out for a corner. The fans in the Kop all 'ooohed' and then cheered – and me skin just trembled. It was only a few thousand, but it was the kind of appreciation I'd been after. When it came, I couldn't stop smiling because of the adrenalin, the ecstasy. And that was just a good bit of skill, what was a goal going to be like?

The game didn't last long, but that moment just encouraged me to be meself even more and to make the most of the fans. After all, that's who you're there for as a footballer. We're both involved in the same game, so I'd always try and catch someone's eye; give them a smile or a laugh. I've always thought, 'They've come to be entertained, so entertain them, get them involved.' Gazza was brilliant at that, and I wanted to give the same kind of feeling to people watching me, just on a smaller level. It wasn't always a conscious thing during games but the showman in me coming out.

It was the perfect way for me to start, already one up and at home in front of our fans. I loved the Racecourse. It was easily the best ground I'd played in by that point, but then again, Colliers Park was better than most non-league grounds I'd been at.

I was in the squad again when we played Rotherham on the Tuesday night, and I remember walking out in our tracksuits onto the pitch at Milmoor. I was impressed and thinking 'Wow, this is a nice pitch' – just before I heard Fergie behind me saying, 'Fucking hell, look at the state of this pitch,' and everyone else saying, 'I know' and agreeing. For me, it was like Wembley compared with the bogs I'd been used to and, although I was agreeing with all me new teammates, all I could think of was how flat it was, how I couldn't wait to get out on it, how much easier it was going to be for me.

Another appearance came – a good half-hour this time – and then we went to Walsall on the Saturday. I was out on the pitch again, taking it all in, all these new grounds, new experiences, as Flynny came over.

'What you think then, Lee?' he asked.

'Oh, yeah, gaffer, nice pitch, nice ground.'

'Good. You're playing today.'

And with that he walked off. It didn't register with me at first, it had been such a throwaway comment that he couldn't have been talking about me getting a first start, making a full debut. I'd only been playing in the Welsh Premier a couple of weeks ago and now I was starting in a League One match?

I turned to Craig Faulconbridge and asked, 'Does he mean that?'

Craig nodded, but it wasn't until the team was written out on the board in the dressing-room that I believed it – and then the excitement took over. No nerves, just excitement.

It died a little when it didn't go to plan at first and we were two behind before we started getting into the game in the second half. There was about half an hour left when we won a free-kick near the halfway line. Fergie took it, Brian Carey headed it on, and as it fell my way I took it on me chest with me back to goal. Then I just did what came naturally – an overhead kick. It sounds strange when you say it, when it's in black and white that your first League goal is a bicycle kick, but when you're out there and in the moment you're not thinking about what you can or can't get away with. It's what I would have done on Ashbury, it's what I would have done down the Doms, it's what I would have done for the Eagle or the Quiet Man. The only other thing I could have done in that position was lay it off for someone else, but I'm a striker, and strikers score goals.

I didn't see the ball hit the net, I only heard the crowd – and it was a different roar from the first one I'd heard at the Racecourse. I knew instantly it was a goal, and I ran up to the away fans behind the goal, turned around and pointed to me name on the back of me shirt just to make sure they knew – to make sure everyone knew it was me.

Kevin Russell got the second with a long-range shot soon after and then, a few minutes from time, I'd taken on a defender, had me shot saved and played the rebound across to Craig Faulconbridge, who knocked it in. 3–2.

I couldn't have asked for a better day, even if I was trying to play it down in the dressing-room as everyone came to say their well dones. The texts started to come through – 'The first of many' was one of the ones I remember – before I spoke to Sangy.

'An overhead kick? Fucking hell, mate, only you,' he said laughing.

But that was the point – it was only me. If I'd gone from Ashbury straight into the YTS ranks somewhere I might have stopped meself, I might have been too nervous to try things like overhead kicks, too worried about taking a risk. But I hadn't had any coaches making me worry about risks – all I knew was how I'd played all me life and that had worked fine so far for me. I'd had me knocks, but they were me own fault because of the life I wanted to lead. I'd had to learn everything meself – through me own choice – but I'd done OK so far, so what was there to be fazed about? Why not just keep going, keep just being me?

I think Flynny felt the same. He was a great character. You could have got beat 3–0 but the next day he'd still be there with a big smile as if you'd won 5–0. He put everyone at ease, and he wanted me to be meself.

Thanks to Flynny, I was getting me first taste of coaching – he and Kevin Reeves were very hands on – but they weren't trying to turn me into a player I wasn't. Reevesy was great – such a fantastic striker in his own day – and under him I began to learn a lot about movement. One bit of advice I liked was how he explained that sometimes strikers moved too much, that it was better to hold the space, let the defender move off you and then make your run. That suited me down to the ground.

I'd never had that type of coaching, something that was trying to bring the best out of me ability rather than adapt it or alter it. They both trusted me and had seen what type of player I was. They didn't put any limits on me, they just let me play.

But only for Wrexham. In that first month, it wasn't long before Joey Jones grabbed me.

'You're doing well, Lee, but you can't play in the parks any more.'

I'd signed me contract, but I was still turning out for the Quiet Man on a Sunday and having a few drinks with the lads after. The drinks I could get away with; the football I couldn't.

'I'm not, Joey,' even though Lee Preston was doing a good job for them – I'd registered under me dad's surname. We'd gone into a different league and had to start out in the bottom division, and I'd already scored 86 goals in 19 games even if teams were starting to not turn up. Playing local leagues in Liverpool, I never thought anyone from the club was going to find out.

'You can't play, 'cos if you're injured you're fucked.'

Joey didn't have to say any more. As much as I was still up for a laugh and to enjoy meself, me mindset had changed. That first goal had started something, and I didn't want to fail now I'd begun to work for it. With the effort I was putting in, I'm not sure how I would have reacted if it had been taken away for whatever reason. So I'd stay behind after training for extra shooting sessions or whatever; I could sense this was happening for me.

And it was still happening so quickly. The following Tuesday came the first goal at the Racecourse in a game against Northampton, the third in a 3–0 win. I should have passed it really and as I ran through I remember seeing Kevin Russell out of the corner of me eye screaming for it, his hands in the air waving at me to pass it. I ignored him to go inside, and his hands dropped in frustration ready to give me a rollicking – before I put the ball into the bottom corner. I'd scored, and I was doing me share of setting people up for goals too, so I wasn't bothered about the stick – and Reevesy had the best answer when Kev told me to put a lottery ticket on for him that week.

'Tell them, Trunds, it's not about luck.'

No. It was about confidence – and I was full of it.

I came home from training the following Monday and I'd gone to see Frankie at his shop, and as we got chatting I was telling him about how we had to go to home games in a suit. I only had one suit meself, so I asked Frankie if I could borrow one of his. He fetched a beautiful grey Versace suit, probably worth about £700.

'I wouldn't mind keeping this,' I told him.

'Tell you what, if you score a hat-trick you can keep it.'

It was a deal. Frankie came to the game, just like he'd been there with me dad for me debut, and there were a few lads from the Quiet Man just behind the dugouts. Twice Oxford went ahead, but I pulled us back – the first a chip off the outside of the foot and then sliding one in after Carlos Edwards had volleyed across the box. They went 3–2 up, but a few minutes later I levelled again with another chip from long-range. As the ball went in, I immediately remembered what Frankie had said and ran straight towards where he was sat in the main stand. Already I could see by his face he didn't know whether to laugh or cry, but just to remind him I puffed out me chest and flicked the collar of me shirt, pretending to do up a tie. To be fair to Frankie, he was as good as his word and I had a cracking Versace suit to go with a first hat-trick ball.

Flynny was obviously pleased with how things were going, but he wouldn't say a lot apart from telling me to keep doing what I was doing. Which was probably the best thing he could say, because I wasn't thinking too much about what was happening – the only thing on me mind was how glad I was to be playing professional football. I wasn't thinking about opponents or what teams we were up against, only about meself and me own game.

And there wasn't any need to be thinking about anything else – if I'd messed up in a match then it didn't matter because no one was expecting anything from me. I was under no pressure to deliver from anyone but meself. It's only when you build your reputation, when you've done things season after season that it starts to sink in more about how difficult it is to keep up with that.

The start I'd had made sure I felt every part a pro, and the Wrexham lads knew it as well. They weren't questioning me, and I wasn't questioning meself. How could I? I'd managed seven goals in me first five starts in the Football League.

The press started taking an interest in me, especially in Wales, where you have this mix of local and national media so the spotlight is that much brighter than at a lot of other clubs. Our league run fizzled out, well short of the play-offs in the end, but we did have the FAW (Football Association of Wales) Premier Cup to play for against Swansea at the Vetch. The teams in the English system had been kicked out of the Welsh Cup, so this had taken its place. It was only a little thing, but it was a big deal for me. It was the biggest competition in Wales as far as I was concerned, and it was live on the BBC, so I made sure me nan had the video on. I scored the first – although Kris O'Leary would later claim I fouled him – and I remember thinking what a hostile place the Vetch was as fans tried to grab me when I was giving an interview on the pitch.

I didn't mind. I enjoyed the media stuff, and I was making the most of every bit of attention that was coming me way. Like *Granada Soccer Night* back home. Not long after I'd started scoring with Wrexham they showed a long clip of me goals, about four or five of them, to the panel on that night – including Mark Wright. Perhaps by then I'd realised he was right, but I was still able to have a laugh to meself as I watched his face.

But the real satisfaction came from the fact people were noticing me, people were recognising me. Whether it was just the name from the videprinter on a Saturday afternoon or the goals on the telly, being recognised just told me one thing – I'd made it.

CHAPTER SEVEN

November

THE CAR PULLS UP at the gates to Sky Sports' studios in Isleworth, just outside of London. The call goes through and someone comes to meet me and take me through to the green room.

It's half past eight on a Saturday morning.

I'm used to the routine by now; it's me fourth time on *Soccer AM*. A lot of people don't get asked at all so it's always a confidence boost when you get invited back.

And it's me first time back in years. The call never came when I was at Bristol, not since before being arrested for the whole so-called anti-Cardiff thing at the Millennium after the Football League Trophy final. I don't know whether that had anything to do with it, whether they wanted to distance themselves from me because of all the controversy, I don't know.

But I'm back. Only I'm not quite.

I've always been invited on when Swansea have played on a Friday night, normally because of the rugby international clashing with a Saturday kick-off. The show would always send a Sky camera to the game to focus on me, to give them something to chat about the next day. It's always given me a buzz to know that going out on the pitch, a determination to try and do something different. To show off, I guess.

Sat in the green room I knew there wasn't going to be a lot to talk about from the Derby game the night before. Not about me anyway. I'd been on the pitch 60 seconds before the full-time whistle blew. Don't get me wrong, it was a great result – Fede Bessone scored a cracker inside the last ten minutes to give us a 1–0 win. It put us third and the highest position the club has been in 26 years, since the John Toshack days at the Vetch.

After the start we've had it's brilliant for the club to be flying high, for the confidence to be there as a team and for it to be coming together for us as a side after all the upheaval of the summer. You could feel it in the dressing-room last night, the belief that we could really do something.

I just hope I'm around long enough to be there when we do.

When they show the clip on the screen I make a joke of the fact me only highlight was chesting the ball and clearing it from me own box, telling them it's the first time I've gone into the dressing-room and lads have been saying, 'Good clearance,' not 'good goal' or 'good skill'. I've never been afraid to take the piss out of meself – you can't take yourself too seriously, especially when I've not normally been one to take life too seriously.

Like a few years back when the show asked me to explain a celebration me and Andy Robinson did at Barnsley where we were waving our arms in the air one at a time. I told them we'd been listening to an old rave song the night before in our hotel room and started pulling out the old dance moves – and that we'd decided to do it if one of us scored, with Robbo getting right into it. They did a sketch imagining the scene in the hotel room, complete with two lads with fake bald caps on in white underpants dancing around to 'On a Ragga Tip'. I think I've been asked to 'do the dance' everywhere I've gone ever since.

It was all good fun then and it is now, so when they ask for me to join in on a sketch based on *I'm A Celebrity* I'm happy to join in and have a laugh. It's part of the fun of going on the show, a mix of football and comedy – no wonder so many lads like it, why so many footballers like it.

I've always enjoyed going on and never feel nervous, just excited. It's the showman thing again, the attention. Who wouldn't want to be on national television? Some people get all uptight about the cameras, the lighting, the make-up, all that, but when I'm on the orange sofa, or anywhere else, it's just a chat and a chance to be meself. They are experiences I never thought I'd have growing up, so why not enjoy them when they come?

I've known Helen Chamberlain for years now, and we had a chat before going on air. Now she's asking me about Bristol City, and I'm not afraid to make it clear to everyone that there's no future for me at the club, just as I'm not afraid to spell out how much I want to stay at Swansea.

'I want to finish my career there,' I tell them, I tell everyone watching. I'm not sure the gaffer will be though.

I've already told him that, told him I want to stay beyond next month, beyond the end of the season, so he's not hearing anything new, although I do mention he's still got what it takes when he joins in the five-a-sides. Which is true. You don't lose it after winning two Champions League medals. He's only 39, so it wasn't long ago he was in the heart of that Juventus side or part of Portugal's World Cup squad, and it's quite surreal to think of him joining in at training down in Llandarcy with a club that almost dropped out of the League a few years back.

He commands respect, which is probably one of the reasons he's been able to do so well after coming in for Roberto. Not many would have been able to stamp their own ideas on things so quickly after the previous manager had done so well – but how can you question a guy who's been at the very top and won it all?

I came in after training one day wearing jeans tucked into a pair of boots I'd just bought.

'Very nice, I like it, Lee,' he said, before turning to our captain Garry Monk and saying, 'Do you think I could get away with that, Garry?'

Monks looked up to him and, spot on, said, 'Gaffer, you can get away with anything – you've won two Champions Leagues.'

The questions come about me not starting games, like they have done from the Welsh press too. I'd already made me point to them – that I wanted to stay, that I was desperate to score in the South Wales derby a few weeks back to try and secure that contract I was after. But I didn't make it off the bench. The derby was the first game I'd looked for when I re-signed, but although I was part of the squad and tasted the atmosphere better than I had from the stands, I never got onto the field until the final whistle, where I celebrated with the lads and the fans. It was a strange one – the disappointment of not being involved in something, the joy of sharing the win with the Swansea fans.

But Paulo was straight with me from the off. There'd been a lot of questions to him about me not playing, too many perhaps, because people knew what I could do from before. But he'd known all about that and that first day told me straight he wasn't going to pick me on me name – and I agreed. It was about what I did for him in the here and now that mattered.

We have a good relationship, an open one, and we'll often talk about football and different things. He knows I want to stay after the loan deal, but I've never forced the issue. The only thing that can do that is getting out there, being a good influence around the place.

Music producer William Orbit comes on before John McCririck, the horse-racing pundit, making sure I don't get another word in on the show. It makes a change for me. I have a go at the game they have in the car park where you hit the ball through a cut-out hole in a giant Premier League trophy, but I miss – as does everyone else – before I say my goodbyes and hope there's a next time for me on the show.

Because while I'm back in the spotlight now, there's still the chance it won't be for long. I don't have doubts about meself, but there are doubts about how long this will carry on for, how long before the worst-case scenario comes and I'm told to go back to Bristol.

It's a strange feeling – I'm back, but not quite. And I know how quickly things can turn. Better than most.

CHAPTER EIGHT

Red Dragon Dreams and Nightmares

THE PHONE RANG – it was Reevesy.

'What number do you want, Trunds?'

My first full season as a pro and already I'm being asked what squad number I'd prefer. No. 10 would be the obvious one, but I knew that was Fergie's and, as well as I'd done in three months as a fully paid-up footballer, I wasn't going to take that off him.

'Yeah, No. 9's fine,' he said, the both of us knowing what I was going to pick anyway. The second-best one, another goalscorer's shirt.

More importantly, it was a sign that I was being seen as a key part of the team now, a first-teamer from the off rather than some kid trying to prove himself, prove that I deserved to be playing at that level.

I still needed to do it over a longer period, but I couldn't have asked for a better start to life as a pro. That didn't stop me trying, mind. I was on the basic wage for a League One footballer and I thought I'd given meself a chance of a bit more after the way I'd started, so me and Neil thought it was worth a go. Not a lot more, but I was mindful that I could be stuck on the same junior wage for another two years.

We asked, but we knew what the answer was going to be – Wrexham weren't a money club. They never had been and probably never will be so that was that, I took the 'No' on the chin because, as well as I'd done, I was definitely in no position to cause a fuss.

But even by this early stage there'd been a bit of speculation, rumours in the papers of this club or that club keeping tabs on me. Nothing major, but it was certainly different from just hearing on the grapevine at Chorley that there might be a scout from so-and-so and there might be a trial in it for me. These were real chances now, real opportunities, not half-promises. Not that I was looking for a way out of Wrexham – I owed so much to the club for giving me the opening I needed. But I was looking for a way up.

Me mum had come home from Ireland when Brooke was born, so I'd bring home the match reports from the *Daily Post* or the *Evening Leader* for her and me nan's scrapbook. They were all good write-ups too, all talking about how I was something different, how I stood out from a lot of the other players in the division, all making me believe that I could go on, could move up again – however long it took.

The only way that was going to happen was to push on from where I'd left off, and that meant a first proper pre-season. The first one I'd even half bothered with had been at Rhyl, and even then what I did on two or three sessions a week or on me own time was nothing in comparison to the full-on version. But, bizarrely, I was bang up for it, enjoying the challenge of it all. Watching the other pros, I'd started to figure out what it took to be a success, and the effort you had to put in on the training ground. And, after a while, the strange thing was that I began to enjoy it. Not so much the actual running, the sprinting, the shuttles, all that, but the satisfaction I got from it. All this time it had been a big mental hurdle of mine, too much hard work and not enough fun, but I was able to enjoy it simply because I could get through it.

I felt fitter than I'd ever been, although Gary Neville didn't think so when we played Manchester United at the Racecourse in a pre-season friendly for Brian and Kev's testimonial. They had just won the Premier League and they had all the stars out – Ryan Giggs, Ruud van Nistelrooy, with me up against Jaap Stam. It was perfect for me, a relaxed exhibition-style environment, and I did well before Neville slapped me on me belly and asked me if it was fat or muscle. I was still carrying a bit of weight and I knew it, so I told him.

'Get rid of it and you'll be playing in the Premier League,' Neville said. Hearing things like that about me ability meant I was as confident as I'd ever been going into the season, and two goals in me first two games back didn't do anything to stop that.

What did, though, was Flynny going. The financial situation at the club wasn't great and when he didn't get the money he felt he needed to spend in pre-season it was clear it had started to take its toll on him. He had done so much for the club, picking up players on the cheap and establishing good teams out of them, all those great cup runs, and had become a very well-respected manager in the game. I've no doubt he had ambitions and I don't know how much more he could have done at Wrexham on the kind of budget the club had. He'd probably had enough by the end, so he and Reevesy both came out and said they were going to leave when their contracts ran out at the end of the season.

It didn't get that far. We'd only won one of our first eight games when it came to a head against Tranmere. You can sense a different atmosphere in the dressing-room when things aren't going well. It's more mental than anything else. The minute a goal goes in it's, 'Oh, no, not again' straight away. When you're at the top you don't get that feeling, you just believe you're going to score yourselves.

When you're at the bottom your heads are down without even noticing it. Players freeze because of the tension and it gets worse and worse. Confidence isn't just a personal thing, it's about confidence in others too, in yourselves as a team. It's massive, and it had taken me so far, but all the ability in the world counts for nothing if the team doesn't believe in itself.

We lost 5–0, all second-half goals at Prenton Park, with a lot of me mates from across the water all watching in the stands. The next thing we know, Flynny's gone and Reevesy's gone with him. I don't think the club would have ever sacked him, so I think the decision was as much his as theirs. Mutual agreement, I think it was officially called – the least he deserved after 12 years there.

It's a weird feeling when it happens, especially to a manager that you like, that you don't want to see go. You feel so helpless, yet it's been you – and ten others – out on the pitch that haven't produced. You don't try any less, it just doesn't happen.

I was gutted, gutted for Brian, this man who had taken a chance on me and given me the confidence to be who I was, but also selfishly gutted for meself. I liked Flynny as much as a person as I did a manager and I felt he liked me. Would the new man? Would whoever came in change me position? Would he have a problem with the way I went about me game? In non-league I would do what I wanted regardless of who came in, for better or for worse. This was different, and for the first time since turning pro I had doubts.

To be fair to Denis Smith, he changed very little. I hadn't heard too much about Denis, but he'd had plenty of experience as a manager with the likes of Sunderland and West Brom before. I was left to me own devices to start with, just told to do what I did and, after Kev Russell and Joey had taken charge for a couple of games as caretakers, I started in Denis's first game in charge – a 1–0 win against QPR. It was only our second win of the season, but it wasn't to last. We had a little bit of a honeymoon period, but then it was six games without a win. I'd be in and out of the side, and I never seemed to be able to get a run going, especially in front of goal. I wasn't too bad, but that was just it – I wasn't standing out. Me name had got around a little, and I'd be marked that little bit tighter – sometimes too tight for my liking. I'd got me first red the season before when I swung an elbow at the centre-back when we were four down against Bristol Rovers. The defender had come looking for a reaction and I'd given him one without thinking of the consequences. Flynny never said much at the time, just reminded me I had to learn. And I was still learning – in a struggling side too, which didn't help, but I still managed double figures in that second season. I could be pleased with that, although even I couldn't help but feel down about the whole season. Flynny had gone and we went down – on the same day we beat Cambridge United 5–0 with Lee Jones scoring all of them and me not involved.

Relegation is tough to take for anyone, but it wasn't the worst thing in the world for me. After all, League Two was still a higher level than anything I'd managed before Wrexham, I was still being paid more money than I'd ever had before Wrexham and I was enjoying the whole footballer's life. I'd never had anyone singing me name before, but now I was getting it every week from the Wrexham fans, who I loved playing for. I loved being on the other side of things, signing the autographs and never daring to say no because I still remembered asking for them meself. I loved showing up to the special events, not because I felt I had to help them out but because I enjoyed being asked. I was walking through the car park at the Racecourse before one match with a few mates I'd got compos for and they spotted a young lad with 'Trundle 9' on the back of his shirt. All me mates were saying, 'Look at him, look at him,' as I tried to pretend it was nothing, that these things were just par for the course for footballers. Inside, I was bursting with pride – it was almost as big a thrill as scoring. If I'd always felt like a footballer on the pitch, I was starting to feel like one off it.

And I enjoyed everything that went with it of course. When you're a lad, you look at footballers and see them with the money, with the nice cars and with whatever girls they want. The money was decent enough, but I wasn't going to set meself up for life just yet and I couldn't drive, but I was happy enough with just girls by this point. I hadn't suddenly stopped going out altogether, even if I had eased off. And I was single again after me and Hayley had split up, so I made the most of the night life and the perks of being a pro. I didn't have to pretend any more, there were no made-up stories chatting to girls, and I would bask in it if someone ever asked, 'Are you Lee Trundle?'

I remember going out one night and pulling this bird and having a quickie around the back of a nightclub in Wrexham. The following Saturday I was walking out of the tunnel for the warm-up when a copper standing on the side of the pitch said, ''Ey, Lee – you put in a good performance the other day.'

'Oh, yeah, cheers. I enjoyed the game,' I said, assuming he was talking about the two I'd scored against Wigan in midweek. He wasn't.

'I was watching you on CCTV,' he said, laughing.

'In that case, bung me a copy of the tape next time,' I said, with the both of us in stitches as I ran off.

It was the stuff any young lad dreams of, and you didn't have to try very hard with the whole VIP scene – even if we weren't exactly VIPs. Not in Liverpool anyway, and Wrexham wasn't the best of places for a night out.

I was still living in Liverpool and getting lifts into Wrexham off a few different lads who would pick me up in Page Moss on the way to Colliers.

It was time I had a car of me own, so I mentioned in an interview I gave to one of the Wrexham papers that I was going to have a crash course so I could pass me test. Not long after I had a letter from a Wrexham fan who said he'd give me lessons for free as long as I got it in the paper that I passed with his company. That suited me fine, so I'd have the lessons every now and then through the season. One night he said he wanted me to come out for a drink with him. I was staying in a hotel in Wrexham and I really wasn't fussed about the idea of going out for drinks with this guy who I hardly knew and who all the lads in the team had started to give me stick about, saying he must fancy me for giving me all these free lessons. I tried to make my excuses when it came to it, even trying to say that I'd forgotten my shoes to wear out – only for him to turn up for that day's lesson with an awful-looking pair of big brogues he'd borrowed off a mate. He dropped me off at the hotel, but I bumped into a girl I'd met who was going to be a Miss Wales contestant. There wasn't much competition between a night out with a driving instructor and a night in with a potential Miss Wales, so it wasn't long before I rang him saying I was too tired and we had to leave it. Fair play to him, though, he helped me pass, so I do owe him a drink.

Then again, I didn't have the best of starts to life behind the wheel. There were a few kids playing at the Doms youth club who I thought were worth looking at – a lad named Joe Feeney, me cousin Frankie Lacken and another lad called Mark Duffy. Just like Tony Kelly had done with me, I wanted to make sure some of the talent round Huyton got a chance to show what they had. Wrexham agreed for them to come in for a bit, and I'd arranged to take them to Colliers in me new Ford Focus. Duffy's mum had just dropped him off by me in Page Moss and told me to be careful of the roads because they were wet, as any mum would. But of course, being lads, we had the music blaring and were not worrying too much about the speed as we headed off. I'd already had a scare the week before when I was driving a couple of lads around, a trialist called Dan Bennett and me mate Joey Dooley. We were just in town when we skidded going around a corner, the two of them in the back shouting, 'Fucking 'ell, Trunds' as they were frantically trying to put their seat belts on in time. I don't know whether it was the tyres or just me because the next week, as I was taking the lads from Huyton in, the car skidded right across the Runcorn Bridge. I'd lost control and we bounced from one side of the barrier to the other, only avoiding other cars by complete luck. It was a horrible crash, and we were lucky we didn't have much more than a few bumps and bruises. I'd burned my hand on the air bag but nothing worse than that, although Duffy did cut himself just underneath his eye.

'You all right there, mate? Looks like you're bleeding,' I said to him, just before he raised his own finger up to check and then fainted when he realised I was right. A nurse who'd been passing checked we were all right, and she helped him come round and asked if he was OK. 'You passed out,' she told him.

'Nah I didn't, I was just resting me eyes.'

I couldn't stop laughing when I heard that, even though in front of me was a six-month-old Ford Focus completely written off. And I'd only managed to get it on Motability because I could say I was me nan's driver.

It was worth the effort – the lads got youth deals and Duffy ended up in the League with Morecambe. Not before another scrape though. I was stuck without a car, so Frankie Lacken's dad – a boxer who was also called Frankie – had a big old Volkswagen Sharan, and I asked if I could borrow it to take the lads in. He agreed, so we were off on our way to the training ground, doing about 80mph along the dual carriageway when there was a rattle, quite a loud one.

'What's that, Frankie lad?'

'I dunno, Lee, I've never heard it before.'

We carried on regardless and tried to ring a few places to come and have a look at it, but no one could get to Colliers before we had to leave to go back to Liverpool. Fuck it, I thought, and we set off again – only for the noise to start up as we were heading along in the middle lane. All of us were looking around to try and figure out where it might be coming from before – bang – the wheel came off the car. I was desperately trying to pull this big thing over onto the hard shoulder as the wheel bounced past us and off towards Liverpool. If it hadn't been for the fact one of the younger Wrexham lads had been a few cars behind and had seen what had happened then God knows how we would've got the thing back, but he used his AA membership to get us towed to Frankie's with the wheel safely tucked up in the back. Of course, we never said anything to Frankie Senior – Frankie got the wheel back on and never said anything, just hoping it wouldn't come off again.

That first crash, the one in the Ford Focus, made the papers. They loved the fact I'd gone to hospital but come back just the next day to play. I did well too, coming off the bench and looking sharp – enough to get me back in the side. I'd started the season – me, Lee Jones and Andy Morrell all playing. There was Hector Sam too, another Trinidadian who had come in, and before long it was clear Denis preferred him up front with Andy, using his pace. It was difficult to take at first, and I've no doubt the young me would've got frustrated and given up on it, thrown me toys out of the pram perhaps. But being around guys like Darren Ferguson and Brian Carey, I hadn't just grown up a lot more I'd also seen how they conducted themselves around the club and around the training ground, and it made me realise that was the way you needed to carry yourself. As much as football is a selfish game, as much as you worry about your own position, you do form a bond with the lads you're in a team with, just from spending so much time with them. It sinks in eventually to all of us it's not always about us as individuals.

With that in mind, me and Denis were getting on OK, and although fans immediately think there's a problem between a manager and a player if he's not being picked, that wasn't the case. It was just he felt there should have been more of an end product to what I was doing, to the tricks and the build-up play. I felt I needed more chances to play and not the ten, twenty minutes I was getting off the bench – even if it was every week.

Of course, I wasn't happy with the situation – although that's not why I turned down a new contract. They'd put a figure down, but it was hardly anything different from what I was already on – one of the lowest wages at the club. Denis had promised to look at my contract the previous summer, but I thought it was cheeky to keep me on practically the same wage I'd been on for two and a half years for another two seasons, especially when I felt I'd done the business for them. At the same time, I wasn't planning on running me contract down – even though whispers of other clubs being interested started, like Hull for instance. That excited me, a club on the up who'd not long moved into their new stadium. But I still wasn't actively looking to go. I liked Wrexham – the club and the fans. I had a lot of time for the whole place because of the chance they had given me, plus it was great to be able to stay at home, close to me family and me mates, and just travel in every day. Besides, at that point I thought there'd be another offer from the club, especially with the way things were going.

Andy and I had really started something up front. Andy had been at the club a while after coming on trial from non-league like me, although he was a couple of years older, and when we got a run together we just clicked. We had a good side with Dennis Lawrence, who played with Carlos in the World Cup for Trinidad, Carlos himself, Fergie and Brian Carey, Steve Thomas or 'Ossie' as we called him, Shaun Holmes, who was a good lad and used to come out in Liverpool with me and Ossie, Hector, Paul Edwards, Stephen Roberts, who got capped by Wales, and Jim Whitley, the ex-Manchester City defender who had been one of Denis's first signings. We were solid at the back with Big Den and Brian, had Fergie able to pass it in midfield, good pace out wide, and then me and Andy in attack. It took a bit of getting used to – I'd always played off the bigger man or got the service from someone else. Here I was taking up a different role, more of a team player and looking to create more. I still got my fair share – 12 before the season finished – and I would have had more if I'd been on penalties. Andy scored thirty-four, but he had seven penalties – and I reckon I won all of those. He was getting the headlines, though, and I couldn't blame him – he was on fire and I was just happy to play my part because we were on course for promotion. I might have felt differently if I had still been on the bench, but I knew my value in what Andy had been doing and what the team was doing – and I was in double figures again for goals anyway. Plus, getting out of the bottom league was a reason to celebrate – but then something came along to ruin all that for me.

During the week, I sometimes used to go and get a sports massage in this college in Liverpool. I happened to be waiting outside for an appointment one day when this girl walked past with her mate. A minute or two later, the friend came back, handing me a slip of paper with a number on it. She said that her mate had mentioned that she liked me and for me to give her a call. Normally I'd have no problem with that, but I happened to be waiting with a group of older ladies and I felt a bit embarrassed. I told the girl thanks but no thanks and that was that.

The next day I was with me mate who lived not far from the college and I happened to see the same girl. I waved 'hi', called her over and apologised for the other day and for not taking her number, explaining I had felt a bit funny about it. She was fine about it and when I suggested we meet up later she agreed. She was a good-looking girl, seemed normal enough, and the plan was to have a couple of drinks at mine before heading out somewhere. But when she turned up at the house, it didn't take long before she was turning the conversation to sex, talking really openly about her fantasies and things, about how she'd love to have a threesome – to a point that she said she might have a girlfriend that might be up for a bit of fun. It was full-on stuff. We met the next day and we both had mates with us, all agreeing that we'd meet at mine later. It was harmless fun, we were all young and single, and when we got back to mine the talk about sex began again, only this time the girl was suggesting I slept with her friend – so I did. It wasn't out of the ordinary, I'd always been confident and comfortable with sex, and I'd always been a bit of a Jack the Lad. The girl stayed downstairs with me mate, just chatting away in the front room, before she said something that startled him – she asked whether he thought Lee was 'ready to settle down yet?' Me mate checked she meant settling down with her, which she did – even though she'd been the one setting it up for me to sleep with her friend. It was all a bit strange and I told her as much, that it was just a bit of fun, as I dropped both girls home.

We had an away match not long after, and when I came back I noticed there was paint over me front door. Me mind immediately went to this girl, so I gave her a call, but she was more interested in why I'd never called her back like I'd said I would. She came round crying, and I started to feel bad about the whole thing, beginning to think it wasn't her, that she wouldn't come back to me house if she'd been the one who'd damaged the door. Stupidly, as one thing led to another, we ended up having the threesome she'd asked for.

By the next morning, I'd decided it was better not to get any more involved with this girl and decided not to call her when I'd told her I would. Later, when I was watching telly, there was a knock at the door. One of me neighbours was stood there, telling me how she'd just seen lads running away and if I was quick I'd catch them. There was white paint all over my new BMW, the first proper car I'd bought. I had my suspicions straight away, but it would happen one more time before I thought I had to do something about it. Her dad answered the door when I knocked and I told him I thought his daughter had put paint all over me car.

'When?' he said. He didn't give it long to reply when I told him it had happened the previous night. 'She was with me last night, in the pub.'

I was curious. 'Which pub was that then?'

He told me he'd been in the Stanley, a pub in Huyton, all night.

'OK, me mate's the manager at the Stanley, I'll go down now and look at the CCTV – if you were in there last night I'll come back and apologise; if not you can reimburse me what it costs to sort me car.'

It was a blag, but I knew it would catch him out. Within half an hour I had a call from the dad to say he'd got it wrong, they were in a different pub and that was that. I left it at that. If he was going to tell lies for his daughter then I wasn't going to get very far.

Soon after that I had a call from the police, telling me there'd been a complaint that I'd been harassing this girl and could I go down to the station. I was happy enough with that. I could tell them what had been going on, and I wasn't afraid to tell them this was a girl I'd slept with and not the kind you'd want to bring back and meet your mum. They were fine with it, sent me on me way and just said that they had to follow these things up if people made accusations.

There was one more attack on me car, even though I'd parked it at me mum's place, and then a week or so later the girl phoned me. It was a Friday and we were playing Cambridge United at the Racecourse the following day. If we won, we'd win promotion. I answered the phone and she told me if I slept with her one more time everything would stop. I told her not to threaten me, but later she called again, this time asking whether I'd thought any more about her offer. I told her exactly what I thought of her offer, but she came back saying she'd been to the newspapers and they would take her story.

'Big deal,' I said. 'So you've slept with a League Two footballer.'

'No,' she replied. 'Raped.' And she put the phone down.

The words cut right through me – I was scared stiff. There can be nothing, nothing worse than for someone to say that to you, to accuse you of rape when you've done nothing wrong.

I knew this was no time for messing around. I headed for the police station and told the officer what had just happened, what she'd said, what she'd threatened. He took it all down, told me I'd done the right thing and told me to just go home when I asked what I should do about this whole mess. I followed his instructions and was pulling out of the car park when I saw the girl walk in – she was going through with this, with these lies.

I pulled the car around and walked back into the waiting room. I could hear her crying in the background. It was the same tears she'd turned on when I'd asked her about the paint on me door. The officer came back in to see me and asked if that was the girl I'd told him about. I said yes, but again he just told me to go home and wait.

But wait for what? I was shitting myself – and over something I hadn't done. I'd never been in trouble before, I'd never got meself a police record – I'd even shit meself stealing a fucking toffee apple. And all the while I waited, I knew I was being accused of rape, something so despicable I couldn't even bring meself to say it.

I'd been a Jack the Lad, as I said. I knew I had a reputation for sleeping with more than my fair share of girls, but I was young and single – that wasn't a crime. The only thing I might have been guilty of was not treating her right – I'd used her for sex. But even then she'd been more of an instigator than I had, talking so brazenly about fantasies, sleeping with me the first night I'd met her. She'd made her own decisions, and I'd made it clear it was just a bit of fun. I'd never made out I'd wanted a relationship, and I always said the same straight from the start with girls, because it was just never worth the hassle in the long run. This was no different, and she'd known that.

I waited at me nan's, unable to tell her. I mean, what the hell could I say to her? I didn't want to worry anyone about anything. Really, I felt I shouldn't have been worrying meself because this must all be a bad joke – but I had no clue how far it was going to go. What I should have been worrying about was one of the biggest games of me career the next morning, looking forward to it even, but that was the last thing on me mind.

I stayed over at Ashbury, which wasn't unusual. I never stayed at mine if I was on me own. I was used to having people around me, used to being at me nan's. She would look after me and made sure I ate well. And then I waited, and I waited.

It must have been about three in the morning when they came. The van came up the road, five officers all in uniform stepping out. I was in the front bedroom and could see them all. I headed downstairs and waited for the knock.

'Are you Lee Trundle?' and before I knew it, they were reeling it all off. 'You're under arrest, you do not have to say anything . . .' words I'd only heard on the television – but this was very much real life. It was difficult to take it all in without being sick, the words 'rape' and 'threats to kill' sticking out and stabbing into me stomach.

The cuffs went on as I was marched into the van, officers searching through me car as I got in. I found out later what they were looking for – she'd claimed I'd gone to her house with a knife. I remember telling one of the officers I was a footballer and I had an important match tomorrow. Someone laughed.

The cuffs were on as I went to the station, me shoes and socks removed and me rights read out to me. Fingerprints, photos, all that, and then into the cell. This horrible cold cell with its light-blue walls, thin blue mattress, no pillow and a brown stitched blanket, the light from outside shining through. The night before the biggest game of me life and I wasn't sleeping. Even if it had been a five-star hotel I wouldn't have slept a wink; I honestly thought I was going to go mad. The fear of not knowing what the hell was going on was eating me up. I wanted to cry but couldn't because me mind was racing so much. I wanted to be angry but didn't have enough energy. I'd done nothing wrong so there shouldn't have been anything to be scared about, but yet it had already gone this far. The thoughts went over and over in me mind, 'I haven't done anything wrong, but are they going to believe me? I've already told them what happened yet I'm still in this cell.' When she'd cried about that paint on me door, I'd believed her. Surely they wouldn't fall for the same tears? I felt sick just to think someone would believe I'd do what she was accusing me of, to be that evil. And that was the thing – being locked up was something I could deal with; having someone say you're a rapist was just hell.

It was morning when I got to phone me nan.

'Lee? What's going on?' I was crying inside. I wanted to tell her how alone I felt, how I was worried I wouldn't see anyone again. I told her where I was, what had happened.

'Arrested? What for?' I told her. She didn't ask me if I'd done it.

'Who's said that? What's she going on about?'

I didn't get seen until one o'clock. I remember because as I walked inside the interview room I looked at the clock. The button clicked down on the recorder and I told them everything, every minute detail, nothing spared. I had nothing to hide, nothing I could say could make this worse, there was no room for embarrassment; it had gone past all that. I didn't have a solicitor with me. I was asked if I wanted one, but why would I need one if I'd not done anything? I thought surely they would see that too. It was only afterwards, when I got a solicitor, I was told how stupid that could've been.

They read her statements out to me – I didn't know what to say. I lost count of the times I fell back into me chair in disbelief at what she'd said. So many things were just false, obvious things like we'd been seeing each other for more than a month, that I was getting aggressive because she wouldn't get serious with me, going to her house threatening to kill her and, then, that I'd raped her and kept her in my house.

They didn't charge me; they released me on bail. It was half-past three. Even at one I thought I'd have half a chance, I might make the bench, get a few minutes as sub. When the clock turned past half two and didn't stop, me heart just sank lower. I was missing the biggest moment of me career for something I'd never done.

I'd told me nan to phone the club to say what had happened, and they'd told the press at the game I'd missed it for family reasons to try and protect me. I knew that was the next thing. I remember being in the taxi going through Huyton and I could see people in the next car talking – they wouldn't have been talking about me but it felt as if they were. I wasn't worried about what Hayley thought because she knew me too well, she knew the type of lad I was, that I'm not the aggressive type, that nothing would have gone on. But then I started thinking about Brooke and people talking about her dad doing this and that, imagining her in school and it getting chucked at her that her dad was a rapist.

I went to me nan's. We used to get the *Echo*'s football pink – the evening football paper on a Saturday – and soon after I got home there it was, splashed on the front. It was all in black and white, with a spokesman for the police confirming a 26-year-old man 'faces four allegations of rape, harassment, threats to kill and false imprisonment'. The police didn't name me, but the papers knew. I'd always wanted recognition, but this was the other side, the other extreme. I'd done nothing wrong, but the paper never said that. The Wrexham score was there – we'd won 5–0. We were promoted. But that wasn't on me mind. I'd started to worry about me career by this point, wonder if I could get sacked, worry that if I did would any club touch me? All because of this one girl.

Everyone was waiting for me at me mum's but I didn't want to go through it all again. Philly took me back to his and me and two of me cousins played cards through the night to take me mind off things. The following morning I went to go home, but I could see the reporters all waiting outside as I pulled up. I knew the names of the papers they shouted at me as I walked past but not the faces. These weren't the football reporters that knew me, these were the news lot – but I wasn't saying anything anyway. Partly because I couldn't, partly because I just wanted to hide and hope it would all just go away before the next day's editions. Our Frankie came round and didn't waste any time.

'Come on, Lee lad, we're going out.'

It was the last thing I wanted to do.

'No, you're not staying in,' Frankie carried on. 'You've done nothing wrong. You're getting out there and showing people you've got nothing to be ashamed of.'

I didn't feel like it, but we went out, only local in Huyton, but I got out. There were people asking me what was going on, what had happened, but not once did I feel like anyone was doubting me. People believed me without me having to ask them to – they were just refusing to believe what this girl had said about me. I didn't have to go around pleading me innocence; they already knew. Older women would come up and say their daughters had all said 'Lee's not like that.' Going out was the worst thing I could have thought of that day, but I'm so glad I did, so glad Frankie made me. I wasn't being judged, I was being supported.

That was Huyton – then it was Wrexham. I went straight to Denis's office on the Monday, going through it all again. But the club were behind me from the off. They were brilliant and one big fear of the whole farce was removed straight away. They'd protected me the best they could on the Saturday, and then on the Monday they released a statement that said they would continue to support me and highlighting the fact that no charges had been brought against me.

And then it was into training. It was probably the best thing for me, to be around the lads again. They didn't have to say too much, they knew what I was like, they'd even known about the hassle I'd been getting from this girl because of the way we all used to swap stories in the dressing-room. I knew they were behind me.

There were only two games left of the season now and we were already going up, back into League One at the first attempt, but we were playing Leyton Orient away the following night, and Denis wasted no time in telling me I was playing. I wasn't in the right frame of mind in all honesty, but it was the best thing the club could do to back me in all this – a greater show of support than any statement.

It wasn't me best game, it was never going to be, but I played and I showed the world I wasn't going to let it stop me – even if some of the Orient fans tried to remind me. I heard it all, 'Trundle you rapist', 'Trundle you nonce', 'You won't be able to score in jail' – that kind of crap. It was sickening to hear and of course it affected me game. It was still hanging over me and it would for the next three weeks.

I'd already played me last games for Wrexham by then, celebrated with my teammates, gone round on an open-top bus, had a medal round me neck – but all with this shit in the back of me mind.

I'd played what ended up being me last game at the Racecourse on the Thursday, scoring twice in a 6–1 win over Newport County to win the FAW Premier Cup. And then it was all over. By the Friday, the police came and said they wouldn't be taking it any further. She'd withdrawn her claims. How that came about I don't know, whether she came to her senses to drop all the crap or what – don't know, don't care. All that mattered was that it was done and the accusation was no more.

Me solicitor made a statement saying how angry I was about the fact she had dragged me name through the mud while she stayed anonymous, even after she retracted what she'd said about me, but there was more relief than anger in me. All I could think about at that time was, finally, it's over.

Wrexham put a statement out saying they'd said from the start I had no case to answer, but it's always a bit lopsided when it comes to these kinds of things. I was front-page news when I was arrested. When it was dropped, the story was a couple of hundred words long. Look around the Internet and there are loads of stories of the arrest; there's one or two about the claims being withdrawn. I can joke about it now, but at the time the only paper that carried a big piece to say I was falsely accused was the *Daily Sport*, not a paper many people buy for its news.

About two weeks after it all ended, I drove past Page Moss and saw her standing on the side of the road. She saw me and laughed as I went past. It turned me stomach. I wonder if she ever thought what she did to me, how I still have that fear that Brooke will have to hear from some kid that her dad was supposed to have raped someone. I wonder if she realises how that will never go away. I wonder if she realises that every time I meet someone new in me life, someone I want to get close to, I have to go over the story again and tell them meself, rather than worry they'll hear it first from someone else and get it wrong.

Mud sticks, doesn't matter how clean you are.

It does make you think how easy it is for people in the public eye to be targeted. Like Dave Jones, the Cardiff City manager, and those false allegations of child abuse made against him when he was at Southampton that should have never even made it to court. Then every week having to put up with the chants – words you can brush off later but at the time just make you sick. If the person involved can get used to it, that's one thing, but what of the family? There's no other way, I guess, but it is hard to take when the people who say these things, who make these accusations in the first place, don't have their name plastered all over the papers or on the telly when they're proven to be wrong.

It's still there now, still in the background, people only knowing half the story. Even now people think I left the area because of what happened, that I was in trouble and couldn't stay in Liverpool. Can you believe that? That I couldn't even live in the area that I'd grown up in, where I was born, that I'd been forced out of me own home? It was a tight-knit community that had backed me from the start, so why would that have been an issue? People just jump to conclusions, no matter if they're wrong or not.

The truth was, I'd already made my mind up I was leaving before any of that happened. Leaving Wrexham anyway.

There hadn't been any movement on a new contract, mainly because the club wasn't in a position to offer me much of a better deal. I know Denis wanted me to stay and by the end admitted I shouldn't have been stuck on the wage I was on, but it was too late. The club had let me contract run down and, after I'd been doing well, there were other clubs interested.

Of course money was an issue. I'd come into the professional game late, and I wanted to earn what I could while I could because I'd missed out on all the years I'd messed around.

But, for a similar reason, I wanted a new challenge too. Getting promoted at the first attempt and having a key role just made me believe even more that I could play at a higher level – and I needed to find a club that could help me do that. Wrexham were going up, but I felt I'd done what I could with them, as much as Denis had been good to me, as much as the fans had been good to me, as much as the club had been great to me. It was just time.

There were a few serious bits of interest as it got to the end of the season, including from Brian Flynn, who was now managing Swansea, who had spoken to Sangy. The problem was, they were playing Hull on the final game of the season and needed a win to stay in the Football League.

Wrexham were at Bury on the final day of the season – a 2–0 win to wrap up third place and promotion. As we celebrated in the dressing-room, I popped me head out of the door and saw a steward.

''Ey, mate, how did Swansea get on?'

CHAPTER NINE
December

JUST GIVE ME the ball.

We're 1–0 down and we're running out of time. I'm running out of time.

There's five games left after this before the loan is over, and I need to show what I can do. I've got those goals against Sheffield United and QPR, but it's more than that now – I need to show I can be an asset, to help take this team where it wants to go.

Just give me the ball.

I've got a chance here. I've got a good 20 minutes to get into things, actually get a feel of the game rather than the odd few minutes I've been having for the last couple weeks.

And all the while I've been in limbo, desperate to stay, dreading going back to Bristol with no clue about what's going to happen when the deal runs out on New Year's Eve. I can't go back, not to go and face Johnson. I can't go and train there and see him every day, not the way he is, not the way he's been with me.

I want this so badly, but I've not been able to get out onto the field where I can show me worth – that I'm worth keeping on, even if only to the end of the season.

The chairman had always promised me there would be a chance, that it would be properly reviewed. But there's no good me just saying I want to stay, that I'm worth keeping – I've got to show it. But I'm running out of time.

We could do with a win here too. Peterborough are bottom of the table, but they've taken the lead. Their big centre-back, Exodus Geohaghon, has launched a throw into the box, the ref's missed a push on Gorka, and Chris Whelpdale has put it in the net. We've been battering them in possession, battering them all first-half, but we do that with a lot of sides. The problem the lads had last year was that they didn't take many chances; this year it's been the same, and we're not creating as many either because we're set up slightly more defensively. It's paid off – we've got one of the best records at the back in the League, but we're struggling in front of goal.

I'd been warming up when the ball went in. I don't think it had stopped moving before Paulo told me to get ready. I was.

Just give me the ball. This is it, just go on and get yourself a goal. Just do what you do.

Albert Serran, another one of the Spanish lads here, plays a ball from the back. I latch onto it. Geohaghon is close, but I'm strong in me upper body, always have been. Gorka is inside, the pass is on, but I've got to be a bit more greedy, be a bit like the old me, I've got to get this goal. The challenges are there, but if I can just turn it onto me left foot I've got a chance, that's all I need.

I've never planned celebrations, if you excuse that daft one with Andy Robinson. Normally, I just do whatever comes naturally, just let the emotion take over. I run straight towards the Swansea fans behind the goal. There's a fair few of them, a long old trek but they're there, in a section on the corner too. I needed to show them I could do it, just as I needed to show everyone else.

They start chanting. 'Sousa, sign him up, Sousa, Sousa, sign him up . . .'

I needed them to get back on me side. In the beginning, the songs would come all the time, but that's not going to happen when you're not playing. I needed to remind them I could still do it.

There's six minutes left, but we can win this. Just give me the ball. Me confidence is there, I'm in that frame of mind, I feel I can do something here. There's still time.

I'm stood with me back to goal, where I'm dangerous. The pass comes in from Jordi Lopez, just right – into me feet just outside the box. Geohaghon is there again, but I've got him. Just get a little space, shift the weight, roll the ball, space for a shot. Bottom corner.

That's it, you've done it. You've shown what you're about, what you offer, what you can do. You've shown you can be an asset to this side. We've got the win.

Surely that's it, surely that's the game, surely that's me contract sorted? Me heart eases – I'm not going to start saying it, but I know I've done what I had to, as much as I could with the time I've had.

But it's not the game. A slip at the back, the cross comes in, Aaron McLean finishes. It's injury time and it's 2–2.

The gloss is taken off it. Paulo had been going wild on the touchline when I'd scored. He is again but for a different reason. Still, we've come from behind and we're still in the play-off picture. Not bad for a side people were expecting to struggle this year.

I phone me mum and me nan, as I do every game, then me dad calls for a chat before I get on the bus, disappointed with the result but not afraid to be satisfied with what I'd managed. They can probably feel the relief down the mobile. The last few weeks all I could say was 'No, I didn't get on' – not easy after the highs I'd had in a pretty short career, not something I was used to or wanted to get used to.

It's a long journey home – it always is when you're playing for Swansea, everywhere is miles away – but I enjoy this one, being able to savour the moment as we go along, being amongst the others, being part of it. I'm me old self. I'd played me part in the game, and the chance is there for more now. I can come out of me shell a little bit more. When I first came back, I didn't want to be too loud too soon, as much as the respect was there. The Spanish lads had called me a legend and I didn't even know them, but I hadn't shown them who I really was before. Now I've given them a glimpse.

The chat doesn't last long. Some of the lads still play cards, but I guess there's only so much you can talk about when you're cooped up for this long. We've all got iPods, personal DVD players, everyone doing what they do to break the trip up. In the old days, there would be a drink and fish and chips; it's pizza now, though. Whether it's any better for you, I don't know, but it's about getting the carbs back on ready for the next game. Besides, the way I've begun to watch what I eat and me diet these days, I look forward to me treat on a Saturday.

There's something else to look forward to. Brooke is coming back for Christmas in a few weeks, coming down with me mum and Pat to spend it with me and Charlotte in the flat. Hayley's always been good like that, taking it in turns on special occasions and different things. I'd been a bit nervous before, worried Brooke was coming down and me being on edge because I don't know whether I'll have to leave again a week later. I still don't know, but at least I know I've shown them the best way I can now and I just need to keep that going. Brooke will love the flat. She can open her presents in the morning before I go training. It would have been awful if she'd been coming down to Swansea to say goodbye to the place – she'd always loved it. She's a proper little girl now, but she used to come down to the Vetch and run out onto the pitch with me, wearing Daddy's shirt. She'd loved it from the start. We both did.

CHAPTER TEN

Magic Daps

HUW JENKINS DOESN'T come across as someone who gets excited very easily. But he was exciting me.

I'd been to see Port Vale, and Tranmere were the only other club with a serious offer I wanted to consider, but Reevesy had brought me down to Swansea to have a look around the place and help me make up me mind. He drove me to Verdi's, a lovely little café down in the Mumbles looking out over the Swansea Bay, something a million miles away from back home. Mind, South Wales didn't seem the most attractive place at first when we passed through Port Talbot on the M4, with its giant steelworks filling the horizon.

'We're not there yet,' Kev had said with a laugh as we drove on.

It was Swansea's little trick – always take the players to the west of the city – preferably on a sunny day – and show them what a beautiful place it is with all the beaches, the views and yet still all close to the city centre with all the shops, bars and things so you don't feel out in the sticks. It's what made Swansea so appealing.

The Vetch was another thing altogether. Stuck behind a few old terraced streets, it was a bizarre place with a tiny old centre stand, a massive standing terrace running the length of the pitch opposite, the terraced away end behind one goal and then, behind the other, a new stand – a two-tier thing that only stretched across half of the pitch and looked like it'd only been half finished. I'd played there a few times with Wrexham, once in that FAW Premier Cup game when I'd realised how hostile the fans could be. There weren't many of them there but, on its own, the long North Bank opposite where you ran out from the dressing-room had a noise louder than most of the other grounds I'd been to. At the end of the previous season, when the club had been fighting to stay in the Football League, it had been packed, more than 8,000 every week in the run-in. Wrexham had averaged something like 4,000, and we were going for promotion.

'Don't worry, we'll look after you,' said Sue the kitwoman, giving me a 'cwtch' – Welsh slang for cuddle – as Reevesy showed me around, and I explained to her I didn't know what I'd be doing, where I'd be signing for the new season.

And one of the biggest reasons for me uncertainty was the thought of leaving Brooke, limiting the time I'd get to spend with her and potentially missing out on so much, not being there for some big moments in her life. That alone was enough to make any decision that much harder. But even just leaving Liverpool was a worry for me. I'd hardly lived on me own, let alone in some strange city hundreds of miles away. I didn't even like sleeping over at me mates' houses as a kid. I'd been used to having me family, me mates around me all the time, and I really wasn't sure about the prospect of giving all that up when there was still the easy offer of joining Tranmere on the table.

Port Vale and Tranmere were a division above too – the same division Wrexham had just won promotion into – and had only just finished outside the play-offs the previous year. When it had come out I was talking to Swansea and was going to leave Wrexham, there were a lot of people saying I didn't have the stomach to move up a level, but that was bollocks because I'd already played in League One.

Money was a factor, without a doubt, and the offer from Swansea was a good one. But there was more to it than just that.

Huw was a Swans fan. He was the club chairman, but he was a supporter first and foremost, just like the rest of the board. They were pretty much all local lads who'd done well with their businesses and stepped forward when the club was in danger of going under. It wasn't some big financial rescue package, they just started looking after the club in the right way. But they still had plans, they still had ambition – only it wasn't driven by making money, it was driven by their love for the club. It didn't take long after meeting him for me to figure out what Swansea meant to Huw, it was obvious from just speaking to him as he went on about his plans for the place, how the board wanted to take the club forward, how there were things in place for it to move up, like the plans for a new stadium. Most of all, he didn't want to hang around in League Two, even though they'd only just done enough to stay up the previous year. Huw used to say we were the only city side left in the market town division. He wanted out and I was going to help him.

It was impressive stuff, exciting stuff, but the reason I signed was the same reason I'd gone down to have a look in the first place – Brian Flynn.

Flynny was the big pull for me, to have the chance to work with him again after those first few months I'd had with him at Wrexham. I'd had to adapt me game a lot more under Denis, but Flynny just wanted me to play. He knew what I could do, he knew about me ability, he knew how to play me, where to play me. He knew me. He was excited about the players he'd brought in on loan to help the club stay up and was looking to hold onto, players like Roberto Martinez from Walsall and young lads like Leon Britton from West Ham and Alan Tate from Manchester United. He told me he wanted to give me a free rein, that I could make a massive difference to the team and that I could be one of the final pieces in the jigsaw. Everything I wanted to hear.

It was all agreed, the club setting up a press conference to unveil me – although strangely they decided to do it in a travel agent's in the city centre because they sponsored the club. Not the kind of top table thing you see on *Sky Sports News* these days with the flash bulbs going, but it was all new to me – and a big deal too. I was on the phone to the lads back home to tell them all about it before making sure I'd got meself a nice new suit, got the hair just right, thought about the kind of things I wanted to say. If I was going to be centre-stage, I wanted to make sure I at least looked the part. The best thing, though, was that I was being made a fuss out of, just like I had always wanted. There were about half a dozen newspaper reporters there, a couple of TV crews, a few radio guys – you didn't just have the Swansea press, you had the Welsh press too, so everything was bigger. For me it was a glimpse of the size of the spotlight you could be under if you got it right.

And everything seemed right to me. Me first home from home was a flat overlooking the Marina, a real bachelor pad a stone's throw away from the city centre and the town's main street for bars – Wind Street, pronounced as in winding someone up. It was perfect, a first bit of flash living to make me feel like a bit of a star and make me feel good about making the move. I still only agreed to a one-year deal, though – I was wary of committing myself for much longer in case it didn't work out, in case I couldn't stick it away from Liverpool. After all, Flynny hadn't lasted long after I'd signed at Wrexham, so I knew how quickly things could change.

But I was made to feel at home from the off. I wasn't the only one in the side away from home for the first time. Lads like Leon and Brad Maylett who'd signed from Burnley were the same, so there were a few of us in the same boat. Then you'd have Roberto who would make a fuss of you, make you feel at home and take you out to eat at different places – but as soon as you did he would be talking about football, talking about the club, about the different players we had and how we were good enough to get out of the division. It was like he was selling the club to me even though I'd already signed. That's just the way he was, the way he is, even – just so passionate about the game and about his team.

But it wasn't just Roberto; there was a passion around the whole place, a genuine buzz about the start of the season, and I think a lot of it was to do with the fact the city had come so close to losing its team the previous year. It was as if everyone had been given a reminder of what football meant to the place. A lot is made about rugby in Wales – as far as I could see, Swansea was football.

There were almost 9,000 at the Vetch for me debut, the start of the 2003–04 season and a scorching hot day, against Bury. But I was trying too hard, I was trying too much to impress, wanting to get the fans' approval from the very first game. There was nothing natural about it. We won 4–2 and I got one – a header, strangely – but there were too many times where I tried to do too much. Still, I'd got an early goal to settle me down, and the lads were buzzing when we went to Cheltenham the following week.

We'd taken a big following because it was one of the closer away trips for Swansea and it was another boiling afternoon, but things turned really flat when we went 3–1 down. We were still playing the football, though, and Flynny was happy for us to go for it, to go and attack. He'd never put any restrictions on us whatever the score was; it was about just going out and playing. We wouldn't do free-kicks or corner routines, we weren't given loads of details of the opposition, not told to sit back – just go and play and make the most of the ability we had. So we did – and about three minutes after they'd scored the third, with twenty-odd minutes to go, I got one back. Then another. Then another – the last coming in injury time. Looking back, it was the game that said I'd arrived at Swansea. I'd shown the fans I could be a goalscorer. I'd shown I could give them a bit of entertainment as I did it, and the way it happened was the boost I needed. It carried on. I got one as we beat Boston 3–0 the following week, got another as we put four past Mansfield.

The more confident I got, the more the tricks came – I was happy to try different things because I knew I'd already got the fans behind me. The way I played was almost down to them – I knew they had faith in me already, so if I tried something and it didn't work, they'd let me off. There were no groans or grumbles if I tried to beat a man rather than pass it. I was in credit with them because they'd seen I could give them something a bit different. I was able to go out on the pitch knowing it wasn't a big deal if I made a mistake – and when you're fearless like that then you don't end up making many. They made it easy for me. The Wrexham fans had always been good like that too, but here I wasn't some trialist who'd done well, some kid from non-league. Here I was a big signing. I'd arrived as a player who'd done it and won promotion in this league, not someone with it all to prove, prove that I even deserved to be a pro. I'd been signed as a goalscorer, and I was scoring goals.

But it was the way I was getting them that was getting the attention, the bit of glamour I was trying to bring to the place with the tricks and the pieces of skill, the kinds of things you're not supposed to see in League Two. It helped with the ground being so compact, the fans being so close to the touchline that they could see the juggles or the flick passes and the wink I'd give afterwards. They could see how much I was loving it. And it wouldn't be tricks for the sake of tricks; they'd produce something, they'd set something up. One of me favourites – and still is – was where I'd have me back to goal with the defender up tight, roll me foot over the ball as if I was going one way but drag it back the other and put it on me left to shoot (it was always me left foot).

The press didn't take long to catch on, and they loved the 'Magic Daps' nickname as much as I did. It came from the pre-season tour of Holland where I'd gone on a bit of a run from our own half, taken on a few defenders, taken it past the keeper and scored. There were a few Swans fans who had travelled over, and one of them shouted something about me having magic daps. I didn't have a clue what they were on about, so I went to ask Kris O'Leary, one of the local lads in the side.

'It's your boots. Daps means your boots.'

It might have had something to do with the fact I wasn't exactly the shy type – I didn't mind coming out wearing silver or white boots, even if I was in the bottom division. A bit different from me Kenny Dalglish Pumas. Anyway, Flynny loved it too – I think he was just happy that I was being meself.

He wasn't the only one – the fans were loving it and so was I, especially when the tricks started getting attention outside Wales. Saying that, it took something special to get people really sitting up and taking notice.

It came in the September. I'd already got eight goals by then, and I was getting me name about the place because I was top goalscorer, but it was a game against Huddersfield that showed why I wasn't just a normal striker doing well. It wasn't a conscious thing. I didn't think before the game, 'Right, I'm going to do the shoulder roll,' it just happened – and things were never really the same after that.

I'd already scored in the first half, cut in from the right-hand side, hit it into the top corner and run straight towards the North Bank where I'd always celebrated me goals. We were in control and knocking it around for fun – which they didn't like. They had one lad sent off for two yellows, and when Kevin Nugent got the second with about five minutes to go we really started to relax and have a bit of fun. I don't know who cleared it, whether it was a goalkick or a long ball from our half, but I can remember the ball coming down out of the sunlight and at the last minute I thought I'd give it a go. I'd messed around doing it in training, and I'd done it in that game against Rhayader, so it came into me head: 'Why not now?'

With me back to goal, I took it high on me chest, began to turn so the ball rolled across the top of me back and over me shoulders and let it drop onto me foot as I spun around to face the goal. I tried to loft a pass through to Britts but the keeper got to it first – but it was worth the go. The fans loved it, and I spent the last moments of the match with a massive smile on me face – even when Ian Hughes clattered me in the corner in injury time, probably because he was pissed off with what he'd just seen. Their manager, Peter Jackson, came out and accused me of this and that after, saying that I was goading his players, that – funnily enough – I was a showboater.

So? That's the way I enjoyed playing football. The fans seemed to enjoy it, the press enjoyed it – they were all saying after how I should send a copy of the video to Cristiano Ronaldo because he wouldn't have pulled it off. Incredibly, a few years later it was voted in the top ten football tricks of all time in a poll I saw on *Sky Sports*, just behind René Higuita's scorpion kick, with Ronaldo, Ronaldinho and even Johan Cruyff all in there. I bet no one said anything to them when they tried different tricks.

The thing is, I wasn't doing it out of spite or just to deliberately take the piss; I was doing it for me, for the fans. Jackson said – and he wasn't the only one that year – that I'd end up getting a kicking. That never bothered me – I'd grown up with it. I remember once when we were playing in the five-a-side in Kirby and I'd kept on nutmegging this older lad during the game. Eventually he came up to me and told me he'd smash me head in if I tried it one more time. The next time the ball came into me feet, I could see this lad's challenge a mile off. So I called it, yelling, 'Megs' as I put the ball between his legs. He was fuming and he squared up to me, and we went face-to-face before he smacked me right in the nose and broke it.

It was worth it. It was the same now – and if other players had to resort to flying into tackles or kicking me up in the air, then that was fine again. I'd be the winner because I'd got a man sent off.

Any tricks I tried weren't done to rile anyone up or disrespect anyone; it was me having a good time. It was what football was about for me, football with a smile, and when I was enjoying meself I'd try different things, different tricks, because when I was a fan that's what I liked to see.

For people to come in, pay and cheer the things I was doing just made me want it to do more.

Flynny was great with it all. 'Why should I tell him to stop doing it?' he said after. He and I both knew as long as it had a purpose, as long as I was looking to get an advantage, then it was worth it. There were times when we were in front and I'd go into the corner and juggle with it, mess around with a few flicks, just to run the clock down, but the vast majority of times, if I was trying a dragback, or a step-over, or whatever, it was to make space for a pass, or to make space for a shot or a cross. It wasn't for the sake of it; I knew there had to be an end product.

And there usually was. We were top of the league and I'd got nine goals, well on me way to beating me best for a season. Of course, the funniest thing about all that stuff after the Huddersfield game was being accused of being a showboater – because everyone wanted to be. 'Showboat' was the name of the segment they had on *Soccer AM* where they'd collate all the best bits of skill from different games, mostly in the Premiership or Champions League. I used to watch it every week – I think every footballer did – looking out for different tricks and seeing who did what and whether you could copy it in training on the Monday. The show had got hold of the footage of the Huddersfield game after hearing about it and rang me up, asking me to talk them through it and explain how I did it. At the end of the conversation they said they'd have to get me on soon – and on I went.

I was buzzing, a lower league footballer, not even pro up until a few years back, being asked to go on the biggest football show in the country, with probably every footballer around watching. I was happy just to be meself and have a laugh and make the most of it. I enjoyed the media side of things, whether it was a quick interview with the local lads at the side of the training ground or a shoot down the beach for Welsh telly or Sky. I enjoyed doing something different, experiencing different things. I thought people just wanted to speak to me because of me goals – which I'm sure they did – but I remember a few of the press lads saying later that they always knew I'd be good for a quote or the radio lads would say I spoke in good 30-second soundbites – perfect for their news bulletins. I wouldn't have known that. I didn't know what made a good quote, I just enjoyed people wanting to speak to me because I was still loving the fact I'd made it in the game – there's not many papers covering you when you're playing for Chorley. Of course I tried to be entertaining when I did it, but that was just me. I remember meself, as a kid, watching different players getting interviewed and always liking the ones with a bit of charisma the best. Who's going to want to watch you if you're sat there being boring? It's another form of entertainment, it's what we're there for.

I was up for all that, and I never minded taking the piss out of meself either – and I think the hosts on *Soccer AM*, Tim Lovejoy and Helen Chamberlain, liked that. It was the fact I was willing to laugh at meself that did me a favour in the end. I once wore a T-shirt which had 'I love Dub' on it, the kind of style that had a big heart on it instead of the word 'love'. Anyway, when I sat down and the shirt crumpled up it looked like it said 'I love DVDs' – and for some reason this tickled them. After that, every week they'd show one of me goals and say, 'We spoke to Lee about his goal and this is what he had to say . . .' – only for them to have a picture of me on the screen and one of the cast members to put this thick fake Scouse accent on and shout, 'I love DVDs!'

I still get it shouted at me to this day – which is a bit random – but I don't mind. I like the piss getting taken out me, I think it shows that you're liked, as strange as that sounds. In football, there's always banter in the dressing-room, as you'd expect with lads spending so much time together, but you never take the mick out of the players you don't like, only the ones you do. If someone in the street ever shouted it at me it's because they found it funny but also because they know me for being a footballer, for the goals and the tricks – and that's not a bad thing to say for yourself. It's when they stop saying it, when you stop going on shows, stop having a laugh that you should be worried by it.

Plus, by going on the show I'd managed to get me montage – the one I'd wanted since knocking a ball around on Ashbury – as they put a whole load of me goals and skills together. I was made up. I'd taken Philly with me, and when we went out in Liverpool that night I think I grew another inch every time someone said they'd seen me on the telly that morning. I wasn't just getting by being a footballer, I felt like I was becoming a star – and I loved it.

It sounds a bit shallow and all that, but every kid when they're dreaming of becoming a pro gets as excited about the fame as they do the football.

And the thing with Swansea was, being so isolated as it was in football-terms, having just that one club for everyone meant the attention was that much more intense than in so many other places. In Wrexham, you had Liverpool fans, Everton fans – plus so many of the players lived elsewhere outside the city. Here the players were always made a fuss of, and I loved being involved with the fans. I loved being stopped in the street or on a night out to talk about the game. It's the same now. Some players don't want to know, they shy away, and it's all down to the individual's personality at the end of the day. But I've always been OK to stop and chat about footy, life, whatever – it's in me make-up and I just enjoy it, I guess. I don't know whether that's to do with the attention thing again or just the fact the thrill and the excitement of making it in football have never gone away for me. Flynny always used to reckon I had a bigger buzz from it than many because I got into the game late, because it took me so long to get there and it could all be over before I knew it.

But I always found it strange that there are lads who hate all that attention, but then would be in their element going out and playing in front of thousands of people. They're not afraid to go and perform when thousands are giving them stick from the stands but can't deal with speaking in front of a few people. I can understand some players don't like it, what I can't understand is them moaning about it, moaning about having to go up to the sponsors' lounge after the game because they've won the man of the match, or speak to the press because they've scored. It sounds strange for me to say it after the way I was when I was in non-league, but you realise it's not all about you. It's not about you playing well so you can be pleased with yourself. It's more than just the teammates and manager and all that. It's about the people you're playing for, it's about the people who watch. I know that's rich coming from someone who blew so many chances to be part of it when he was younger, but I'd always been about making the most of the moment – and I was enjoying my moment in the sun with Swansea.

Like before, I was standing out and I was loving it. It wasn't just the goals and the tricks, it was the whole thing. I'd wear the white boots and all the flash gear – the whole showman thing again. But then I'd always try different clothes. I'd always been the first to wear the new stuff back home, and I'd not been afraid to express meself that way. If I liked it, I'd wear it and not worry what people thought. It was different with me hair. There was only a short back and sides for everyone in Liverpool, and dyeing was for women in Huyton. So I don't know whether it was the moving away and wanting to show I was going to be flamboyant, I can't remember, but I decided to have it spiked and long at the back, like a kind of mixture between a Mohawk and a mullet. Dyed blond too. I had plenty of stick for it, some of it well deserved too, looking back, even though I was convinced at the time it looked good. I suppose it couldn't have been that bad because the papers were full of stories about hairdressers in Swansea having to cope with demand for lads coming in and asking for a 'Trundle' – and one kid who got sent home from school because he'd copied me.

The thing is, if you're going to be like that off the pitch then you've got to do the business on it. But I was flying; it didn't seem like I could do anything wrong when I got out there. Ask any striker, when you're in that kind of frame of mind, when you've got that kind of confidence, you don't feel like anything can stop you.

I remember one game against Yeovil down the Vetch just after Christmas. They'd been doing well and it was a big game, almost 10,000 in the ground and things were a bit tight before we won a penalty when Andy Robinson was brought down. I was on pens and had the ball in me hand waiting for the ref to calm everything down and then I noticed Chris Weale, the Yeovil keeper, walking up to me. I'd end up playing with Wealey at Bristol, but here he was trying to have a bit of a chat and put me off.

'So, where you going to put the ball?' he asked.

I had a big grin on me face. 'In the goal, mate.'

He smiled too. 'Which side then?'

Looking him right in the eye, with a wink I said, 'Give it a minute and you'll find out.'

Wealey started laughing and went back to his line – and I managed to put it away to his left. I got another later on too, a last-minute winner, which made it 16 goals in 21 games. Whatever people thought of me being cocky or arrogant or whatever, you couldn't argue with that.

The club weren't complaining either, and I'd already signed a contract extension by then. They'd come to me within the first three months with a better deal – an extra year on top of me original contract – and I was more than happy to sign it. I'd realised I'd done the right thing coming down here, and as much as I was missing Brooke, having to wait for me mum to bring her down at weekends and school holidays, I'd settled in Swansea.

I'd had genuine worries about settling, but the lads in the side and the spirit we had helped put a big dent in any concerns from the off. I was living away from home for the first time, but there were a load of us in the same boat, including Andy Robinson, who I'd already met before when he'd been on trial at Wrexham. Robbo was from Birkenhead – a Jedi as we used to call them – and he was a good lad as well as being a top player. He'd done well at Wrexham, but they'd ended up offering him something stupid like £200 a week and he wanted to try his luck elsewhere. He went to Tranmere but it didn't work out and he ended up playing local leagues and working for his dad's removal company before Flynny gave him a chance with Swansea. He'd had a great start, and we were getting on like a house on fire. He was quiet when he was at Wrexham, not even hanging around for food at the training ground, saying he was going home whenever I'd ask him to stay and chat. But we'd been put together to room in Holland, and it didn't take him long to come out of his shell. I used to love me music, so I'd brought a few CDs, including an oldies one with 'Too Busy Thinking About My Baby' by Marvin Gaye on it. It was one of those that stuck in me head and I would sing it everywhere – and it wasn't long before Robbo was joining in with me like a double act. By the end of the tour, we were both blasting it out until there was a bang on the walls and a Dutch voice coming through, 'Don't you two know any more songs?'

We'd just clicked. On the pitch, we'd have a good idea what the other was thinking, perhaps because we'd got so close off it. I don't think it was just the Scouse thing – even if he was a plastic one – perhaps it was more to do with the similar backgrounds we had in coming into the game so late. But it was also because I found him hilarious and he was easy to take the piss out of. We were in Fairwood once, the university pitches the club used to train on in the Gower, and he was reading the paper in the canteen. He was looking at some picture captions, the joke ones, and there was one with a zebra on a Kawasaki motorbike trying to get away from the lion chasing it. He turned to me and said, ''Ey, Trunds, d'you reckon that's a camera trick?'

'Fucking hell, Robbo,' I told him. 'I know Birkenhead's rough, but I don't think I've seen zebras nicking motorbikes before.' He claims to this day he said it as a joke, but the colour of his face when I started laughing me head off showed it wasn't.

It wasn't just Robbo I got on with, though; there was a load of us, all lads together with similar mindsets and no big-timers.

And one of the things we liked to do together was have a drink. Like I said, we were young lads away from home – most of us single – and we used to meet up quite often because there wasn't much else for us to do. The majority of us used to live down the Marina, where the club put us up in flats, so we used to meet in a pub called the Pumphouse at the end of the waterside. Every Saturday night after a home game we'd be there, have a few drinks and then head over to Wind Street, where we'd hit it hard. We weren't afraid to celebrate, and the ways things were going with the football we had plenty to celebrate. You had people coming up wanting to chat about the game, say well done or bad luck, buy you a drink, which for me was a great way of coming together with the fans. There was a good nightlife in Swansea – and still is – so there'd be plenty of clubs to choose from – and plenty of girls for us to try our luck with. Not all the best looking all of the time, of course. I remember once me and Brad Maylett were in a club called Time when I spotted a girl at the bar who wasn't the best. I gave him a nudge and said, 'Look, it's Neil off *The Young Ones* over there.'

He started pissing himself at this girl, who looked the spit of the hippy student character with the long brown hair, but she'd caught what I'd said, and it obviously wasn't the first time someone had mentioned it to her.

She came right up to me and said, 'Did you just call me Neil from *The Young Ones*?'

'No,' I said before pointing to Brad. 'I was just saying to me mate, Neil, look at those young ones over there.'

'Oh, all right,' she said and everything was fine after I bought her a drink.

It was more about us being out as lads, as teammates, than chasing girls, though. And it wasn't just Saturdays, we'd have a good drink on a Sunday too. Well, all of us apart from Roberto, who was teetotal. He was probably the highest-profile player we had. He'd played higher up the leagues, was a bit older, and he was well known because of all his work with Sky on their Spanish football coverage – but he never came across like that. He wasn't one to look down his nose at us or anything like that; he'd be the one making everyone feel settled and part of things. He'd be one of the ones wanting to go out, wanting us all to be a group, and he was always a massive part of things off the field. He didn't need a drink to enjoy himself, he'd still be right in the middle of things and the first up on the dance floor. Of course, sometimes he'd be the one to say to you it might be best to go home or whatever, but even on a Sunday, our day off, he'd stay there all day, still chatting away when the rest of us must have been getting more and more drunk and harder to understand.

We'd lose track of time when we were out. I remember once seeing Karl Connolly go off to the toilet at one point during the day and not coming back. Karl was another new lad but he was a bit older than the rest of us, Flynny signing him after he'd done well for him at Wrexham before. There must have been at least half an hour gone before someone asked where Karl had gone, and I went off to the toilet to see what had happened only to find him sat there on the toilet, fast asleep with his kecks round his ankles.

Then there'd be a session on the Wednesday. We'd finish training and go to a pub called the Bryn-Y-Mor, have a bit of a pub lunch together and then be on the ale all day, playing killer pool and having a laugh. On a heavy one, we'd stay out and head over to the Adelphi on Wind Street for karaoke. We'd all be there – 'And now, next up on stage, it's Alan Tate!' – everyone would get up and have a go, have a laugh.

We were having a great time and this was brilliant for me – playing football, producing the goods on the pitch and still being able to have a laugh and a drink. There was nothing wrong in that as far as we were concerned – the results on the pitch were backing that up. Looking back now it was a case of me slipping back into old habits, but I was training harder than ever and the way I was in front of goal then I was hardly going to question meself, I don't think anyone would've.

It was having an impact on me weight, though. I'd never watched me diet and it had caught up with me when I started at Swansea. I was probably at me biggest then, even though I'd started to try and eat the right things. It was just I was eating too much of them. We didn't have any food put on for us after training, so a load of us would go to a restaurant on St Helens Road called Paco's. I never ate breakfast, so by the time we'd get there I'd be starving and have a massive pasta dish with meatballs and everything else, thinking that was what was best for me. Now I'd never eat that amount of carbs, but in those days I'd go back at eight in the evening and have another big dish, on top of snacking at home with tea and biscuits. Throw in all the pints of lager I'd drink on a night out and it was just adding up and up. We never had body fat tests then like we have now, and as much as I was thinking that I was doing the right thing, you didn't have the same education about it all as you do now.

It wasn't an issue for me because I was having me best ever season, but I was getting stick off others, off the away fans. It wasn't the first time; I'd got it when I was at Wrexham but, especially after the whole *Soccer AM* thing, the more people knew who I was the more I became a target. I never took it to heart because I just saw it as them trying to get at me because they were scared of me as a player and of what I could do. Besides, whenever away fans have a go it feeds a bit of a fire in you to do well.

I don't think the kit did me any favours, though. People used to be surprised when they'd see me out or back at home and say how they thought I was smaller than I was on the pitch – but I used to wear me shirt hanging out with me big baggy shorts. Plus, we used to only have one shirt size for everyone – large. Look at pictures of little Leon Britton back then and you see the shirt's drowning him – it was a way of the club cutting down on costs.

I have to say though, I never thought I was as big as I was when I saw meself on telly playing for Swansea. We'd played Rushden in the first round of the FA Cup and we'd battered them 3–0, even though they were in the division above, with me scoring the first – chesting down a ball from Kev Nugent and putting it in the bottom corner. Because the BBC had the rights, BBC Wales had their own *Match of the Day* with full extended highlights of the game. The video was in ready because you never expect to see yourself on *Match of the Day* when you're down in the bottom divisions, whether you're doing well and scoring goals or not.

It's another one of those things you dream about as a kid, but winning and going through had given me the chance of making it a reality, especially when we pulled a side from the Conference – Stevenage – in the next round. We beat them at the Vetch, me scoring the second after they got it to 1–1 in the first-half, so we went into the third round fairly easily. Like everyone in the lower leagues, you're hoping to get a big name if you've made it into the third round, but when we came out with Macclesfield at home we all thought we'd have a good chance of going through again. They were in the same division as us and nothing special, but I was up for it – it was me first chance to play in the third round and I knew if I could score I'd get meself on telly that night. In the end, I did more than that; I'd had one of those games where everything I tried came off, every time I got the ball I seemed to beat a man or get meself a chance out of nothing. The main thing was, though, that I got me goals – one a low shot just before half-time, the second a peach of a free-kick from 20 yards. One of me better ones.

They picked it out on *Match of the Day* and picked out some of me best bits of the day, with Mark Lawrenson having a little dig about me not being the quickest – 'Trundle by name, Trundle by nature' I think he said, as well as saying I looked like a Teletubby, but to be fair to him he also said I had too much ability to be playing in League Two.

I was desperate for a Premiership side in the next round to prove it, but we ended up with Preston, a team one division down from the top flight. It still got a lot of publicity, though, because here were Swansea, a team who were 90 minutes from going out of the League the year before, playing in the fourth round of the cup with half a chance of an upset thanks to the game being at the Vetch. Plus you had the whole thing with Flynny and his record for cup upsets – he'd got a reputation for knocking top division sides out of the cup with Wrexham, including that win over Arsenal in 1992.

But there was a lot of attention coming onto me. I'd been named player of the round after the Macclesfield game, and I remember Sky doing a big build-up between me and the Preston striker at the time, Ricardo Fuller, calling us the two form goalscorers in the country. The BBC came down too to do a big piece with me and Lawrenson for *Football Focus* after the comments he'd made on *Match of the Day*, and with him being a Preston fan too. They were great, playing up the whole back story of me coming out of non-league and not looking like your typical lower league striker, but I stopped them when I thought they were stepping over the mark. We were filming down on the beach and they wanted me to boot the ball in the air and shout ''Ave it', like the Peter Kay character in the John Smith's ads that were on at the time. Like I said, I'm more than happy to have a laugh and not take meself too seriously, and they must have thought a lot of me to be screening this interview nationwide on a Saturday afternoon before the game, but I felt they were trying to make out I was some fat pub player.

I knew, though, the game was me real chance to show what I was about, that I wasn't some novelty act. Plus, there was a little bit of edge to it for me after not getting what I thought was a fair crack with Preston when I was at Chorley.

But it was also a big test for us as a side. Preston had been around the top end of the Championship for a while, getting to the play-off final a few years earlier, and had plenty of players who've since gone on to play in the Prem; lads like Fuller, Dickson Etuhu, who's at Fulham now, David Healy, the Northern Ireland striker who scored that goal to beat England a while back, and Graham Alexander and Tyrone Mears, who were up there with Burnley.

They were 50 places above us in the League before kick-off, but we fancied our chances with guys like Britts, who'd been superb all year, Roberto, Robbo who was banging them in for fun and Izzy Iriekpen, another ex-West Ham youngster Flynny had brought in to play at centre-back alongside Kris O'Leary. The fans believed we could do something too, and we had a massive crowd there with an amazing atmosphere. It might not have been the kind of stadium I'd imagined meself playing at when I was kicking around on Ashbury, but the noise was the same.

It was a great opportunity for us, a game where we had nothing to lose. It was my kind of stage.

We flew at them from the start, as most lower league sides do in those sorts of games, trying to unsettle them in our own backyard. It didn't take long for me to get through – less than a minute I think – and I couldn't believe how it had opened up for me. I cut inside and the shot was on, but I ended up making it easy for the keeper. I tried to compose meself a little and tell meself there'd be another chance, but things were getting very tight very quickly. I was being marked by Claude Davis, the Jamaican international, and he wasn't messing around, having a go in me ear from the start. There'd been a lot of him in the press about how he'd kept

Ronaldo quiet playing against Brazil not long before this game, so I don't think he was taking kindly to me trying to get the better of him. It was getting niggly between us and I came off worse. I kept me eyes on the ball as it was coming towards me in the air, but he caught me right on the side of me face and straight away I heard a high-pitched boom. There was a bit of a pop and a flash. I wasn't knocked out, but I knew I'd been hit. We tangled again not long after, with me getting a yellow for leaving something in there for him, and I was probably lucky it wasn't more than a booking.

The knock was me bigger worry, though. I left it until half-time, but as I ran off I felt the side of me face and it was obvious there was a dent where me cheekbone should've been. In the dressing-room, I called over our physio, Richie Evans, to have a look. He didn't take long to tell me it was broken.

'Evo, I'm not coming off,' I said without giving it a second to sink in and with a fair bit of desperation in my voice. I told him it wasn't hurting me and although Evo was trying to tell me it was probably best I came off, both he and Flynny knew that wasn't going to happen. We were matching Preston, and I wasn't going to give up on the rest of the lads, especially the way big Roger Freestone was doing in goal and Kris O'Leary in front of him. Kris was having a stormer despite getting no kip all week because his missus had just had a baby.

I got back out there, but the chances just weren't coming for me. In the end, the possession they were having started to take its toll and they went ahead about 15 minutes into the second half – Etuhu from a corner if I remember. Flynny changed it around a little and brought James Thomas on – another local lad who was a hero in Swansea after scoring the hat-trick against Hull to keep them up the year before.

And it wasn't long before we took the game to them and got back into it. Britts was brought down about 20 yards out, and I fancied the chance from the free-kick. The only problem was that it was on Robbo's side – we had an agreement that I'd curl them from the right with me left and him from the left with his right. A quick 'fuck off' told me all I needed to know, but I wasn't bothered when he put it in the top corner.

There were ten minutes left but there was only one side in it and we were pushing for the win rather than settling for the replay. The ball came into me feet and I managed to get a bit of space before putting it out wide

A child of the '70s – as you can tell by the wallpaper.

Our very own Wembley: Ashbury Road, where football started for me. Not in this photo, though – that's me on the left, off to the school play with a lad called Carl McHale.

The 1986 FA Cup final street party. That's our window behind us, with me Kenny Dalglish flag taking pride of place.

I was always a snappy dresser . . .

A kids' tournament run by the Eagle at Knowsley United's ground. I'm the fair-headed one in the second row, with me mate Tony Blythe on me left. Me cousins are on the left: Michael McMullan (crouching), Kenny Carey and Paul McMullan, with a certain Steven Gerrard in front of them.

Me and me mate Kenny outside Anfield. Getting a few seconds with players like him and Ian Rush meant everything to me, and it's one of the reasons I always make sure I make time for fans.

Double winner and player of the year with the Eagle. I must have thought it was time to start practising me autograph, because I signed the back of this one.

Playing for Liverpool reserves at Melwood, with me mum and me nan, Josie, wrapped up warm in Berghaus jackets – a Scouse speciality. I signed for Burscough shortly after, the first of me six non-league clubs.

Just gone 10 p.m., 7 May 2000 – the moment everything changed. Holding Brooke for the first time.

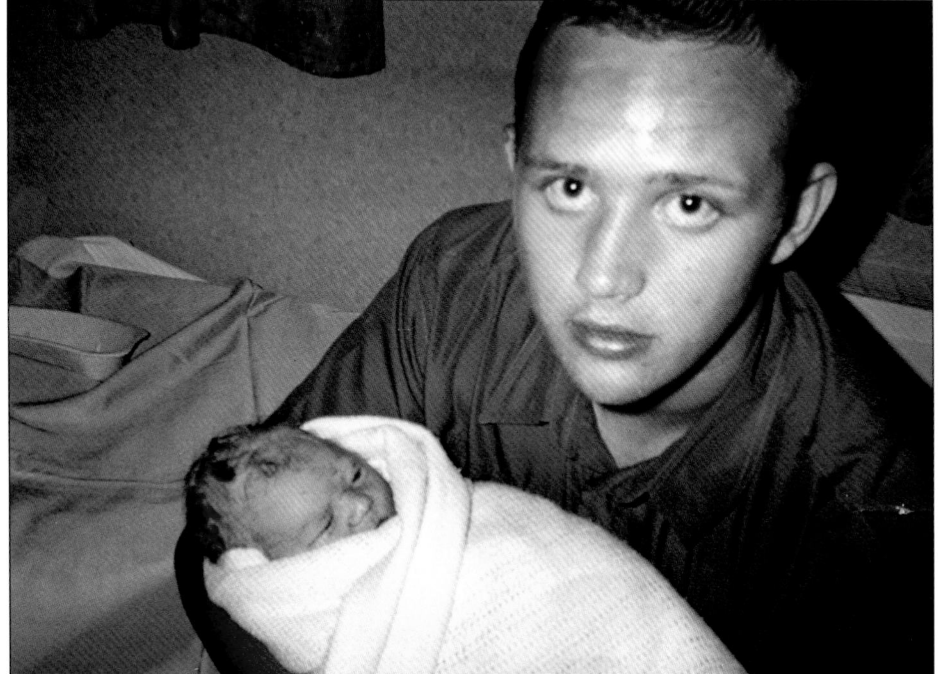

Starting as you mean to go on. Celebrating with the FAW Premier Cup with Mark McGregor, Steve Thomas, Craig Faulconbridge and Danny Williams less than three months after turning pro. (© Les Evans)

On the ball for Swansea against Preston in the FA Cup, complete with Magic Daps. (© Huw Evans Picture Agency)

Showing my love for the club – and a bit of belly at the same time! (© Huw Evans Picture Agency)

'An excellent player' and Patrick Vieira. Getting an ego-boost at the PFA dinner from the man who was about to lift the Premier League title. Left to right: Graham Lewis, Steve Daley, me, Vieira and Phil Dears.

I was always happiest with a ball. Taking a break from the fitness and formations for a bit of fun.

Daddy and mascot before the first game at the Liberty, against Fulham.

Take a bow, son! I always felt appreciated at Swansea. (© Huw Evans Picture Agency)

The T-shirt that caused all that trauma. (© Getty Images)

One of the biggest moments of me career – and I knew it. Scoring the goal that took Bristol City and me to Wembley. (© Getty Images)

Ninety minutes from reaching the top – but it just didn't happen for us that day and the Premier League slipped away. (© Getty Images)

That first goal back in a Swansea shirt. I think the face says it all. (© Huw Evans Picture Agency)

The last game of the season, against Doncaster. Finding the net with our final chance. (© Huw Evans Picture Agency)

The fans haven't realised yet, but I clearly have. The goal that would take us to the play-offs is disallowed. (© Huw Evans Picture Agency)

And the disappointment sinks in at the final whistle. (© Huw Evans Picture Agency)

Me and Charlotte in Vegas – although I'd already hit the jackpot with her. The best thing to come out of me move to Bristol.

Me and Swansea. (© Chris Barroccu Photography)

to Michael Howard. Now, normally I sit out of the box to see if anything comes out and try to hit one from the edge of the box, but I took a gamble and I ran on. It paid off when Thommo headed it on right to where I was standing. I could have headed it meself, perhaps should have, but I knew I had time so I took it on me chest and shot first time and put it past Jonathan Gould, the Preston keeper. Besides, a volley looks better than a header, doesn't it.

I went wild, running off to the North Bank. The sight was just incredible, to see the old stand full and then to see every single one of the fans bouncing in the air. In the centre stand I knew me mum, Brooke and our Frankie were all there to see it and share the greatest moment of me career so far. A goal like that in a game like that – there was no feeling to beat it. I didn't want to come down from the high so we were out straight away, even though Evo was telling me I needed to go to hospital to have me cheek checked out.

'There's nothing wrong with it, I'm all right,' I was saying, more concerned with making the most of the moment and getting on the ale. He let me off and I was to meet him at Morriston Hospital the next morning, luckily not being able to stomach any breakfast before I got there. The X-ray confirmed the cheekbone was broken in two places and they wanted me to have the op straight away. It was the first time I'd gone under for surgery, but I wasn't nervous about it, probably because me mind was still replaying the game over and over as the buzz carried on. It was different when I got out the next day, when the pain started, the adrenalin, alcohol and anaesthetic all wearing off.

But the excitement of the fact we were in the fifth round and all the coverage we'd got from the win was enough to get anyone through it. It had been the big upset of the weekend, and the papers and the telly were full of us, full of me, and I was happy to tell anyone who'd listen how I wanted Liverpool in the next round. Away of course, so I could play at Anfield – and then knock 'em out at the Vetch in the replay. I got close but not quite – we drew Tranmere away. I was gutted – I was desperate for a big team and to have our cup final, but we'd missed out again. All the lads watched the draw together and you could sense the disappointment – we all knew that when you're in the bottom division you didn't get many chances to play the top sides, to make impressions or to savour the big-ground experiences. Ours had just gone. Slowly, though, we started getting more upbeat, that we could beat Tranmere, that we'd have a great chance of making the quarter-finals. I'd read we'd already got further than any Swansea side had in 24 years, and now we could be the first club from the bottom division to get to the quarters since Cambridge in 1990.

There was no danger of me missing it either, broken cheekbone or no broken cheekbone. Flynny told me to go off and get rested up, and Evo had made sure I could play by getting me a mask made, a bit like the *Phantom of the Opera* one Gazza wore playing for England a few years back. I hated it, it kept slipping down all the time, but it was worth it if it would get me playing.

And it did. I'd missed a lot of the build-up because Flynny had sent me up to Liverpool to get away – ideal for me because it meant I could spend a fair bit of time with Brooke while I got the chance and sort of come back down to earth a little bit. I took it easy because I knew how big this could be if we got it right, if I managed to have one of those days. After all, you get to the quarter-finals of the FA Cup and people have got to take you seriously as a player, as a team. Flynny knew it was important for us as well, that it was a big opportunity for all of us as players, so he pulled out all the strings to get the preparation just right. A few days before the game he booked us all into the Carden Park in Cheshire, this big country hotel a lot of teams have used, including Wales and England, and had us all feeling like Premiership players. He made sure we felt relaxed by putting different things on in between training sessions, some lads going off to play golf together, others going for jacuzzis or massages – all the luxuries were laid on. Reevesy had sorted out different team-bonding exercises for the night, and by the Saturday we felt ready to take on the world.

By the Sunday it felt like the end of it.

There's not been many games that have been harder to take than that one, probably because it was so early on in me career and because it had been built up so much. I mean, even now I've never got as close to the quarter-finals. It was different from when I'd lost to Macclesfield in the FA Trophy all those years ago because when you know you've been beaten, when you know you've been outplayed, that they were better, then you can take it – however big a game it is or what the stakes are. Here we at least matched them, we deserved another chance; we didn't deserve to go out.

I was gutted, probably for the fans as much as anything, because I didn't deliver for them. When I'd stepped off the bus at Prenton Park before the game, all I could see was black and white and thousands of fans in these cut-out Zorro masks the *Evening Post* in Swansea had printed. We'd gone ahead. Robbo scored, but, being a Tranmere fan, he didn't want to celebrate; me being a Scouser I made sure I did the celebrating for him. We didn't go for it as much as perhaps we should've, and after they got one back with a penalty it was pretty even – until Iain Hume won it with a 25-yarder. There was one chance, with three minutes to go, but I just pulled it wide and I knew that was that. All that season, I couldn't help but think what would have happened if we'd gone through – Tranmere played Millwall in the quarters and only lost after a replay, then Millwall ended up getting to the final.

Us? We were at Boston the following Saturday. I remember it well because I almost didn't play after I'd left me mask in the hotel and had to wait until just before kick-off for someone to fetch it for me. I had a good reason for leaving it, though. In some of the interviews before the Tranmere game I'd explained how Gazza was me hero, how I loved his way of playing and how I tried to be a bit similar. He must have heard about this because when I answered me mobile that afternoon, he was on the other end.

'Nah, it's not, shut up.' I took a while to be convinced it wasn't one of the lads on the wind-up. It wasn't. He'd been on *Soccer AM* where I'd asked one of the crew to get me his autograph because I was such a big fan. He'd asked for me phone number in return, and here he was telling me how he enjoyed watching me play and to keep doing what I was doing, 'no matter if anyone tries to tell you different'.

It was the biggest motivation that I could've ever asked for. I'd meet him in person later down the years, getting a hug and a kiss off him as he signed his book for me and Philly after a signing session in Liverpool. He's had his troubles after football, but what he did on the pitch was something that always inspired me.

Saying that, after speaking to him and all the hype from the cup games, it wasn't easy facing the reality of it all – and that was that we'd slipped off the pace massively in the league. We had a load of games in hand, but we weren't playing well, our confidence was down and it was all catching up with us. Not just the cup run which, you have to say, was a distraction, as it would be for any side going from League Two to all the big build-up games like that brought.

But the biggest thing that caught up with us was the nights out. It's easy to say now, but at the time we didn't think it was a problem. Flynny didn't turn a blind eye to it, but I don't know whether he knew the full extent of things – though I do remember near the end getting a call from Sangy saying that Flynny had been on to him because our day off had become a recovery day from going out so much. We reined it in a little after that, but he hadn't come down hard. No one said we weren't to go out – and no one was saying anything when we'd been doing well.

We certainly weren't questioning it, but if we'd known what was coming we would have stopped.

There was something like ten games left when the decision came, pretty much out of the blue. We'd lost to Macclesfield and it looked as though that had been the final straw, and the announcement was made that Flynny and Kev had left the club. We hadn't been doing well, but we were still tenth and eight points off the play-offs – it wasn't unthinkable that we could have gone on a run and still have made it. But the club had said that they had wanted them to commit to Swansea by moving to the area and that it wasn't negotiable.

But looking back now I can't help but feel guilty about it all. None of us helped him with the way we were going out so much. People would have known; people from the club would've known because of the type of place Swansea is – the city is like a goldfish bowl and you would only have to be walking down Wind Street and you'd get a call from someone asking what you were doing out.

But we'd be out on a Saturday, an all-dayer on a Sunday, usually a Wednesday too, and then on the next Saturday it started all over again. Perhaps if someone had pulled us in and told us we were taking the piss we would have cut it out; if we'd thought Flynny's job was on the line then it would have stopped. We all loved Flynny and we would never have deliberately put him at risk.

Of course, at the time we didn't think we'd had anything to do with it – none of us did. It was only later, when they tried to put a stop to the nights out, that we realised there'd clearly been a message from upstairs that it had been a problem at the club.

A lot was made of Flynny living away and not coming down, not travelling back with us on the coach from away games as if we were running wild, but it wasn't the case. It was only the odd time he'd stay up north if we'd played up there, and a lot of the players would do the same if they were from nearby.

The club came out and said it wasn't to do with the form we'd been in, but it still seemed a strange one. Yes, some of the fans had got pissed off with results because they knew we had a good side there, and the board were probably feeling a bit the same, but Flynny had taken the club from just staying in the League into a good healthy position with a good cup run along the way. We were above mid-table, not the kind of position where you'd normally see managers leave clubs, and we still could have just about scraped the top seven. Just.

Brian had done well on a bit of a budget too; lads like me, Tatey, Roberto, Robbo, Izzy and Britts all coming in on frees and staying with the club for a fair few years after. In fact, he'd only spent money on one player – Paul Connor – and that was only the week before he left. All right, he'd probably spent a bit on wages and things like that, but we had a good team there and I remember doing a piece in the paper straight after, saying he should've been given more time. The chairman came up to Fairwood and explained what had happened and his reasons for the decision and, to be fair to him, Huw was always good like that, being honest and up front with us, letting us know the facts when something happened.

That didn't stop me being angry about it all. I was upset, and in me head I was remembering what happened the last time and wondering how this was all going to work out – Flynny had been the major reason I'd joined in the first place. I wasn't the only one; Robbo was a bit of a mess because he was another – like me – who Flynny had given a chance to.

Alan Curtis, the former Swansea and Wales player, and a legend down the Vetch, came in to take over as caretaker. I don't think he really wanted to, but he was like that with the club – he'd do anything for it and stepped in when they needed help. The first game after Flynny was Scunthorpe at home and we battered them 4–2, with Conns getting two. We all played for Flynny that day, even though it was too late.

The whole thing took the gloss off the season for me, especially because I don't think I would have done as well if Flynny hadn't given me that licence to just go and play. As much as I've been lucky to have ability and something different about me game, getting told to just go out and perform and show everyone what I could do gave me the confidence to go on. In fact, it probably helped me long after he'd left Swansea.

But even after what had happened, it had still been a great year for me on the pitch personally, and I'd been voted into the PFA team of the year. I got invited to the awards night, a big black tie do near the end of the season at the Grosvenor in London, with about four other lads from the squad. None of them wanted to go and I wasn't going on me own, so I made sure the club accepted all the invites, got our names on the tables and just took a load of me mates from back home along. It was me, Philly, David Green, Stephen Daley and Graham Lewis, all dressed up in our best suits and looking the business. Looking at the seating plan, we had a table with the Norwich City lads, so we went along to take our places before it started. When we got to the table, a fella called Mike Milligan was chatting away to the Norwich lads. He wasn't down to sit there, but he used to play for Norwich and had obviously just come along to the do. Because of that there were too many to sit down, but I made sure me mates all had seats. This Milligan fella turned to us, looked at me mates and said, 'Are these all players, then? Who are they?'

So I began to introduce them: 'Andy Robinson, Michael Howard, Karl Connolly . . .'

'That's not Karl Connolly, I know Karl Connolly,' he said.

But I wasn't in the mood for this. 'So what if it's not?' I said. 'The lads from Swansea said I could use their seats, they've got seats so they're sitting down. Where's yours?' This might have been me first awards night, but I wasn't overawed by it – and I wasn't going anywhere.

But to be fair to him he said, 'No it's all right, I was just wondering. We can get another chair,' and he ended up getting a round in and we had a good night together, especially because Norwich had won the Championship title that year and were going to the Premier.

The PFA do isn't just for the Football League, though, and the place was full of top players. As we were going outside and back to the hotel after, Patrick Vieira happened to be walking out at the same time. Me mates were desperate to get a photo, so I asked him if we could have a picture and he stopped for us. I hadn't introduced meself. I wasn't big-time enough to try and tell someone like Vieira, who was about to captain Arsenal to the title, who I was. But when we took the photo, he said, 'By the way, I think you're an excellent player.'

I said thanks with a massive grin on me face, and the minute he went all the lads were bouncing, 'Did you hear him? Did you hear him?!' None of us could believe it. For him, being at the very top of the Premier, to even notice what I'd been doing way down in League Two was difficult to take in. I'd become a big name in me own division and in Swansea, but I wasn't walking into places like that thinking I was something I wasn't, like I was anywhere near the same level as those guys. Instead, you go back to childhood, looking up to these lads who have won titles, played in World Cups, done the lot. I wasn't in awe of the occasion because I had a right to be there, but I was in awe when I saw these players in the flesh, just as any kid who still has dreams would be.

I had another glimpse of the big stage around that time. Swansea had gone out of the FA Cup, but I still got me day at the final. Winning Player of the Round meant I got a VIP invite to the Millennium Stadium for the Millwall–Manchester United game, all expenses paid. I took Philly with me and we went up to Cardiff on the Friday and had a meal at some posh restaurant with all the top people at the FA. I'm not sure what's the normal done thing at these dos, but Philly is the type of lad who will be himself no matter who he's with and have them all laughing, telling different stories. It was the same thing here – all these guys with Football Association blazers having a good drink and a good laugh with two jokers from Huyton. They put us up in a hotel and then we were driven to the city centre for the match, where all the hospitality was laid on for us at the stadium before the game. Everywhere you looked there were ex-players, legends who'd won it all in their careers – and me. I couldn't believe where I was, pinching meself to remind me what I was doing there. I was buzzing from just having me name in the programme, even if it wasn't on the squad lists in the centre pages, and then I was introduced on the pitch with the rest of the winners. There were a few from non-league from the qualifying rounds, a few more from the lower leagues, then guys like José Antonio Reyes, Freddie Ljungberg and Tim Cahill – big names. They called me name out over the Tannoy as they showed clips of me goals on the big screen, and I couldn't believe the reception I got. I don't know what I was expecting, but it wasn't that. All right, it wasn't a roar, but it was a good cheer – even from the Manchester United fans, who might have given me a hard time for being a Scouser. And from 70,000 people at an FA Cup final, that's not something you get every day. Even if it wasn't me playing out there, I'd still got an amazing taste of the big time. Even walking to the ground earlier, fans from both sides were saying hello, that they liked me skills, and it all showed me that I was making the right impression, doing the right things at Swansea. After all me goals, after the whole *Soccer AM* thing, it showed me I was in the spotlight. Now it was about staying in it – and the work I'd have to do to make that happen.

CHAPTER ELEVEN

January

Saturday, 9 January 2010

'SHE LOOKS LIKE you.'

But me mum isn't on about just Brooke's looks. She's seen her play every week since she started with Liverpool Girls, and she swears she pulls the same expressions as me when I'm on the ball. The same mannerisms, like sticking me tongue out without realising it.

I haven't been able to watch her much since she signed for the Centre of Excellence in the summer, but it's great just to be a dad for the weekend.

Normally I'm fuming when a game's been cancelled, and we were all up for the match up in Middlesbrough, but there's no way I would have been able to make it up here if they'd not called it off yesterday.

Of course, she's a centre-forward, but she's a natural blonde, unlike me in me old days. But me mum's right – she does look like me when she's out there, just playing for the fun of it. She'd only played on the street before, messing around, but one of Philly's little cousins, Faye, played for the Under-10s Centre of Excellence last season and Brooke was interested when I suggested taking her to the trials. Now she's loving it.

I don't know whether the similarities out on the pitch are natural or whether she's just picked up things from watching me so much, from being me mascot for as many games as I could bring her down to Swansea, running out at the Liberty with a No. 10 and 'Daddy' written across her back.

Not that she's seen much of me playing recently.

And it's another reason why it's so good just to be 'Dad' for the day, to be watching her play rather than worry about what's going to happen with me. I should be happy. I am happy. I got what I was after. I got the extension to the loan deal and I won't be going back to Bristol City.

I probably knew in meself it was coming – those goals against Peterborough helped show I was an asset. I was still on the bench when we played Plymouth a few days later, but I got another, the only goal of the game – even if I did have a little bit of a hand off the defender. I had stick for claiming it, but it's in the books as mine, as me fifth in eight appearances.

But now I'm out again, even with Beattie injured I'm on the bench and getting sniffs here and there. The side's doing well. If we're not winning games like we did up at Sheffield Wednesday we're getting the points like at Reading and Palace.

It was after the Palace game – the last game of me loan deal – that I finally got the nod. It was the staff party at the Liberty and the chairman came over, telling me he'd spoken to Paulo and that I'd be staying until the end of the season. I might not have been starting as much as I wanted, but that was the news I wanted to hear. This was where I wanted to be, even if the manager saw me as an impact player. In me heart, I'd already set meself for staying, but it's never enough in football until you hear it for yourself.

All that doubt that'd been hanging over me disappeared – but it didn't stay away for long. Now it's about making sure I stay past the end of the season. I'm confident I'm good enough to – but can I show it as an impact player? Can I show that with ten minutes off the bench?

Some fans have already started saying I'm not fit enough, that I can't last – but how would they know? Me body fat's the lowest it's ever been, I'm the fittest I've ever been, but the only way to get properly sharp is by playing matches. Not ten minutes, not reserve games, proper matches.

I look out at Brooke, chasing around with a smile on her face, wearing the red of Liverpool like I did once, wanting the ball, and I just wish football could be like that again for me. I still love it, I still love playing, I still love training when I'm on the ball, but all the worry and the pressure and the wondering and the uncertainty . . . It's difficult not to let it take over.

It's freezing, but it's good just to leave all that behind for the day, to remember how lucky I am. Lucky that I've got Brooke in me life, lucky that I've got me mum, who's swapped taking me to matches to go with Pat and take Brooke every week instead when I can't be there. Lucky that I can provide for Brooke.

That's what it's all been for. It's been tough – you can't give someone a cuddle over the phone when they're upset – but all those times I've been away I've tried to make sure she'll be all right at the end of it. I mean, she's not known any different. Since she was eight months it's all she's known. It's not as if I walked out when she'd been used to having me around. Like me own dad, I guess. But I've tried to make sure I've always been there, even if I couldn't always actually be there.

And what I've done in me career, she'll benefit from when she grows up – it's why even if there's nothing for me at the end of this season, if I can't show Swansea I'm worth keeping, she'll be all right. We both will.

The final whistle goes. Liverpool have lost, but she's done all right and she's scored – and that's just fine by me.

I'm smiling. Yes, it's frustrating not knowing what's going to be around the corner. But since when has anyone known anything for sure in football?

CHAPTER TWELVE
Trundlemania

PEOPLE DON'T BELIEVE me when I say it, but players are often the last to know when it comes to big news at our clubs. It's just assumed that we get the heads up from the inside about who's coming or going. The truth is, unless one of the lads lets it slip that he's off or this or that club are in for him, we find out when the fans find out.

And there'd been no rumours about who was going to replace Flynny, not among the lads anyway. I knew Mark Wright – yes, him – was one of the people who were given an interview, but even then I didn't find out until afterwards – and it probably would have been the end of me if he'd got it.

Instead, the first I'd heard about our new gaffer was when we were introduced to him by Huw, all sat together in the sponsors' lounge at the top of the East Stand. When I say sponsors' lounge, this was the Vetch, so it was nothing special; it was basically a pub's function room decorated with a few programmes from down the years and different pictures of various Swans players.

I didn't know a lot about Kenny Jackett apart from what a few of the lads had told me: he'd been a top player for Watford when they were in the First Division under Graham Taylor and he'd gone into coaching after he'd retired with an injury, working his way up to Taylor's assistant. He'd left his job as No. 2 to Ian Holloway at QPR, which seemed a bit strange because they were just about to get promotion to the Championship, but he'd obviously wanted to be his own man and fancied a go with us. Huw told us what was happening, and Kenny came into the room, Roberto doing his bit as captain and introducing him to all the lads. As he came towards me, I stood up, just like the rest of the lads had done, and shook his hand. One by one, Kenny went around, until he came to Tatey – who just sat there.

'Where I'm from, it's rude to sit down when you're being introduced to someone,' Kenny said.

But the way Tatey was, being so strong-minded even for a young lad, he just sat there, refusing to budge. It showed how things were still a bit sore with all of us after Flynny had gone, but it was pointless being bitter about it; it had happened, it was gone, it wasn't Kenny's fault and it was just a matter of getting on with it now. It was different for me from when Flynny had left Wrexham and Denis came in, I felt much more attached to Swansea as a club. Like I said, Flynny was a huge part of that but living in the city, seeing the fans as I was out doing me shopping or out on the town, I couldn't help but get caught up in the affection for the club itself. When I was at Wrexham – and like a lot of players do now at different clubs – I'd travel in and travel out. The only time you'd meet the fans would be on a match day. When you're living in a city, walking through town every day meeting friends and hearing them talking about the club and how much it means to them, you get involved even more. As much as I had a soft spot for Wrexham as me first proper club, they never got close to me heart like Swansea did because of that.

But I wasn't daft, I knew none of that counts for anything if the manager doesn't fancy you. But because the fans – and the board – had known how well I'd done that season, I was confident I was going to get a chance under Kenny. I felt I'd established meself pretty well, so there wasn't any need to feel threatened – not yet anyway. Still, all the talk seemed to be about whether I was going to fit in to this new regime. Kenny had been described as this disciplinarian in the papers, people talking about how he was going to get into us and make his mark, and a lot of people were assuming I wasn't going to like that.

In his first week, he arranged to see us all one-on-one. He already knew a lot about us because I remember the chairman saying how Kenny had gone through the entire squad in his interview, talking about our strengths and weaknesses and where he thought he could improve us – as individuals and as a squad. I walked into his office, sat down – and he didn't mess around.

'I've heard you like a night out,' he said in his cockney accent. Kenny'd played for Wales and his family were from Swansea, but he'd lived all his life just outside London.

'Yeah, I don't mind the odd one,' I told him. He asked when it was I went out, probably already knowing what the answer was going to be.

'Well, we'll usually go out on a Saturday after the match, we'll go out on the Sunday on our day off . . . then we might go out on a Wednesday too.'

'Don't you think that's a bit much?' he asked.

'Not really,' I said, straight-faced. 'Some weeks we'll go out on a Monday too, but we've cut that out.'

He must have started to wonder what he'd got himself into, and he didn't waste any time trying to knock the going out on the head. It must have been a big issue with the board, because every player had the same questions.

Kenny wanted to stamp his authority early on, but that was fair enough – and there was no backlash from the lads, which probably says something. I think we all knew deep down we'd been pushing our luck, that if we were going out that many times we couldn't have been at our best. We didn't stop, but we eased right off from then because of what had been said, because it had been spelled out to us; we weren't going to rebel for the sake of a night out here and there.

There was about a month of the season to go when Kenny officially took over and nothing to play for apart from the FAW Premier Cup. He couldn't have been in charge more than a week when we went to Rhyl for the semi-final, and he picked pretty much a full-strength side for the game, including me up front. It was good to go back to Belle Vue, to see some old faces and the ground where it had all kicked off for me, but walking out on the pitch was a different story. We'd had some lovely weather and the pitch was rock hard, but as we went back into the dressing-room to get changed Kenny was going on about how he didn't want to see any of us with 'moulds' on. It was bizarre – if you'd played out there with studs on they'd be going through your feet. Perhaps it had been what was said to him through his career, or that he wanted to add a bit of steel to us, a bit of fight. After all, we'd shown we had the ability in the side, but perhaps he thought we needed to get tougher to get out of the division. But I'm not sure how wearing studs on hard pitches was supposed to solve that and, looking around, I wasn't the only one thinking it. I'd managed to sneak me moulded boots on anyway, but it didn't matter what we were wearing, we were still crap. We lost 2–0 and we deserved to – all live on Welsh telly too. Not the greatest of starts for Kenny.

Being honest, it was probably still playing on our mind about Flynny, because it had come as so much of a shock – no one had braced themselves for him going, no one had wanted him to go. It wasn't a case of not playing for Kenny, but it was just a lot to adapt to at a point in the season where it was all a bit flat anyway.

It was another five games before we actually won again, up in Darlington in the last but one game of the season, and the whole way the year ended was tough to take after the way things had started. It must have been tough for Kenny too, trying to judge players, see what he'd got, where he needed to strengthen with such a lull around the whole place and everyone just waiting for the season to finish. We'd brought in a few players on short-term deals who weren't good enough, and it was obvious there was going to be a big clear-out in the summer. A lot of people thought I might be part of it, that he'd cash in on me to get some money to buy a few others, and it didn't help matters when he dropped me for the final game of the season, a nothing match with York.

It had been the first time I'd been bombed since I'd signed for Swansea, and I wasn't sure what to make of it, whether he was just seeing what others could do or what. I didn't say anything – I didn't have to; the fans did it all for me. It was a tradition for the fans to run onto the pitch for the last game and the players to go up into the centre stand to give them a clap and throw some kit into the crowd. We were all up there when they passed the microphone to Kenny and asked him for a few words. He started off but then ended up sounding a bit like a schoolteacher, telling them all to be quiet as the fans started chanting me name – 'Lee Trundle, My Lord, Lee Trundle . . .' to the tune of 'Kumbaya'. I was part embarrassed because here was me new gaffer trying to lay out his plans for the future and the fans were only interested in me, but of course I was chuffed – they'd made their feelings clear, that they wanted me part of things.

As far as I was aware, so did Kenny, but that didn't stop the stories flying around in the summer. There'd been a few sniffs after the cup run from some top clubs, Portsmouth being one. There was a lot in the papers about Harry Redknapp being keen on me, and when I spoke to Richard Duffy, a young lad Harry had bought from Swansea, he admitted he'd been asked about me. Then Joe Jordan, Harry's No. 2, had come down to watch me a couple of times, although it didn't come to anything in the end. I wasn't expecting much in the summer because of the way the season had faded – and I wasn't looking to get away because I was happy in the city, enjoying me life. Besides, I'd only just signed that new contract.

At the same time, whenever the national press would interview me they'd ask about playing at a higher level – Did I want to? Did I think I could? – and I wouldn't hide me ambition.

But I was talking about top level, Championship, perhaps even Premier League, dream stuff – not just to any old place for the sake of it. But there I was, getting ready for the new season and reading that I could be off to Northampton. The papers ran quotes from their boss, Colin Calderwood, saying I'd been offered to him, that Swansea were trying to offload me. It was all a bit strange, with more stories coming out later that I'd also been offered elsewhere. Kenny denied it when the local reporters got hold of him, saying that he wasn't interested in selling players because he wanted to build a squad. I still asked to see him to get it sorted out and try and find out what the fuck was happening. He looked me in the eye and just said it wasn't true – and I took his word for it. I thought it was more to do with all the rumours of me and Kenny not getting on all coming to a head, because anyone would have known there was no way I – without trying to sound too disrespectful – was leaving Swansea for somewhere like Northampton at that time.

Perhaps there was some truth in it, I don't know. It would have been easy for me to be seen as Flynny's lad, the focal point for the rest of the lads and the whole going-out scene. Perhaps he thought stamping all that out would be easier if he got rid of me. I don't know, but when he said I was part of his plans, that was the issue done and dusted as far as I was concerned. There were no calls from Sangy, none from the chairman – and I knew if I was being offered around, I would have heard more of it than just one manager's quote in a local paper.

Still, I knew if I wanted to make a mark under Kenny I'd have to play by his rules, and he'd made it clear he wanted all of us fitter for the following season. He'd brought in a dietitian from the Welsh Rugby Union to try and help us, brought in a new fitness coach, but he didn't set us any programme through the summer – it was down to us. I gave it a go, lost a fair bit of weight, and I was ready for what he was going to throw at us in pre-season. I'd even grown to like the hurt from all those box-runs he'd make us do – where you'd jog four sides of a box, then three with one sprint, two with two sprints, and so on. If I was hurting, I knew it was because I needed it and it would make sure I was ready to start showing me worth all over again.

I had to bide me time for that, though. I'd picked up a knee injury out in Holland on a pre-season tour, and I missed the first few league matches – none of which were the greatest of games. I scored on me first game back, twenty minutes after coming off the bench against Cheltenham, but we'd only managed a draw, meaning we'd picked up just one win from our first four. That, on top of the way the previous season had finished, meant we weren't even out of August and the pressure was already on Kenny. It was harsh. He'd built almost a new side with a load of new lads coming in, lads like Garry Monk, Sam Ricketts, Adrian Forbes, Kevin Austin and Willy Guéret all coming on frees, but the fact was that he had to deliver.

I remember going to QPR in the Carling Cup where the home fans started singing Kenny's name for all the work he'd done for them – and our fans sang 'Take him back, Take him back, Take him back . . .' A few of us were looking at each other wondering what the hell was going to happen, because as much as it wasn't nice to hear, once the fans are against you you've had it. Football's brutal sometimes; if you don't get results people will turn, no matter what you've done in the past.

The thing was, though, it wasn't just about results. One of the reasons I'd settled so well at Swansea was that they wanted football played, wanted to be entertained, to see the ball passed. It's not often you get that in League Two, but that was the situation and I'd made the most of it. Under

Kenny, it was becoming pretty direct. He'd also dropped Roberto, completely bombed him from the squad, and that didn't sit well with anyone. Roberto was a massive fan favourite and had been since the survival season where he'd helped the club stay in the Football League. He'd developed a special bond with the supporters because of that, and every game you'd hear his name sung no matter what. He was a classy player, able to pick a pass and make sure the supporters got the kind of style they called for. Kenny was the long-ball merchant from the outside, a pupil of the Graham Taylor school of tactics – in the fans' eyes at least.

The QPR game was a turning point, though. I think Kenny backed down a little after that, looked at his squad and saw the footballers we had and changed things a little. Roberto came back in on the Saturday for a game against Cambridge, I scored, we won 1–0 and that was that – we went on a run and were top of the league by October. I think there was a compromise which got the best out of us; we weren't going long, but we were being a bit more direct and a bit more disciplined in every way. Not just off the pitch, but on it too – Kenny knew exactly how he wanted us to play and he wanted us to know it too. Whereas Flynny was more about being off the cuff and being let off the leash to go and play as free as you wanted, Kenny was big on shape, set-pieces, those kinds of things. Training could be pretty boring going through different routines or different scenarios, how to set up if this happens, where to stand for this match or that, but it was adding to our game. We had the talent – we could all see that – but this was making sure we got the most out of it. There was more of an emphasis on defensive work too, but Kenny never tried to rein me in or over-coach me. I was still allowed to go out and play, to go and try things, and he knew I was brave enough to do it. Like when we played Southend, who were up there with us at the time. It had been tight when we'd gone 4–2 down in the last few minutes, and I decided to have a go from the restart, hitting the bar from the halfway line.

My goals didn't come as easily as they had done the previous year, a mixture of being more of a marked man and the way we'd changed our game – I'm not sure we would have kept six consecutive clean sheets under Flynny. Close to Christmas, I went six games without scoring, the longest I'd been on a drought since joining Swansea, but to be fair to Kenny, he backed me.

Because of that me confidence was still there, and it showed when I got three all at once to break the run, and Kenny was backing me big-time, telling me to keep on playing the way I was. I was still coming up with the tricks and the turns – Sky almost used the whole game against Kidderminster at the Vetch for one 'Showboat' one week – and I still had the fans right behind me. I'd go into every game knowing if I performed I'd get a goal, set something up, make something happen. I felt I was better than anyone I was coming up against. It wasn't disrespectful, or at least I wasn't being dismissive of who I was playing against, but I knew I could be at a higher level. I knew if I was on form, if I kept believing in the ability I had, in what made me different, I could come out on top. It may be an arrogant thing to believe but that was me – and every player has to have that about them, that faith in themselves. Otherwise you fail before you've even started. It was the same when we played sides from a higher division – like Preston the year before, like when we took Reading from the Championship to extra time in a third-round replay – I still had that raw confidence: 'I'm better than you, give me the ball and I'll show it.' It doesn't matter if you are right or not, it's believing in it.

It wasn't just me, we had a lot of players who shouldn't have been in that division, and we didn't want to mess it up like we had done the year before. Fall away again and there was every chance lads would have moved on, meself included. Plus you had the pressure coming from leaving the Vetch for the new stadium the club was building with help from the local council. There wasn't anything said from the board, but we all knew what was at stake – a 20,000 stadium in the bottom division would have looked daft. On the other hand, have a good year, go into a new league and the ball could start rolling for the club. Kenny must have felt that pressure, and you could definitely feel the expectations from the fans – every game at the Vetch was turning into a cup final.

But that had its advantages. I remember one match against Bristol Rovers, the closest game Swansea had to a local derby while Cardiff were in a higher division, and their manager, Ian Atkins, was going mad because he said the referee had buckled at the end of the game when there was a shout for a penalty. To be fair, if I was a linesman standing on the touchline by the North Bank I would have given anything they asked for – and he gave us two penalties for one that day. There were only three minutes left when I saw the leg of the defender come out and I took it. The ref pointed to the spot, but for some reason I just smashed the penalty straight down the middle and the keeper saved it. I had me head in me hands and all I could hear was their fans screaming – but then the noise changed and Brad came rushing up behind me telling me the ref had said to take it again because the keeper had moved off his line. Straight away I livened up, knew exactly where I was putting it and started celebrating the moment I hit it. It was all kicking off; the away fans were going nuts – not helped by Andy Gurney, who was from Bristol and used to play for Rovers, right in front of them giving it large. Atkins wouldn't shake hands with anyone after the game and was mouthing off, but the fact was his side had tried to kick lumps out of us that day and we stood tall. Lads like Gurney, who'd come on a free from Swindon, helped with that. Gurns was a good older pro who you knew would have your back. Then you had big Kevin Austin, who played at full-back. Every week you'd see a winger knock it past him and Kev shielding the ball for about 50 yards because he was too big for them to run around. We all had to learn how to take a kick in that league, and I'd often have to suffer the knocks because I was being targeted. But as long as it didn't get personal then you'd have a smile at the end, shake the hand and it's done. You had to get used to the physical side of things, but the key thing was no one would be able to intimidate us, and lads like Gurney and Kev gave us a real toughness.

And we needed it. I remember one game against Boston where we really showed we weren't going to be messed with that year. We'd gone 2–1 up through me and Robbo, but they pulled one back with about twenty minutes to go and it was getting tense. There'd been niggles all match and you could sense it was going to go off – and it did when I won it in the last minute with a penalty. Their manager, Steve Evans, came marching up to me at the final whistle. I went to shake his hand but he wouldn't, calling me a cheat because he thought I'd dived. I hadn't; the defender had been daft enough to dive inside the box, I'd gone past him and caught the leg – I made sure I went down, but it was still a foul.

'You fucking prick, what's wrong with you?' I asked him. He thought better of it and offered his hand, but it was still all going off. This was the same ground I used to think was great playing in the Conference, now I was walking off thinking I couldn't wait to get out, with the way the home fans seemed to want our blood. There was spitting and a lot of abuse, and even their manager was accused of making anti-Welsh comments to Kenny. But it didn't matter – we'd won, we'd pissed them all off and if it was us against the world, then great. Tatey thought so, hammering their door as we walked through this tiny tunnel at York Street.

'Fucking have some of that,' he was shouting, still pumped from getting the win. All of a sudden, their door flew open and some of their players came out looking for a fight, but the corridor was so small you couldn't fit more than three people standing next to each other in it. There were two teams trying to get at each other but no one able to do anything because there was no space. It was like a cattle pen. They had big Jason Lee playing for them at the time, and I could see him standing at the back – I didn't fancy me chances with him much, so I can remember looking around for a smaller lad and leaving him to Kev or Big Willy Guéret if it did kick off. They accused us later of kicking their door in, but I think an investigation showed it had come off from the inside – probably because they were so keen to get at Tatey. And it didn't stop there – our coach had been damaged by their fans too, so it was a pretty eventful day. But we'd got the points and proved we couldn't be pushed around.

It got us in trouble once or twice. We'd played Shrewsbury earlier in the year and both Monks and Robbo had been sent off within two minutes of each other. Monks tells a great story of how he'd been taken into a dressing-room and kicked the door because he was so frustrated. While he's sat there just about calming down, the door flies open again and it's Robbo with the same steward who'd been trying to cool him down.

Robbo got sent off again that season – for a headbutt in a game at Bristol Rovers – and with three games to go that was him out of the run-in. He had that side to his character, that fiery temper, but it made him the type of player he was. He was committed, he'd get stuck in and wore his heart on his sleeve. Add that to the ability he had and he was a very good midfielder. Sometimes he'd go over the top, but you took that for the type of player he was.

All of us knew what he was like, Kenny included, and sometimes you couldn't help but smile at him. We'd gone through a bit of a bad patch where we'd fallen away from the top a little. The senior boys in the side decided to get the lads together and have a proper night out and get a bit of team spirit back. So we all met up on a Sunday afternoon in a pub called the Lounge on Wind Street and decided we were going to start playing drinking games. We ordered a bottle of peach schnapps for the table and every time someone broke the rules they had to down a shot. The longer we went on, the more rules there were: only calling each other by first names, drinking left-handed, those kinds of daft things. It kept going. One bottle went, then another, and we'd all had a fair few by the time we went to leave and asked for the bill. I took a look and realised the lad behind the bar had tried to charge us by the shot instead of just the bottle like we'd done before at the same bar. If you can imagine how many shots are in a bottle then it was extortionate. I tried explaining this to him and ended up asking to speak to the manager on the phone, but Robbo decided he'd had enough and was giving the lad a bit of abuse, swearing his head off and everything else before we decided it was better to leave. On the Tuesday, Kenny called us in and we all sat upstairs in the pavilion at Fairwood. Straight away he asked us to explain ourselves. So we did, telling him about the lad behind the bar overcharging us.

'I meant what were you doing out on a Sunday,' Kenny said, realising we were missing the point a bit. 'And you, Robbo, threatening the barman.'

Then Robbo piped up. 'Gaffer, I wasn't threatening him, all I said to him was "'Ey, mate, that's not fair".'

The place went silent – and then we all pissed ourselves laughing, Kenny included. I don't think those words had ever come out of Robbo's mouth, let alone said so politely. He was rough around the edges, but he was a diamond for us, scored some important goals through the year, and now we would have to do without him for the last few games, including the last ever game at the Vetch.

We were still relying on other results to go up automatically, but it felt as if winning in the final game at the old ground was more important than promotion. The place, as rundown as it was, held a lot of special memories for a lot of people, and there was big pressure on us as a group of players to do it justice. There was a massive build-up: singers on the pitch, the Welsh national anthem, good luck messages from various celebrities, legends being introduced before the game, people like John Toshack and the side he'd taken from the bottom division to the top flight at the start of the 1980s. Because of the move to the new ground, it felt like this was the start of something for the club, and we had to play our part. I was loving it, of course, all the atmosphere, all the build-up – it was like a cup final, and my type of stage.

We got a great start, Adrian Forbes scoring a beaut about ten minutes in – and then we pretty much hung on. The fans were tense, so I tensed up too and didn't get into the game as much as I would've liked, something I was desperate to do at a ground that had been so good to me.

But the most important thing was that we still had a shout of promotion. Results had gone for us elsewhere and we went to Bury knowing if we won and Southend dropped points we were up. It was unlikely, but we took close to 5,000 fans with us that day – just incredible. We walked out for the warm-up and we couldn't believe it, it was like a home game; the Swans fans were rammed in one end behind the goal and right across the pitch in the stand opposite the tunnel.

They didn't stay there for long.

Kris O'Leary put an early ball over the top, Forbesy chased it, nodded it on and hammered it into the back of the net: 1–0 up after about 30 seconds and the fans went wild, running onto the pitch from all over the place. It took a good while for them to get back off, but they were rushing on again when they heard that Southend had gone behind. It was tough to stay focused, especially when Bury were sending men forward and having a right go at us. I can remember turning to one of them and asking what they were playing at, to relax because they had nothing at stake. I don't think they liked the fact we'd practically invaded their ground – their directors had taken the cash by giving Swansea the majority of the stadium – and they wanted to spoil the party. They weren't happy with the fact that our fans kept on spilling onto the pitch either. The more obvious it was we were going up, the more the fans would creep onto the sides before it got to the point where the ref called the managers together to try and get it sorted. A few of their players and their bench started to complain, telling the ref to call it off, but there was no way we were letting that happen. Gurney was straight in there and, as it turned into a bit of pushing and shoving, he headbutted one of their lads and warned there would be more of the same if they didn't back off. It was a farce, but there was no way the ref could call the game off – there would have been a riot. I'd been subbed off with 20 minutes to go, so Kenny sent me behind the goal to try and keep them off the pitch. 'They'll listen to you,' he said. I wasn't so sure about that and I was practically begging them to stay off until it got to the point where the ref could blow up. When he did, I don't think I've ever run as fast, trying to make sure I got to the tunnel before the fans got to me. They'd all come on for the last game at the Vetch and it was a bit too much for me, people grabbing me, trying to get bits of kit; I'd felt claustrophobic.

We did want to celebrate with the fans, though, and when we got into the dressing-room area one of their directors told us to go up into the centre stand. We all piled up there with the champagne, spraying the fans below, bouncing up and down, all pushing to get near the front. Robbo, who had travelled up even though he couldn't play, was swinging off the front of the stand, and some of the lads had stepped over the barriers and were trying to get on top of the roofs of the conservatories that were just below.

The police had started to get involved by this point, although I'm not too sure why – I think they said they were concerned about the safety of the crowd, but the crowd were having a great time partying on the Gigg Lane pitch. Our big French goalkeeper Willy Guéret had stayed right at the front when the police and stewards started breaking it all up, and Willy was someone who didn't like being pushed – whoever it was doing the pushing. He gave a push back and, after getting a warning from the copper, did it again. I don't think anyone thought he was going to get arrested, but there he was – with his top off having already thrown it into the crowd – our goalkeeper standing on the top of the stand at Bury in handcuffs. The fans went mad, chanting 'Free Willy' at the police as he was led off; the whole thing was just surreal.

The stewards came up to us all and ordered us back down the stairs because there was a real worry things were going to get out of hand. So we headed downstairs, still not sure what the hell was going on. All we knew was that we had been promoted. Of course, seeing our goalkeeper carted off had put a dampener on things, but it didn't take long for none of us to care. We must have been worried about him for all of a minute.

I was back in the same dressing-room where I'd run out to find out how Swansea had got on against Hull in me last game for Wrexham – I was back in the same place and back in League One. I'd got 23 goals, better than I'd done the previous year, and I'd played in 42 of the 46 games. And yet I'd still done it me own way, playing football the way I'd always played it. It hadn't been as sensational as the previous season, but I'd known that it was more about me moving up now. It wasn't about sacrificing the way I played to get there, but I knew I couldn't be taken seriously much longer if I was hanging about in the bottom division.

That was all for another day though as we celebrated at Bury. Kenny was on top form, asking one of the old Swans lads in the press, David Giles, if he could recommend any good goalkeepers in case he couldn't get his out of jail.

We went to pick up Willy together, but only after getting the coach driver to make a quick detour to Tesco to pick up slabs of ale for the four-hour journey home before pulling up outside the police station. We'd all been singing different songs as we started to enjoy ourselves, and it must have been a pretty strange sight for anyone passing, but eventually out he came, still in his football kit. There was a huge roar when he got on – he'd been given an on-the-spot fine and he wasn't going to live it down from us as we asked if he'd been too scared to take a shower in the nick and all that.

Even Willy had found the funny side to it, and we were having a great time as we made our way home before Kenny strode up to the middle of the coach. We were playing the FAW Premier Cup final on the Tuesday and he wanted to remind us.

'Right, OK, lads, well done, but there's a big game in midweek, have a good night but take it easy . . .'

He hadn't finished talking before he was covered in lager – it wasn't the time for lectures and he probably knew it. Besides, I'd already been on the phone to the manager at Crobar, one of the dance clubs in Swansea, making sure they were expecting us, all 20-plus of us dancing the night away in our trackies until the early hours.

The FAW Cup game was a few days later, but that was a celebration in itself – a second final game at the Vetch. We were playing Wrexham, the first time I'd gone up against them since leaving, and although I couldn't believe it when I heard a couple of their fans singing 'Trundle is a rapist' after all I'd been through with them, nothing was going to spoil the night for me.

We went one behind, but I was right up for it – a game against me old club and the chance to get the last goal at the ground. I'd had thirty-one, every one of them celebrated in front of that North Bank, but to get the final one would have been special. It didn't happen though; the best I could do was force an own goal for the first and then set Robbo up for the second. It didn't matter too much, especially as I refused to let Robbo take the credit for it, saying only the last league goal counted and Forbesy had already got that.

People knocked that competition – it doesn't exist now – but it was a good excuse for a party that night and the fans were loving it; another chance for a pitch invasion and to grab more souvenirs from the old place, ripping down whatever signs they could – a few had even brought spades to get bits of turf. I've seen some clubs who've moved grounds put everything up for auction, but this was the best way – it was the fans' place after all, so let the fans take what they wanted. I always felt the club had a special relationship with their supporters, and the fact that no one was batting an eyelid as thousands of fans walked out of the ground that night with their seat under their arm just summed it up for me. It was the city's club, and it was there because of the fans. We were all in it together, and with the move to the new stadium we could feel a door opening for all of us.

The new stadium was literally called the New Stadium for a while – at least until they found a sponsor and called it the Liberty Stadium – but it felt like home from the start. We'd been taken there when they'd just finished the shell of the building – no seats, and diggers still on the pitch, but you could get a feel of the place, the size, and start picturing yourself walking out there with a full crowd. I was dead proud of the place before I'd even played there, driving me mates past it every time they came down just to show off. It was a step closer to the top for me, even though I hadn't moved anywhere. I felt I was closer to the Premier just by being in this new environment. There weren't many new grounds in the lower divisions, but I always felt an excitement when I'd gone to Reading and the Madejski in the cup or to Hull's new place and felt I'd raised me game. Just thinking about it happening every week had me buzzing for the new season.

I wanted to really fly, wanted to hit the new division from the start. I felt more professional just from having this new ground to play in, and I wanted to go there and make sure I impressed from day one. So I did something about it.

I'd always do some training in the summer, or at least some exercise just to keep me ticking over, but it would normally be a kickaround with the lads, five-a-side just to have a game rather than with any fitness in mind. It's not the same – in football when you're tired you can stop, ease off for a bit and carry on when you get your legs back; it wasn't the proper training I felt I needed this time. I started back on the running, but I was never a fan of just jogging round the streets until you got bored, so our Frankie suggested I go with him to Huyton Boxing Club for something a bit different. And it was: circuits, skipping, press-ups, bag work, pad work – all different from what I was used to, and the intensity of it all really got me blowing. It was tough and it wasn't much of a rest, but Kenny had told me he wanted to see an improvement in me fitness and I gave him one. By the time I came back I'd lost almost a stone in weight and it was noticeable – although just shaving me head because I'd had enough of the mad hairstyles made a difference on its own.

Still, I was the fittest I'd ever been, coming in the top four in the tests in that first week back instead of the bottom four, coming third in a triathlon out of all the lads when not so long ago I don't know if I'd have managed to finish it. It was a good job too; Kenny took us off to RAF St Athan for a week of pure fitness work, and it was like being in the army. Evo had designed our schedule and it was a nightmare, staying in this tiny room on camp beds, up at six for a session before breakfast and not finishing until nine that night, when we'd do some pool work to finish off. There were four sessions a day and it was horrible, even if we all knew it was for our own good. And I guess that was the difference between the old me and the new one – the penny had finally dropped about what it was going to take if I really did want to make it. I would have walked out of that camp before, I would have been arrogant enough to say I didn't need the fitness. Before, I'd never been bothered about it too much. I'd stepped it up a gear to get into football, but I'd got along with me ability on that base level. Now I wanted to take it up a notch, I wanted to do meself justice. I can remember telling meself I'd come this far but if I wanted more it would take more. Not by compromising the way I was or who I was, but taking away the reasons why I couldn't go all the way.

There were those who didn't believe me. I wasn't even on the betting list for top goalscorer, despite the fact I'd been up there in League Two for the past two seasons and had scored at this level before. I'd always loved seeing me name come up on *Sky Sports News* when the top scorers' panel would flash up – that hunger wasn't going to vanish just because I'd moved up one division.

And I was convinced that was all I needed – that hunger to do well because I knew I already had the ability. That's why criticism didn't bother me, especially back then. If the bookies didn't fancy me, fine, it wasn't about proving them wrong, it was about proving meself right. It didn't stop me telling some of me mates to put a few quid on me at long odds though.

I should have got up and running after the first game too. We'd played a couple of friendlies at the new place before the season started properly, the first a game against Fulham in a testimonial for Alan Curtis. To run out for the first time was amazing and to do it against a Premier team was perfect. But playing in Curt's testimonial meant a lot too. He was a legend at the club, helping it to the First Division under Tosh, but it was the way he played that made him stand out. A lot of people used to say there were a lot of similarities between him and me, and he would always be there to offer advice, about how to handle certain situations, and I definitely looked up to him. It's why I've still got a photo framed from that game – Curt in his No. 7 shirt clipping a pass through to me. I didn't get me goal, though. I'd been saying all week how much I wanted to score the first at the Liberty after not getting the last at the Vetch, but all the lads had been giving me stick, saying they weren't going to pass to me to make sure I didn't get it. Marc Goodfellow did, and I'd have to wait for me chance to open me account at the new ground.

It came when we started the season against Tranmere – but I never took it, one of their defenders clearing off the line in the first few minutes. I had a penalty too after I'd been brought down just before half-time – but I missed it. They'd just missed one through Jason McAteer, but mine was crap – I'd changed me mind at the last minute and ended up rolling the ball to the keeper.

Anyway, the honour had gone when Bayo Akinfenwa, one of our new signings, got what turned out to be the winner. Bayo wasn't like your average striker – I mean, what strikers are 17 stone? You definitely wouldn't have wanted to have got on the wrong side of him because he was a big lad. But he wasn't fat like many people thought – his body fat was pretty low, considering, and when he took his top off he was solid. He didn't help himself because the way he walked was as if he waddled – but that was his strut. He was funny like that, coming from London but speaking and acting like he was American. He had a really different background, playing all over the place – even in Lithuania – before ending up in Swansea. I think he'd been a bit of a wild lad when he was young, but he'd turned to religion and he'd always be saying his thanks to God but without pushing his beliefs onto anyone else. It was strange, if you just took him on first appearances you'd think he'd be a right angry head, but he was more of a gentle giant than anything.

He was big into his family too – and it was a big family. I remember, just before Christmas, he'd been allowed to go back to Nigeria where his grandmother had passed away, but he'd missed his flight home and it took a while for the club to find out what was going on. You couldn't make it up, but we made the most of it, making sure Kenny got a Christmas card that he read out to all of us at training: 'Dear Gaffer, having a lovely time, weather's great, don't know when I'll be back, lots of love, Bayo.'

But aside from all that, he was probably the best strike partner I had at Swansea. He was strong as anything and he was great to play off – he was the big man I wanted, not just in the air but with a lovely touch, and he set me up with a hell of a lot that season.

But not that first day, that was me setting him up – chesting the ball from a throw-in, flicking it over me head, hanging it on the back post and watching two defenders shit themselves when they saw Bayo go in for the header.

It was just what we needed in the new division, and it didn't take long before we were flying as a side again. The whole new stadium thing had given everyone a lift, not just me, and we were full of belief that we were good enough to challenge in this league even though we'd only just come up. How can you not think like that when you go and beat Bristol City 7–1? I managed two that day to make it five from five, but Kevin McLeod was taking the headlines away from me. He'd got a hat-trick in the Bristol game and was coming good for Swansea after struggling to get over glandular fever when he'd first signed. Macca was a top player. He'd started off at Everton and had played a few first-team games so everyone knew he had ability, but it was only now that he started to show it. He was a bit younger than me and Robbo, but Kenny used to love talking about his three Scousers, all with bad haircuts and bad dress sense as he used to tell us. I'm not saying I was perfect, but the other two didn't do me any favours for not getting the mick taken out of us. Like when we flew to a game for the first time. We were playing Hartlepool away and the club sorted out a deal with a local airline so we didn't have to spend seven hours on the bus just getting there. It's standard for a lot of clubs nowadays, but back then, and us being in lower divisions, it was all new. We'd been told to bring our passports as the form of ID everyone needed for domestic flights, but Macca thought they were taking the piss so didn't bother. They had to use his Macros card and a player profile from the club programme just to get him on the flight. We got there an hour later, but the minute we were on the tarmac Robbo was phoning his mates back in Birkenhead.

'All right, mate? I've just landed . . .' just so the lad on the other line would ask him, 'Oh, so you've been on a plane,' and Robbo could brag about flying to a game. He must have made five calls, all saying the same thing.

Anyway, the club was showing how professional it was starting to think now we'd moved out of the Vetch – and it worked, because we got a decent draw that day with the two I got taking me past fifty for the club. I wasn't stopping, though, and with the side showing we could challenge in the division I was having a great time.

Me confidence was just massive. Ask any striker, they'll tell you sometimes you just go through periods when you're in the perfect frame of mind, you're in that zone where you know as soon as you get a chance to hit something, you hit it because it's going in. It's like the Midas touch – you just know whatever you're doing is going to come off. It might last for a week, a month – with me it felt like it was lasting forever – but when you're there you make the most of it. You hit shots early, you'll take on the world because you don't fear anything. You feel untouchable.

I was going into games feeling teams would fear me and that me teammates had complete faith in me. That was probably the biggest thing – they knew what I could do, they trusted me and they knew I could produce for them, that I could create a bit of magic in a tight game or when things weren't going our way. Some players don't like that, don't want to have that responsibility, but I always felt better when that pressure was on me and I felt it brought the best out of me. To know that someone is depending on you is brilliant and can shake you out of a bit of a lull, make you pull your finger out and perform. If one of the lads shouted over during a game, 'C'mon, Trunds, we need something here,' then I'd love it. It's on your shoulders, but it wasn't something that weighed me down – it lifted me up. To know I had to be there for teammates, I thrived on that.

Some days it wouldn't come off, I wouldn't get it right and I'd get told like anyone else, but when it happens no one has to say anything because you know yourself you should have done better. The lads used to take the piss because whenever I went on a run and messed up or knew I should've passed to someone I'd never look up at them – all they'd see was me with me hand up or giving them a thumbs-up with me head down. I'd get stick for not giving it or going it alone, but at the same time they knew they had to let me try things because that's what made me different, that's what made me dangerous. Sometimes it was worse than others, though. I remember one game at the Vetch when we'd broken quickly. I'd pulled the keeper out of position, and Roberto was in with only the defender in front of him if I passed it – but I'd shot meself and missed. We watched it back on the video the next day and you can see Roberto shouting at me to give it him, then with his arms up – by the end he had both hands in the air waving frantically like he was giving out an SOS signal. He never got many goals, Roberto, so I don't think he spoke to me for the rest of the week.

With me profile rising I'd get plenty of stick on the pitch from the other side too, but I could laugh at most of it. I never minded the centre-backs who would try and use it against me, say they were going to make sure I couldn't do a photoshoot if I tried something or that they were going to do this or that to me. None of that bothered me, but I'd hate the ones who'd try to talk normally, as if we were mates down the park. I couldn't stand it, it used to put me right off – I'd rather the pinches and the break-your-legs chat than, 'Oh, all right, Trunds, how you doing? Saw you on the telly the other day,' that type of thing. I guess part of the reason was I wouldn't want to get into them too much if they were being all pally.

But I wasn't thinking too much about defenders at that time. I wouldn't go into a game worrying how to beat them – I was going into games wondering what I could do to them. Me confidence was showing through and people were really starting to take notice. I wasn't some novelty act from League Two any more.

We played Southend around the October at Roots Hall – we were both right up there in the table and we needed a win to go top. It was a big game and, because it was an international weekend and there were no Premier League or Championship games, it was match of the day on the Football League show on ITV. They had done the big build-up, saying it was me versus Freddy Eastwood, who'd done really well for them, and making a big deal of us both climbing up from non-league. I was right up for it, the big occasion and the chance to show a bigger audience what I was all about. A chance to show that I'd stepped it up since that cup run under Flynny, that I was more than just tricks.

And I rose to it. I hammered the first and then I set Bayo up for the second – getting the ball in the box, keeping it tight to me, getting around three men and getting a shot out of nothing before he put the rebound in when it was cleared off the line. I was man of the match and even got applause from the Southend fans – it was just one of those days where everything I tried came off, every piece of skill. The local press lads were saying to me after that there were a lot of national reporters there and all they'd wanted to do was ask Kenny questions about me – but it was at times like that, when I could feel more eyes on me, that I always seemed to come good. I mean, it's always better to do something in a game that people are going to talk about if you want to get talked about yourself.

It wasn't just the newspapers. Andy Townsend was there for ITV and he came out after and said some good things about me and that I deserved a chance with Ireland. I'd always made a big thing of wanting to play for the Republic because me granddad was from Inchicore. Flynny had made a few calls to Brian Kerr, their manager, when I first got to Swansea and started scoring, but I'd heard nothing. After the Preston game in the cup, Lawrie Sanchez, the Northern Ireland manager, had been on to Flynny asking if I was eligible for them, but I didn't qualify – and I only wanted to play for the Republic anyway. Wales had asked too, and I loved the fact I'd had international sides checking out if I had any connections – you can't get much bigger recognition. When Andy Townsend picked up on it, I thought it might help me, especially as he was a former Ireland captain, having played for them in the World Cup, and now quite a well respected pundit. I was still in League One, but I was proving I wasn't a flash in the pan, and he reckoned the extra time at international level would actually suit me. And that's the thing. It might sound daft, but if you're confident, you can be thrown in at any level – and that was the case with me. I'd gone from non-league to the top of League One, raising me game all the time. If they'd put me with international players I would have lifted me game again. Look at Sam Ricketts – he'd already been called up for Wales after being in League Two with Swansea and showed he could handle it.

And at the time it really was a case of why not? I was the top scorer in the division – in fact, with 17 in 17 games I was top scorer in any division. Ireland's strikers were Robbie Keane, Clinton Morrison, Stephen Elliot and Gary Doherty, so I felt I had every right to be in contention – Keane was the big name and Clinton Morrison was scoring at a higher level, but I could have fitted in there.

But nothing came – not a B squad, nothing. There were a few League of Ireland players in the squad at one point, and I just couldn't see how that was a better standard than where I was. I got me hopes up again when Steve Staunton took over as Ireland manager the following year, someone who would have known about me from his time at Walsall in Swansea's division. He gave an interview saying I had a chance if I kept on scoring; I kept on scoring but I never got me chance. It killed me because I was desperate for it – not just to get international honours but to play for Ireland. It wasn't bullshit. I just wanted that one call-up, just one chance, but it never came and it's one of the big regrets of me career. It would have capped it all to have played for them because it really was a dream for me since I was a young kid where me mum and me nan would speak about me granddad. I watched them in Italia '90 as a kid, playing on Ashbury in the emerald green shirt when everyone else had England ones on. I know it's easy for people to write off all that saying I'd only mentioned playing for them because it was me easiest way to get an international cap, but when you're a kid you don't think like that. When you dream you don't dream about playing for Ireland because you don't think you're quite good enough to play for England. You play for who you want in your dreams. I dreamed about playing for Ireland because I wanted to play for Ireland.

But if Ireland weren't taking me seriously, at least other clubs were. It was in the October and I remember the phone going. It was Sangy.

'Sheffield Wednesday are going to put a bid in for you. D'you fancy it?'

I knew Wednesday were a big club, and although they were only a division above, they had plenty of history and were playing in front of 25,000 every week at one of the top old grounds.

'I'm not interested.'

I didn't even give it time to sink in. Huw let me know about the offer when it came in officially, but I said the same to him – I didn't even want to hear what they had to say – which suited him and he could turn it down without any fuss. You have to give the board credit for that, because £750,000 – which is what Wednesday were offering for me – wasn't a small amount for any club in that division, but they stuck to their guns and said it wasn't enough.

A lot of people were surprised, because I think they'd assumed I'd be off the first chance I got to move up. But to me it didn't make sense. We were top of League One and not looking out of place; they were near the bottom of the Championship and could've easily been relegated. The last thing I would've wanted to do was leave and in six months' time find meself back where I'd started. The way I saw it, there was a chance for the ideal scenario – getting to the next level with Swansea. I loved the club and I loved the city, and I wasn't going to underestimate the value of that by jumping for the first offer that came in.

I did think there would be more, that this bid was the first of a few. With me profile and the goals I was scoring and the bid from Wednesday getting so much coverage I thought there were bound to be more – but it never happened. It didn't disappoint me, I wasn't looking to move and it was well before the transfer window opened in the January so the timing of the whole thing had come as a bit of a surprise anyway. And I hadn't turned down Wednesday just to hold out for the next one, to hang on in case a Premier club came in – I just took that one offer on its merits and turned it down because I believed in me heart I was better off staying.

To be fair to Huw, he made sure it was worth me while to stay. He and Sangy got on well back then; they would speak all the time about this and that, and Neil had already floated the idea of image rights to him. Sangy'd always be talking about different ideas and when he mentioned it to me I told him I'd be right up for it if he could pull it off, not really expecting him to. David Beckham and Michael Owen were probably the only two players I'd really heard of with a similar deal, where you either get a cut of everything sold with your name on it or just get an up-front fee. We had a case, though – if you walked into the club shop me face was everywhere. Apart from me shirts with No. 10 on the back, there were posters, pictures, dolls, birthday cards, mugs, bedspreads, all sorts. I think I saw one figure that said 85 per cent of everything that was being sold at the club shop had me name on it. There were even knickers, thongs to be accurate, with me face on the front – although if I ever saw a pair of those on a girl I would've kicked her out of bed. Even I don't think I could handle me own face looking back at me, although I did sign a few pairs – just not while anyone was wearing them.

The whole thing was different, to say the least, but I think Huw wanted to reward me loyalty a bit for turning down Wednesday. He could see I was happy at Swansea and that I wanted to do well for the club, so we agreed and sorted out a fee which allowed the club to market me image however they wanted. The papers loved it, with *The Sun* and the *Daily Mail* lapping it up, especially when we had the press conference to confirm it with the new brand – LT10. They put out a range of clothing soon after, sweatshirts, tops, shorts, T-shirts, all with the logo on it. The press were calling me Wales's David Beckham – although I don't think I could've got away with wearing a sarong down Wind Street. Still, it was great publicity for me and for the club who – from going from the Vetch and the bottom of the Football League – suddenly started looking like a really progressive and ambitious side.

Not that any of that stopped the stick I got from the lads, going into training the next day to see LT10 written on all the Tubigrips. They sold the clothes range in different shops in town as well as the club shop and, although I don't think I would have gone out in any of it, I was gutted I never kept anything. I've been a bit lax like that over the years. All me Swansea tops have been given away to fans and different people, and it's only recently I've started keeping the tops I've worn in big matches. The thing is that they mean so much to the people I've given them to, whereas

I'll always have me own memories and the experience of being there in the middle of it, something that the fans can never have. I don't need a top in a wardrobe for that, as nice as it will be to look back on when I'm done. That said, perhaps it's better that me shirts are on someone's wall, in a frame, whatever – not because it means more but because it shares a little bit of what I was lucky enough to have.

One thing I did keep was the Swansea edition of Monopoly they brought out with me on the front – and I can tell you there's a few of them knocking around Huyton after the Christmas they first went into the shops. Even now, if I'm in HMV and I see it on the stand I'll stop and have a little look and pinch meself, that I can be so associated with a city to make it onto Monopoly. It's crazy, especially being from Liverpool rather than South Wales.

But that was what it was like at the time – crazy. I wanted the world to slow down because everything was happening for me so quickly. I'd had an offer to appear in a play at the Grand Theatre and was bang up for giving it a go until we couldn't agree a schedule. I seemed to be on every paper you picked up, in the front or in the back, photo shoots, fashion magazines, the lot – and I was making the most of it. And if it wasn't me, it was Gavin Henson – the Welsh rugby player who was at the Ospreys. He'd had a massive year with Wales and the Lions, and he was a bit like me in not caring what people said about what he wore, the different haircuts and all that. One of the papers tried to make something of it, running a poll to find out who was the most popular at the time. I won it, but I would have swapped it for his six-pack any day.

Everything had just exploded for me, and it was getting to a point where I couldn't ask for much more. I'd even got a nice new place in the west of the city, which was definitely an improvement on the front bedroom of a council house back on Ashbury. Part of me deal was for the club to look after me accommodation, so I went around looking for something perfect for a young single lad to impress – and I found it. It didn't look much from the outside, a bit like a bungalow in the nice part of town, but there was a downstairs into this plush living room that I'd fitted out with all the mod cons, a dining room at the side that I'd turned into a games room with a pool table. Out the back it had a huge conservatory, the same size as the house itself, with a huge swimming pool and a sauna on the side. The balcony around the back had views over the beaches and it really was stunning – a bachelor's dream.

I had plenty of chances to show it off too. I'd have huge parties. I remember one pool party with everyone in Hawaiian shirts. Plus, there would be a new girl to bring back every week, every night almost. When I'd first go out on the pull back home it was a case of chasing after them, buying the drinks, talking for hours to try and get lucky – here it was girls chatting me up. I couldn't believe me luck at times – and neither could the lads from Huyton every time they'd come down to see me. I'd go out on the weekend, pick up different numbers which would sort me out for a different date for the week and then start over at the weekend. In the space of one season I went out with a Miss Wales, a Miss England and a Miss Great Britain – I'd have gone to Scotland and Northern Ireland to complete the Grand Slam if I'd not been so busy. There was a lot of talk that I went out with Imogen Thomas, a former Miss Wales who ended up on *Big Brother*, but we'd only met once or twice and it was nothing serious. I'd get invited to a load of different events, different dinners and dos, and I'd pick up a different girl at each one – even if they knew I wasn't looking for a girlfriend. I'd always made that clear and especially after what happened at Wrexham I was quite wary at times. Not long after it happened I'd always send a text to the girl the next day saying I'd had a nice night and hoped they'd enjoyed themselves, waiting to get a text back saying they'd had a nice night too so I knew there could be no way of anyone saying anything like that again.

But I wasn't going to let that ruin me life and stop me enjoying me freedom as a single lad. After all, it was any young lad's dream to have girls chasing after him. When you'd talk with your mates as a kid it would be one of the reasons you wanted to become a footballer.

But the main reason for wanting to be part of this game was still for the highs you got on the pitch – and when it came to that I was living the dream.

The fans had really started to believe something special was happening with the side, and when it came to our first game under the floodlights, on a Friday night against Yeovil, we sold out the Liberty for the first time. We'd been getting good crowds, bigger than Cardiff City up the road were getting in the division above, and the stage really was set for me. After the bids and the transfer rumours, and then all the image rights stuff, I was all over the national papers and they had begun to send more and more reporters down to our games because of the interest. People were calling me the most talked-about player outside the Premier League and, if you looked in the press and on the telly, it was probably a fair shout.

I knew there were people down to watch me against Yeovil, and the atmosphere building was turning it into something a bit different from the usual. The Liberty had a different feeling from the Vetch, like any new stadium would compared with an old-fashioned ground – after all, it was the type of place to bring your wife and kids, whereas you probably wouldn't have wanted them anywhere near the Vetch.

But Friday night games always used to bring the best out of the fans, the lads all having a chance to meet after work and get a few beers in because the missus had let them out. Our games used to get shifted to a Friday quite often if it clashed with the rugby, but whereas it would knock other clubs' attendances, ours would go up. Through the roof in fact. There was always a buzz around because it was the start of the weekend for a lot of the fans, with Swansea being a working-class place – and the buzz carried onto the pitch.

The Yeovil game was the biggest crowd I'd played in front of at the time, and I knew I needed to shine – and I knew I was going to. Sometimes I've sat in a dressing-room before a game and thought 'this is made for me' – and every game that's happened I've gone out and done it. It's that confidence again, but it's something that's in your gut rather than your head. It's something you can't force, something you can't turn on when you want to. It's just there.

It was there that night. It had been a tight game, but we were starting to cause them problems. They had a lad called Efe Sodje at the back, a Nigerian international, but I knew he would always fly into the tackle. I went for him – dropped the shoulder to go past and waited for the foul. I didn't waste any time with the penalty because I just wanted to hear the noise with that many people there, all wanting me to do well for them.

I ran towards the stand behind the goal and kissed the badge on the centre of me shirt. It was something I'd started in me first season at Swansea, but it wasn't something I'd done before then or something I'd planned. I can't remember what game exactly because it was just a case of doing what the emotion tells you – and it was telling me how much it meant to score a goal for the fans. I'm not sure when it comes to different players, whether they do it to try and win fans over or what, but for me it was because I'd been swept up by the whole Swansea thing, being among the fans and feeling part of them.

Everyone was on top form, and we were showing why we had a good chance of a second promotion, of getting to the Championship and really starting something at the club. But we needed a second – and this was my night.

The ball went loose to the right of Chris Weale's area in goal for Yeovil and he came out to clear it – only for Bayo to start closing him down, which I can't imagine being the best of sights for anyone. Wealey didn't scuff it, but he got a bit too much height on it and it headed towards the halfway line and the touchline – right by me. I can remember seeing him backtracking to his goal and getting into his six-yard box but still being slightly off his line. As the ball came down, I knew what I was going to do – control on me chest and have a go. It dropped out of the sky, I took it on me chest, let it drop halfway and boom – made sure I hit it with enough height to try and get it over him. It was perfect.

I didn't have to run, I knew what'd I'd done, I knew I'd delivered. I just stood there, put me arms in the air, closed me eyes and stood there, taking it all in. This was me moment and I wanted to lap up every part of it. It was a few seconds before everyone got to me and started jumping on me, but those seconds are still in me head, still there when I close me eyes.

CHAPTER THIRTEEN

February

IT DOESN'T TAKE long for the news to get around.

I'm sat in the canteen at the gym, having something to eat after training, when a few of the younger lads catch on.

'Didn't fancy a holiday this year, then?' one of them asks.

I've been booked in to take one of me coaching badges at the end of May, the UEFA B licence, in Cardiff. Normally, it'd be the time of year I'd be off on holidays, off to Vegas or somewhere, right after the last date of the play-offs.

Not this year.

Monks and Kris O'Leary have got their confirmation through too, all of us wanting to take the first steps on the coaching ladder. You need all the right badges these days if you want a job in football, so it's best to get them while you're still in the game rather than waiting until you actually need them.

The stick comes about me getting on, but it's not too bad. Because the fact is, I am one of the older ones. I look around the room, the lads spread out over different tables in the lounge area, and I realise I'm the oldest there. The closest is Shefki Kuqi, the Finnish striker who's not long signed for us; he's about a month younger than me.

Me. The oldest player in the squad.

I don't see it that way. Me and Monks get the banter about being the old men, but I'm still the one messing around in the dressing-room, having a joke on the training ground. I'm like a big kid at times, that's me personality, and I'm still just as comfortable chatting with the younger lads as I am with the older ones. I've never wanted to be one of those senior pros that keeps himself to himself and away from what's going on – I want to be involved with everything.

And when you come into the game at 24, it's difficult to accept this isn't going to last forever. I'm still only in me tenth season as a pro. If I'd been 18 when I made it, I'd be 27, not 33. But that's why I applied for this course.

I'd been thinking about it earlier in the year, and every week that goes by when you're not playing, the thought gets a little bigger. Tony Pennock, the youth coach at Swansea, helped set it up for me, I sent the forms off and now I've got the go-ahead to attend the course up in Cardiff.

Some lads get involved in it all a lot earlier, but I couldn't have. It's not just the fact I probably would have messed around, not taken it seriously enough, but I didn't take enough notice of football. Not since I was a kid had I properly sat down and watched games – I just saw the highlights on *Sky Sports News* or knew who was doing well. The older I've got, the more I've begun to watch. And properly watch, looking at different players and how they move, how different teams set up, when different managers make different changes. It's not been something forced, not something I've felt I've had to do, it's just something that I've taken more of an interest in.

Paulo's No. 2, Bruno Oliveira, comes around the tables to hand out our info sheets. Paulo's big on watching games too, and every week we have sheets with a full rundown of the team we're playing that week, every player's strengths and weaknesses, who they pass it to, who passes to them, who gets the ball most, every little stat. Nelson, our analyst, goes through every minute detail and it all gets handed to us to use if we want. It's a long way from Flynny, and some lads just don't bother with it, they don't like thinking too much about what the other side are going to do and just want to concentrate on themselves.

But you still have to read the sheets. Every Friday we'll go through the video clips, and Paulo likes to make sure we've all done our revision homework – he picks three players and gets them to talk about the strengths and weaknesses of the other team and where we might be able to get in. It's a bit like being back at school. I guess if you want to use that information, then it's up to you.

I tell Paulo about the course and he's pleased for me, agreeing it's better to have the badges in place for when the time comes. I don't know when that will be, mind. I'm not writing off me playing days, and only last week I was man of the match when we beat Peterborough after coming off the bench early on.

But I've always felt I could give something back, and I want to be ready when I get that chance. I don't know anything else, I don't know any other trades, so of course it's a way to make sure I stay in a job when the time comes. But I reckon the way I came into the game, the way I play, it all gives me a different outlook from other coaches. I never had proper coaching when I was a kid, but when it was there, when I went to trials or training sessions back home, it always seemed to be about trying to force you to play a certain way. It shouldn't be like that, it should be about fine-tuning, adding a bit of experience to go with the instinct. Plus, the bad experiences I've had would help me be a better coach; it would help me encourage others not to do the same.

I know I could be a manager one day. People may laugh, knowing me as the type of person I am, but why not? There are different types of manager like there are different types of players. One way isn't the only right way.

But I also like the idea of doing what Alan Curtis does with us. He's a legend at the club, and he has a really hands-on role with the youngsters, bridging the gap between the youth set-up and the first team. Whatever I do, I just want to be ready for that new environment. If I get stick for it, so be it. But I think the reason I'm not getting any is because they know it too.

After all, every manager has to start somewhere – even the best in the Premier League.

CHAPTER FOURTEEN

Paying the Penalty

I KNEW HE was there, because a few of me mates had seen him outside. They'd even tried to ask if he'd come to watch me, but he'd just smiled.

Everton weren't playing that Saturday and with us playing only over the water against Tranmere, their manager, David Moyes, was at Prenton Park. Was he there to watch me? I don't know. He would have at least known who I was after those lifts he'd given me to Preston when I was still at Chorley. But if you read the papers he was having a look at me; Everton were after a striker and I was being mentioned in the same breath as Nicolas Anelka as a potential signing for January.

I was being linked with Charlton in the Premier, Southampton too, but Everton were the side that had caught me eye – as it would with anyone. I'd been a Blue ever since our Frankie started taking me to Goodison, and I'd still go whenever I got the chance. In fact, the day after Moyes was at Tranmere I went to Goodison to watch the game against Newcastle. Whenever I'd done interviews about who I supported I'd say Everton and that I had done all me life – I didn't want to go into all that happened with me and Liverpool and all that. Plus, I thought it was a good tribute to Frankie. He'd been a big influence, someone who'd been a big believer in me and kept on telling me I was going to make it as a pro, that I was too good not to. I'd looked up to him for a long time, and I knew saying I was a lifelong Blue like him would have made him dead proud. What he would have felt like if I'd actually signed for them, God knows.

He was chuffed enough to take his mates to watch me play against them for Wrexham. It was a League Cup game in me last season at the Racecourse. I was gutted not to start with everyone watching, but I came on, did well and had a great effort that hit the bar. I didn't steal the headlines, though – some 16-year-old kid called Wayne Rooney scored twice, his first senior goals.

A lot had happened since then and it was incredible just being taken seriously as a target for Everton. Whether that was only by the fans rather than the manager or not, it didn't matter – to be linked was huge. It wasn't just the fact that I'd grown to support the club, but it's different when it's your home town team. Swansea as a city and as a club had taken me in as one of their own and it felt like home, but when you've grown up in that city it's different. Kris O'Leary used to say as much with Swansea, and you could just tell the buzz he'd got because he was the home-grown lad. I was desperate for it, it would have been everything for me. People would say I was kidding meself if I thought it could happen, but people told me I was kidding meself that I could even make it when I was still at Southport. I didn't listen to them then, so I wasn't going to start listening to them now.

The problem was I never helped meself against Tranmere. Knowing people are watching me normally puts me in the right place to go and perform, but maybe finding out so soon before kick-off affected me or played on me mind a little too much, I don't know. All I know is that I didn't do much. I wasn't crap, but I didn't have the kind of game that would have had people talking about me, and I knew that was what I needed.

It didn't stop the talk of me going. All the lads back home and different people I'd see out in Liverpool would come up and ask, which made me more anxious to find out if I was going to hear anything.

I don't think any Swansea fans would've held it against me if something had happened. I'd been straight with them and never hidden the fact I wanted to give it a go at the top level – and they knew I wouldn't leave for just anyone after the way I turned down Wednesday.

Plus the way everyone was talking it was as though it was certain I'd be off in the January. Every interview Kenny did was full of questions about me going, how he'd cope without me goals, who they might bring in. Somehow – and I'm never sure who comes up with the figures – it had been accepted that I'd cost £1.5 million, but if someone had come in with a £1 million offer I don't think the club would've turned it down. Swansea had moved a long way since the new board had taken over, but because things were run so tightly that would've been a massive amount at the time.

But the offer never came. It was strange, because I was half waiting for things to happen, to get this opportunity, yet at the same time I was happy with me lot. I wasn't going in to the chairman's office every day wanting to know if anyone had been on, I wasn't getting Sangy to phone this club or that club to try and sort something – I was loving being at Swansea and loving me life. It's human nature to want to progress and, being the age I was, I was in a rush to do it. Then there was the fact I'd come into the game late and I wanted to catch up with the money side of things ready for when I finished, knowing all this could be over before it'd even begun. But I wasn't going to lose any sleep about not getting what I wanted, because I knew I had plenty to be happy with at Swansea.

The speculation was flying around, but I never got ahead of meself, didn't start to picture meself leaving or anything like that. I'd been used to seeing me name in the papers, so it was nothing new, even if it had stepped up a level. The lads, though, they thought I was gone – they couldn't see how someone wouldn't take a punt on me because how could you ignore what I was doing week in, week out?

Kenny must have thought so too, because he'd started looking for replacements. I guess he couldn't afford to hang around and wait for it to happen because we were now becoming one of the favourites for promotion. Izale McLeod and Grant Holt were mentioned, but in the end Kenny brought in Leon Knight.

There was a real buzz when Knighty came in. He was an exciting player, and although he'd had a bit of bad press for his attitude since leaving Chelsea as a kid, he was a player who got the fans talking. He was like Jermain Defoe in the way he played, and signing him sent a message out that we weren't messing around in this league.

I'd been injured at the back of Christmas – which can't have done me chances of a move any good – so Knighty went straight into the side and got a hat-trick on his debut. People started talking about me being under threat, but I never thought like that. Knighty was a different option, someone who added another dimension to our game with his speed. I don't know what other players felt like when new lads came in, but because I felt like I'd established meself as the No. 1 striker, everyone else could scrap it out between them and the side would benefit from the competition. I'd loved playing with Bayo, and I was looking forward to seeing what me and Knighty could do, but for some reason Kenny wouldn't give us a run together. I think there must have been once, twice at the most, that we both started games up front, which got more and more frustrating as we started to drop the odd point here and there.

But Kenny hadn't stopped spending. He brought in a few others and then broke the club record – £300,000 – to sign Rory Fallon. Rory had done brilliantly at Swindon, scoring a lot of goals for them, but in a very different role from the way we played at Swansea. He was the target man who liked to get on the end of crosses – we were more about getting it into feet. It didn't suit him and he didn't really suit us, so it was strange he'd come in the first place. Perhaps Kenny had wanted to give us another way of playing, but it was seeing us go more direct again, going longer, even though we'd showed we could do well just by playing football.

It was tough on Rory. He had the whole baggage of being the record signing, and the fans didn't take long to get on his back – especially when he didn't score for 11 games. The strikers were all being rotated, and I don't think it did any of us any favours as we tried to get our rhythm back in the league. We were edging down from third, to fourth, to fifth, to sixth; from four points off the top, to five, to six, before it came to March and we were ten points off first and looking for second spot instead.

We did have a day out at the Millennium Stadium to look forward to. We'd gone on a good run in the Football League Trophy – the cup for teams below the Championship – and with the game being held only up the road in Cardiff, the final against Carlisle was a massive deal for us. It was strange when we beat Colchester in the area final, because we were more excited about playing at the Millennium and that side of things rather than winning the competition, but it was still a cup final and every cup final is special, from Sunday League to this one. It was live on Sky, with the local papers giving it the big build-up, special team photos taken and getting our tailored cup final suits – even if they were these terrible black pinstriped ones with a big pink tie. Willy had picked them out, thinking he had an eye for fashion just because he was French, but they were awful – although I do admit when all the lads were there together on the morning of the match with the flowers in the buttonholes, it did look a bit special.

And it was special. I mean, a lot of people take the piss out of the competition, but try telling that to the fans that were there that day, try telling that to all the lads' families that had come from all over to see us play at one of the best stadiums around. I walked out onto the pitch for the warm-up and already there was black and white wherever you looked – there were 43,000 fans there that day and about 30,000 of them were from Swansea. There were loads of me mates from Liverpool down for the game too, plus me mum had come with all me cousins, so I'd made sure I'd asked where their tickets were going to be beforehand, frantically trying to work out where their seats were during the warm-up. I was getting panicky because I couldn't find them and we were due to go back in, but I spotted them at the last moment and made sure I made a note of it in me head. This was going to be for them.

People often wonder what it's like in a dressing-room before big games like that, but the truth is, I wouldn't know either. You just do what you have to do, in your own way, to make sure you're ready. Some lads stay quiet, some have got to be loud, but Kenny had said everything he needed to say and by now the music was blaring and we were in our own zone, focused on what we had to do, on our own game, in our own world and oblivious to what else was going on around us.

Especially for this one; I was having trouble getting to grips with meself let alone starting to worry about everyone else. Sat there staring at the floor of the changing-rooms, I'd gone very light-headed very suddenly. It wasn't just me head, me whole body felt weightless. It wasn't nerves, because I was desperate to get out there, but I just felt drunk, probably on the excitement of it all. It was pure adrenalin running through me, the thought of running out in front of that many people, in front of so many friends and family – all those people who believed in me. Me mum was there watching, only this time she wasn't standing in the rain with all the dads on the touchline, she was sat at the Millennium Stadium. All these thoughts, all this excitement – I just couldn't keep it in.

I went off at 100mph, desperate to make something happen. Three minutes into the game, I did. Charging around the field, I closed down their keeper, Keiran Westwood, and his clearance deflected off me back to just outside the penalty area. Robbo had been the same as me before the game, like a caged animal, but now he was loose he was everywhere, and he sprinted after the defender, nicking the ball away from him. I could see Britts chasing onto it, so I pulled meself away at the back post, still only just inside the box, knowing he'd be looking for me. He was. The ball lofted over, inch-perfect, and I knew what I was going to do. Chesting it into me stride, the ball dropped to me waist and I smashed a volley with me left, me whole body in the air as I hit it, me full weight behind the shot.

Straight away I turned away from the goal and I looked up – they were all there. Normally I'm all smiles when I score, but when I look back at this game I'm almost angry when I'm celebrating. I was screaming at the top tier, letting all the emotion flood out. I knew it was special, and it's probably me greatest goal, what with the occasion and who was there to see it. On top of that, just the technique of it is something I'm proud of. How many players would have tried to have taken that ball down and place it or pull it back? The way I did it, there was only one place I could have hit it to beat the keeper because the angle was so tight, but that's where I'd put it. Would I be able to do it again? I don't know, it was instinct. How could you replicate the day, the fans, the occasion, the emotion? It was about that moment – and that's always when I've been at me best.

It's quite funny, when people remember that game, they remember that goal and forget it wasn't the winner. Carlisle were from the division below, but they were decent, especially their striker Karl Hawley, who'd done brilliantly for them that season and made Willy pull off a great save early on.

Even with the early goal it was very tight, and five minutes from half-time they got one back. I wasn't panicked. Sometimes you get these games you just feel you're going to win, that when they score it doesn't matter because we'll get one more. The problem was, though, I was knackered. I don't know whether it was the atmosphere that had drained me or the nervous energy I'd had in that early spell, but there wasn't a lot left in me legs, and I was starting to worry that this was going to be it for me – there was no way I could have taken extra time. I wanted to finish it – and the chance came. Tatey came through with the ball, playing it into me feet. I spun it up, turned me marker and flicked it to the right where Bayo was running through. As he always did, he kept the defenders hanging off him and lifted the shot over the save, the ball bouncing into the net. He ran over to the corner and started dancing – taking the piss out of me and Robbo – as the Swans fans went mad.

It might have been a nothing competition for some, but with Sky covering the game it had all the razzmatazz you would expect – the proper stage set up on the pitch for the presentation and then the fireworks going off as Roberto lifted the cup. We had our team shots and then we went off around the pitch, taking it in turns to hold the trophy and milk it all. It was like any other big cup final, with all sorts being thrown onto the field and everyone wearing scarves, daft hats and whatever else. I was on me own on the side of the pitch when a T-shirt got thrown in front of me. I shoved it on for a few seconds without really paying much attention to what was on it. When I did look properly as I took it off, there was a cartoon picture of a Swansea player pissing on a Cardiff shirt, the kind of thing you'd see up and down the country with different teams. I'd seen loads of them in Liverpool with Liverpool–Everton, Everton–Liverpool, Liverpool–Man Utd, on all sorts of things from T-shirts to car stickers. I thought nothing of it.

I made me way to behind the goals where the rest of the lads were, including Tatey. He had hold of this big Welsh flag and I held it up with him. As ever, he was acting the clown with his big jester's hat on and as I looked across to him I noticed what was on the flag. In big capital letters, in this thick black paint, someone had written on 'Fuck Off Cardiff'. I dropped it – I knew that it wouldn't be the best idea to be waving it around.

But that was that, and what with everything going on, I didn't think twice about it. The celebrations carried on in the dressing-room before we got changed and went out to the press where the only question anyone was asking me was about me goal. None of them had seen the pictures.

We headed back to Morgan's Hotel where there'd been a big party put on for us all, the champagne flowing for all the family and friends. Martin Morgan, who owned the hotel, was a big supporter of the club – and is now on the board – and had looked after us, and everyone was enjoying themselves, all the staff at the club posing with the cup. You had the likes of Jermain Defoe there, who was mates with Izzy Iriekpen and Knighty, all me mates from back home asking if he was going to sign for Liverpool that summer. We were having a great time. Even when Tatey came up to me to tell me the police wanted to speak to us it didn't spoil things.

'What for?' I asked.

I thought he was taking the piss. Me phone had been off, so I hadn't gotten any of the messages some of the press lads had been leaving to try and get hold of me. They'd all seen the pictures. I was still taking it with a pinch of salt. It had all been heat-of-the-moment stuff. I hadn't even known what was on the flag, and the T-shirt wasn't offensive, was it?

I stayed out drinking. By the time I got the taxi back to mine in the early hours I knew the papers would be out, so I made sure the driver swung by a garage to pick them up. I was buzzing from the goal and wanted to see the photos of us all celebrating together, of us lifting the cup or of me goal. They were all there, in the back pages, but on the front was something else. I thought it was going a bit far – but it was only just starting.

The FAW had got involved, saying they would investigate what had happened, and everyone was coming out to have a go at us – the PFA, the Football League. It was all kicking off. The club had already told us we had to go in the next day to see the solicitor, that they were going to issue an apology and that we weren't allowed to speak to anyone about it.

That was tough, because I wanted to put a few things straight – like when it was being suggested it was all premeditated, that I'd gone out there with the T-shirt under me top, or that I'd planted it with a mate and that I was supposed to be inciting fans. But that was all bollocks. As far as I could see, how could I be inciting fans? It wasn't on telly, I wasn't posing for pictures to wind Cardiff fans up, it was in front of our fans – and I didn't even know what was on it. Even when I did, I thought it was a bit tongue in cheek, a bit of a laugh and that was that.

Then you had Sam Hammam, the Cardiff chairman at the time, coming out saying that I'd be to blame if there was violence between supporters the next time the two sides played, that I'd done it because Swansea – who he called Cardiff's 'kid brothers' – had an inferiority complex.

The press day the following week was bedlam, with a lot of unfamiliar faces at the pitches down at Jersey Marine in the east of the city where we'd started to train. I wasn't speaking about it, neither was Tatey, and Kenny did all the talking for us. People were waiting to trip us up, and there was enough bother as it was.

One of the radio phone-ins had been full of different people arguing about what had happened, having a go, calling us every name under the sun, and the front page of the Cardiff local paper had a big headline on it – 'Ban this Idiot' – with a nice big photo of me holding the flag. In my eyes, if I was being accused of inciting anything, shouldn't they have been too, for going so over the top? The frustrating thing was that they only had a picture of me, cutting out Tatey on the other side. It felt as if I was being singled out because I was doing well, being the goalscorer, being the high-profile one. I'd allowed meself to be an easy target and they were loving it.

The police said they'd had complaints so they were obliged to look into it, and we really got that impression when we were made to go up to Cardiff a few days later. They'd sent us to one of the smaller stations, away from the city centre, and it was there we were formally arrested for public order offences, where the fingerprints and all the other business was done. I think they knew there'd been no malice in any of it, but they were following the law as they were supposed to. I remember going through all the procedures, them showing me a photo of me holding up the flag and confirming it was me stood there.

'And could you confirm who is holding the other end of the flag?'

Tatey had the flag over his face but straight away I pointed.

'Him.'

He still jokingly calls me a grass to this day, even though his fucking jester's hat poking over the top of the flag and shorts with his squad number on underneath would have given it away anyway.

The officers at the station had been fine. They hadn't treated us like scum or anything like that, and it seemed to me that they knew more had been made of the whole thing than perhaps it should have. I just think that with all the fuss that had been made of it, all the attention it had been given, something had to be seen to be done – so it was.

I think the club probably felt the same, and although we got bollockings for being so daft, Kenny never said much about it. He was coming under a lot of pressure to fine us there and then, but with the police and the FAW taking action, I think he reckoned we were getting our lesson.

We were bailed and given cautions later that month and eventually we had our case heard by the Welsh FA, although not until the end of the season, getting a one-game ban on top of the week's wage we were docked.

It took a while for the whole thing to die down, though. It never played on me mind or anything like that, and Kenny stuck with us, playing us both on the following Saturday against Port Vale. That was great because while everyone else had been trying to vilify us, to get the cheer we did from the Swans fans as we ran out put things into perspective. If anything, it might have brought me closer to the fans. Not for what happened but because of the reaction – I think they saw it as being as over the top as I did.

Then the death threats came. I was looking through the post I'd been sent at the club and I'd opened up an 'In Sympathy' card addressed to me. It was around the time of the first outbreaks of bird flu and there'd been a swan found dead from it in Scotland. In the card, the message read: 'The next dead Swan they find will be Lee Trundle.'

Did it bother me? I pissed meself. I mean, it was funny and having grown up in Huyton, you know the only time you have to worry is when people aren't saying they're going to do stuff to you. If someone is looking for you, the last thing they do is let you know about it. There'd been a few threats of different kinds, but all of it was taken with a pinch of salt – after all, they'd probably come from kids still in school.

I kept it all under wraps, though, and I wanted it all to go away. I'd kept a low profile, but when I agreed to help someone out and do a signing session at a shop in town, the owner must have invited the press because there were photographers everywhere, the Welsh TV news were there, lads from the Cardiff papers. I was signing something for a little girl in a wheelchair but he'd let all these reporters in and was then saying he couldn't do anything about it – but it was his shop, he could've chucked them out.

This time I didn't want the spotlight on me. I wanted people to be talking about me goal that day, about winning the cup, about how far we'd come as a club. Instead, the only thing anyone was interested in was what happened after that game. I was man of the match and scored one of the greatest goals of me career, but it was all about the flag rather than the football – and it still is to some. It overshadowed everything that day, and that's the real shame of it all now I look back – for me and for the Swansea fans who couldn't enjoy the moment more.

We had a great chance to grab some more success though, to really stick two fingers up at everyone who'd piled in on us at the first opportunity, and that was to win promotion – even if we were doing our best to throw it away. We'd really taken our foot off things, and we'd gone from taking 42 points from our first 21 games to picking up 24 from the remaining 22. We'd lost our confidence as a side, and me own had taken a bit of a hammering too. Knighty hadn't gotten much chance to start since he'd signed and Rory had suddenly started scoring, so I was out of the side. Perhaps because they were Kenny's signings he felt the need to start with them by now to justify bringing them in.

But then, when I got me chances, I wasn't taking them. We played Southend on the last but one game of the season. They needed a point to get promotion, but we really needed a win just to make sure we got into the top six. They got what they wanted, we didn't, and I remember walking off down towards the dressing-room after being subbed towards the end, Rory getting both goals in a 2–2 draw. One fan near the tunnel leant over to have a go at me for storming off, telling me I wasn't bigger than the club.

'Fuck off.'

It was nothing to do with that. I wasn't pissed off because I'd been taken off; I was pissed off because I deserved to be taken off. I was pissed off because they were going to celebrate promotion on our pitch when we'd blown our chance to do the same. We were a good enough side to win automatic promotion, yet we were hanging onto the top six by our fingernails. The season had started so well – I'd hit the heights and had people linking me to Everton – now I was on a run of six weeks without a goal and out of the side.

It came down to the last game, away to Chesterfield, to make sure we finished above Nottingham Forest and stayed in the play-off places. Knighty and Rory got the starts they deserved and did the business – Knighty got a hat-trick, Rory got the other in a 4–0 win, and we were in the play-offs.

I was out for the semis too, where we beat Brentford over two legs, and with Knighty getting the two in the second-leg I knew I was going to be on the bench for the final. I started to wonder what was affecting me, which itself was probably having an impact on me game. But then I still felt, come the final, there was a chance for me to make me mark, to make me point. It was the big stage after all.

I couldn't hide the disappointment when it came to it – it was a hell of a come-down for me having gone from No. 1 to the bench. But all the way through that game, with the fans all back at the Millennium, I thought I was going to score, that I was going to hit the back of the net just as I did last time here. They went ahead in the first half, but Rory got us back in it with a brilliant overhead kick. Then Robbo worked a bit of space, took a shot, and the keeper spilled it behind him to make it 2–1.

We were battering them, but they got one back just after the hour mark, and I set off to warm up behind the goal in front of our fans. Kenny called me over and a roar went up as it looked like I was about to come on. The lift it gave me was huge, to know all that excitement was because they thought I could do something, that I could change the game. But I couldn't. A couple of times I worked some space, I'd beat a man, but the shots went wide, and as we went through extra time we just couldn't hit the back of the net no matter how many times we tried.

It was penalties, and I was straight up to take the first one. I knew I was going to score – even if it wasn't quite like I'd imagined it – but there were no nerves, no doubts. I had every confidence in meself, but I couldn't say the same for the others. I had faith in them, but it didn't mean I wasn't nervous then, even though I'd done me bit. There had been a few who'd shied away, who'd said they didn't want one – but you'd rather that than someone take a pen in those situations when inside they're not right. Britts scored, Bayo didn't, hitting his well over. He was a mess, crying on the floor and just not wanting to speak to anyone.

It wasn't over yet, but it would be soon. Owain scored our next, but Tatey had his saved and that was that.

If it was obvious about Bayo, Tatey seemed to hide it well, but it did affect him. He never does show much emotion, but it got to him. I remember him telling me how he went to Ayia Napa on holidays after the end of the season and, as he was walking through the main square, one of the pubs was showing a replay of the game on the big screen and he had to go through it all again. No one blames you when you miss a pen – even the best players in the world miss them – but when it's you, none of that matters. You blame yourself, and I'd never want to go through missing one in a situation like that.

Tatey was in tears in the dressing-room, but most of us were. I'd been in tears on the pitch, slumping to me haunches when that last kick was saved. I stayed out on the pitch when they lifted the trophy; me and Robbo together, both stood there crying. I wanted to take it all in, feel the hurt and bottle it, use the disappointment to make sure I never went through it again. I wanted to remember how bad it felt.

When I did come back inside, I couldn't face the rest of the lads. Normally I'd be the one to pick a lot of them up, being chirpy or whatever. How could I do that now? Normally it's 'Don't worry, lads, three points next week . . .', but there was no next week, that was it. The best way to describe it is like a funeral – horribly quiet, with no one wanting to speak because they're afraid of crying all over again. There's people there, but the room is empty.

I needed to be on me own. I headed for the toilet, locking the door behind me and just sobbed, feeling like a whole season had been wasted, that the way I'd played at the start had been for nothing. Roberto heard me and began banging on the door, shouting, 'Trunds, come out.'

I opened the door and Roberto was stood in his suit, tears in his eyes. He wasn't even in the squad that day, having been bombed by Kenny for a while, and he knew he was on his way out. He was out of contract, and it could have been easy for him to be bitter about it all, to have a slight smile at the way things had turned out after being forced out of the side and away from the club. Football is a team game but it's also a selfish one – but that wasn't Roberto, that isn't Roberto. He wrapped his arms around me, and we both let it all out.

Monks had managed to keep it together after the game, but then he had to go give a urine sample for the drugs test. He was furious and was kicking off because he'd been asked just after one of the worst moments of his career before he calmed down and followed them into the room. It's pretty difficult to go after the game when you're that dehydrated and it took him ages, just sitting there, before he finally started crying. He told me later he could see the tester just looking at him thinking, 'We've got a guilty one here' because he'd been so reluctant and angry at first and was now in such a state. But that's what the play-offs do to you; it's an all-or-nothing situation – and you never expect to get the nothing.

The bus back to Morgan's was miserable. After the Football League Trophy final, we'd all been singing, Rory playing his guitar; this time we just sat. I don't think anyone said a word the entire way home.

It was just as bad at the party, a few players saying goodbye – including Roberto. He knew he was gone, and I'm not sure what the reasons were. OK, Kenny wanted a different kind of player in midfield, but Roberto brought quality to the side and he was a great captain whether he was in the side or not. I don't think we would have had to have gone through the play-offs in the first place if he'd been in the team. There were a lot of suggestions from the outside that Kenny felt threatened by Roberto, that he was undermining his authority. But although I don't know if they ever saw eye to eye properly, none of us had seen any real issues between them. Of course Roberto had his views, and we always knew he was going to be a manager someday, but he'd never confront anyone if he thought they were in the wrong; he was a proper pro and that wasn't his style. If he'd been voicing his opinion in the dressing-room or questioning what Kenny was doing, I could understand it, but nothing like that happened. Whether Kenny thought that was the case I don't know, but the next day Roberto was gone.

As were Forbesy and a few others. I was off too, but only to America for me holidays. Me, Macca and Monks were supposed to be travelling right across the US – New York, Miami, LA, Las Vegas. I didn't get very far before I booked a flight to come home – I just couldn't enjoy meself. People were telling me to drown me sorrows, but I couldn't get over it.

I don't think any of the team did properly – and I think Kenny knew it. He brought in a sports psychologist, but we were all making a joke out of it rather than listening to what the guy had to say. I've had them since and I think it depends on what type of person you are if you take it in or not, but it's never done anything for me. If I thought too much about what I was doing, about where I'd come from in such a short space of time, I'd freeze. I could see Kenny's point, though – there had been an expectation on us to walk the League, a sense that we had deserved to go up and that we'd blown it and this was the way to put it right.

Except it doesn't work like that. Don't get me wrong, we were all dying to get out there and get going – especially me after being banned for that first game for the flag business – but things never did get going. We'd pick up a couple of good results but never put on a run. We'd lost Monks after the second game of the season when he injured his cruciate knee ligament. Quite badly too – they thought at one point there was damage to the nerves, so it could have cost him his career.

Kenny had brought a few lads in like Tom Butler and Darren Pratley, good players, but something wasn't clicking for us, and the chairman was putting the pressure on. He'd already said that we had to deliver promotion and called a couple of our performances pathetic. I'd been out with a knee injury, but when I came back Knighty was scoring for fun and I was out.

But then it all blew up. Kenny came in one morning and told us that was that, Knighty wouldn't be playing for us any more, he wouldn't be training with us any more, he was gone. Only he wasn't, he'd been transfer-listed and was being made to train on his own. We weren't given a reason why, other than what we were reading in the papers – a build-up of incidents and a problem with his attitude, I think Kenny called it. There'd been nothing that was obvious to me, but it must have been something because he'd been doing well and no one's going to bomb a player for no reason, especially when your side's not getting the results.

There were all sorts of rumours going around, like he'd got himself in a mess financially, that he'd got into trouble in London, but it was all just rumours, nothing concrete. He'd had a bit of a reputation – he'd fallen out with his manager at Brighton before he joined us – but the one story people would swear was true was that he had had a scrap with Robbo in the dressing-room at half-time during one game. We fell about laughing when we heard that one. He was fiery, though, Knighty, and he wouldn't back down. He was only short, something like 5 ft 5 in., but he'd fight the world if he had to. I remember one argument he had with Bayo coming back from a game on the coach, telling Bayo he wasn't scared of him, and Bayo – all 17 stone of him – telling him to leave it, leave it, before he finally snapped. It took four of us to pull Bayo back and just thank God we had Kev Austin there to help out. But I liked Knighty; he was one of those you just had to know how to take. There was talk about his attitude and being a bad influence on the squad, but he was sharp on the training ground and was a dangerous player for us – but Kenny must have had his reasons and that was that.

Rory was next to go, sold in the January just 12 months after he'd arrived. It just hadn't worked out for him, and I felt sorry for him at times. The fans never took to him, and that can have a massive effect on the way you play – just like it had a positive one with me.

Rory loved a night out too, and he's admitted he was wild when he was with us, hitting the party scene hard. He's calmed down since, and we joke with Tommy Butler that he finished him off – the pair went to Vegas and it got that bad Rory couldn't speak and Tom had to phone his bird for him to explain. Rory just said,'That's it, I've had enough,' and he gave it all up and went and found God, which must have been a hell of a header.

I'd found someone too – a first proper girlfriend in God knows how long. I'd met Liz McClarnon in the summer when I'd been out drinking with a few of the lads in Liverpool. It was this fairly exclusive place called the Newz Bar, and she walked past the booth we were sat in. I'd only known her from seeing her on the telly when she was in Atomic Kitten, but I put me arm out to stop her. I asked her where she was going and she told me she was moving to the upstairs part of the bar, so I told her I'd be up to meet her in a few minutes. The lads were giving me plenty of stick before I'd even tried – who did I think I was, trying it on with a pop star? But I went up and began chatting away, and we ended up going to a Chinese restaurant I knew that had a karaoke downstairs – although neither of us got up to sing.

The first proper date was a George Benson gig. I already had two tickets because I knew I'd be taking someone, I just didn't know who when I bought them. It just happened to be Liz, who just happened to be famous. At the end of the day, she was a normal girl from a council estate in Liverpool, and that's why I think we got on.

Not that the lads back in Swansea saw it that way, winding me up because they'd never known me have a girlfriend as such, and now they were trying to say I'd only gone out with her because she was a pop star. But I liked her. I ended up loving her. It was exciting – but not for the reasons people might expect. Yes, I liked the spotlight, but I just didn't get her whole showbiz thing – it was all false to me. It was completely different from the football kind of fame that had a genuine thing about it – if you played well and you played for their team, people liked you; if you didn't, they didn't. I only went to a couple of her events in London, but they would be full of people saying, 'Oooh, you look amazing,' and yet the moment they were gone they'd be saying how much they couldn't stand them. I never bothered with that side of it too much even if the papers made a big deal of it. That didn't worry me, they were always going to – I'd got a bit of a profile of me own because of what I'd been doing and Liz was obviously very well known, so the media were always going to latch on to that. And I'm not ashamed to say we did the whole glossy magazine shoot. I mean, if people are going to get photos of you walking down the road, why not get it done properly and get some money for it?

Of course, I got even more stick for that, but I didn't mind – I deserved it. Besides, I was happy. Brooke was happy too, even though it was the first time she'd known me with a serious girlfriend. I told Liz as soon as I met her that I had a daughter, just as I have done with any girl I really like, so they can make a decision there and then if they're still interested. If they're not, neither am I, and that's it. But Liz was great with Brooke and got on really well with her, taking her to concerts when Atomic Kitten did a couple of comeback gigs, and plenty of other girly things.

It got serious pretty quickly, but it meant I had a problem when we decided it was daft her not moving in with me, seeing as she was spending so much time commuting to and from Swansea. I was still living in West Cross, the same bachelor house that I'd taken so many girls back to, and inviting a serious girlfriend to live there just didn't feel right. It wasn't just the memories of the place and what I'd got up to there, but I'd still have girls putting photos through the letterbox with their numbers on the back, or knocking on the door because they knew where I lived. It was all a bit too much, so I got a place in the grounds of Clyne Castle overlooking Swansea Bay.

But if things were settling off the pitch, you couldn't say the same about what was happening on it with Kenny. We'd had a few highs – like beating Sheffield United 3–0 in the FA Cup at Bramall Lane when they were in the Premier League. I'd missed the game because I'd been sent off in the last minute of the game against Huddersfield the week before, swinging an elbow at Gary Taylor-Fletcher after getting fed up with him pinching me. In fact, we didn't have much of a side at Sheffield, with a load of injury problems, but the lads got the win.

The thing was, it didn't lead to anything. We lost pretty tamely to Ipswich in the next round, and we were still outside the play-offs. It was frustrating for everyone – us, the fans and Kenny himself probably. I think he said later on he found it difficult to lift us after the play-offs and that was a big problem in that season. After all, beating a Premier side showed we had the ability, but I'm not sure Kenny believed he could get it out of us week in, week out any more. Sometimes things just go flat with managers and teams – you can't put your finger on it, sometimes things just run their course. That's why you can look at Sir Alex Ferguson at Manchester United and know it's something special, because it's incredible to be able to keep things that fresh after so many years. But I think that's the exception to the rule; I don't know whether players just switch off from hearing the same thing from the same man, but it happens. And it happened with us.

We lost to Oldham in the February and the press lads went for Kenny. He – and Huw – had said they wanted promotion, but now the top two was out of the question and the play-offs were beginning to look shaky too. We kept on thinking a run of wins was around the corner, but they just never came and Kenny took a bit of a hammering. Still, he seemed ready to carry on, to keep fighting – only to walk out on the Tuesday.

We'd heard the whispers on the morning, but we didn't believe it until the chairman came to the training ground and said Kenny'd gone and gave his reasons, one of which was that Kenny thought some of the lads had stopped trying for him. Tatey wanted them named, but Huw refused – and he was probably right. If there were lads who'd given up on the gaffer, then they knew who they were. I wasn't one of them; despite all the fuss made when he took over, I got on with Kenny and there weren't many lads who didn't.

And I found it hard to take this 'not trying' business – most players want to do well for themselves and won't risk hindering that to make a point about a manager. And inside the camp, no one was saying 'Fuck Kenny' or anything like that – the majority of us were sad to see him go. Looking back, though, he just couldn't get us going again after the disappointment of the year before, and perhaps it was a case of not being able to take us any further as a team.

Things had fallen apart a bit. Off the field, lads seemed to be in shit every other week. You had all the nonsense with me and Tatey and even Willy, which was one thing, but the year before, Robbo had been arrested for kicking off with a bouncer in a club in town. He was out with his missus one night and going into a nightclub when she was stopped after her bag had been searched. They'd taken her into a back room as though she was selling drugs, and I don't think Robbo took too kindly to it. He lost his rag and ended up having to go to court for a public order offence, Kenny having to get him out of the nick the morning after it happened. Izzy had got arrested for a fight in town, and then you had Knighty being transfer listed and the same happening with Macca. It was harsh on Macca because I always felt Kenny was on his case; he'd known him from when they were both at QPR, so Kenny knew he had the ability to be a real asset for us. But it backfired a bit and even when Macca hadn't been out drinking, he'd still get it bad from Kenny. Macca never helped himself though, and he'd do daft things, like putting nights on in a club because he fancied himself as a DJ – and then doing it a night or two before a game.

There was Ijah Anderson, a player Kenny had signed on a free in his first year, who got banned for six months for testing positive for cocaine. No one saw that one coming. The drug testers turned up at the training ground, and one of the lads being done at the same time was saying how Ijah was asking, 'If someone was smoking pot in the same room as you, would it show up on the test?'

All of that happened in Kenny's time, and it couldn't have been easy to deal with in his first job as a manager. Add to that the pressure of us not doing well and the money he spent – big money for a club like Swansea – and is it really a surprise it all got to him?

It was tough because he hadn't dropped his standards; he was still as big on discipline as he was when he first came in, but perhaps that fear factor had gone, because the results weren't there. It was the same way of managing that had brought us the success – it just wasn't having the same impact on these particular players. I thought at the time he'd do well elsewhere – and he's proven that with Millwall.

As for meself, I was just hoping that whoever came in would want to play football so I could get going again. I was still on course to hit 20 that year, I'd still kept meself in the headlines and I'd proven I was no one-hit wonder for the fourth season in a row – but I wanted to kick-on again.

And as soon as Roberto's name was mentioned I knew he could make it happen. Joe Royle was mentioned, and Dean Saunders and Gary Megson were supposedly close, but Roberto was the name that stood out a mile. He'd been playing at Chester and was still only 33, but he was born to be a manager. I hadn't agreed with the way he'd been forced out, and I thought if he couldn't be a big part of the club as a player, he could be in this way instead.

Plus, he had the respect of the lads straight away. Those who hadn't played with him had heard us talk about him often enough, so all of us were buzzing when Roberto was officially announced as our new manager. The only problem was getting me head around calling him gaffer. I'd been used to having banter with Rob, going on lads' holidays to Magaluf together, and now he was me manager. It was uncomfortable to start with, but that didn't last long. In fact, by the time the first few training sessions were out of the way and we all saw first hand what he was planning with us we would have called him anything he wanted. It was like a breath of fresh air for me. I wasn't daft enough not to see that Kenny had done brilliantly for me and for the team. He'd taken us from League Two to within a couple of penalty kicks of the Championship, but this was something else for me. Training was all about the ball rather than shapes and set-pieces, games were about bringing the ball through the midfield and into feet, into me.

The first game didn't go quite to plan – a 0–0 draw with Leyton Orient – but I was back scoring soon after and a win up at Carlisle on the last but one weekend gave us a shot of making the play-offs.

We had to beat Blackpool on the final day, and by a couple of goals too – so we went for it. It wasn't to be, in the end. We lost 6–3 in a bit of a wild match, Andy Morrell, of all people, getting four and eventually helping Blackpool up through the play-offs.

But we were on the right track again, and we felt Roberto was ready to take us somewhere – and I wanted to go with him.

CHAPTER FIFTEEN

March

NO ONE'S SAYING a lot. No one needs to be told. There's a strange calmness about the place.

You'd expect boots and insults to be flying around the dressing-room after losing a game 5–1, but there was no ranting or raving from anyone. It's not the time.

'Just put it right Saturday, 'ey, lads.'

I try my best to keep things positive, but I think everyone's got the right perspective about the result. No one wants to get beat, no one wants to get beat badly, and no one wants to get battered like we just have against Blackpool. But it's one result.

It's going to sting for a couple of days, but we're still in with a chance of the play-offs, still in with a chance of the Premier League.

A lot of people are going to say a lot of things about this game, but the fact is we were eight points clear of the chasing pack with eight games to go, and now we're seven points ahead with seven to go.

It could be more. It should be more. There've been games where we've come off just feeling cheated.

Like at the end of last month against Plymouth, where our keeper Dorus de Vries saved a penalty with two minutes to go to keep it 1–0, only for the ref to order a retake because he came off his line.

Or two weeks ago, when we controlled things at Forest and somehow they missed a clear foul on Darren Pratley in the box at 0–0 – then we conceded in the last minute.

We've had a few sickeners like that, playing Newcastle off the park and then them equalising in the last few minutes. And perhaps that's why this doesn't feel so bad – we deserved to lose this one and that's that. Put it behind us and move on.

When you feel a referee's decision has cost you, that's when it sticks in the throat and the frustration begins to get to you. We were all there in the corridors at Plymouth, not enough room for us in the tiny dressing-rooms at Home Park, huddled around the laptop to see where Dorus was when he saved the pen, and all getting even more wound up when we saw his foot still on the line.

It's difficult to get over because you can't do anything about it. If you're playing badly and you get beat, you only have to look at yourselves. It's the injustice, and when it keeps happening that's when it gets harder and harder to take. Everyone expects it once or twice a season because the calls go your way eventually. When are ours coming?

It was the same against West Brom at home a week ago, all desperately looking to see if Angel Rangel had tripped Giles Barnes for the penalty that swung the game their way or if he'd dived. We'd still been in with a shout of automatic promotion up to that point, and we'd had every right to believe we could do it too. We've played some great stuff, like against Newcastle where their boss, Chris Hughton, has called us the best footballing side in the league.

We were anything but in this match.

We can blame the pitch at Bloomfield Road – because it was a disgrace – but it was just one of those nights where everything went right for them and nothing went right for us. It was shit, but it wasn't the end of the world.

'For fuck's sake, lads, we're still fifth in the fucking Championship. Come on, let's get these wins to get us over the line and that's all that matters,' I say as the lads start getting changed, just wanting to get home as quickly as possible.

But it's true. No one expected it of us after the start we had, and if there's a bit of doom and gloom it's only because we've made the expectations rise. Getting in the play-offs will be an amazing achievement however it comes – who gives a shit if we've taken a battering along the way?

Paulo is the same. He hasn't come in slamming anyone; he knows it's one of those nights. He may have played for Inter Milan and Juventus, but he'll have had them. Not many, I'm guessing, but he's had them. He tells us all to keep our heads up, to look at what we've done this season and what we can still achieve.

I don't take long to get changed. I've spent all night on the bench again, not even getting a nod when we were 3–0 down after 50 minutes. We needed something to happen for us, but Gorka Pintado came on for Kuqi and Paulo stuck to one up front. The system's worked for the gaffer before, so it's difficult to argue, and he's kept me involved in almost every squad – but he won't look at changing things, and I've fancied a run with Kuqi ever since he came in. Big, strong, keeps things in and around the box – perfect partner material. But two up top doesn't seem to be an option at the moment and, besides, this isn't about me.

I want to earn a contract and I want to help this club achieve something – however it comes. I'm not getting many opportunities, but I'm not letting me head drop – nor anyone else's.

I sit at the back of the coach, motor running, waiting for the last of them to get changed. I look at some of the lads coming on, Tatey and Britts are both there, lads who've been involved since the ball really started rolling for the club. None of us need telling. Forget about Blackpool – there's eight games left to take our chance. The Premier League is still in reach – and who'd want to turn that down?

CHAPTER SIXTEEN

Bristol – So Near and Yet So Far

I DIDN'T THINK anything of it at the time.

'Bristol City?'

Darren Way was sat next to me on the coach just after finishing a session on our pre-season in Sweden. He'd played for Gary Johnson at Yeovil, and he'd heard that he was interested in me.

'Yeah,' he nodded.

It was the first time anyone had mentioned it to me, not even Sangy had brought it up. I put it down to summer speculation; I mean, it wasn't the first time me name had been linked with another club. Pre-season had only just started and it's when agents and journalists are at their best – or worst, depending which way you look at it.

Roberto had taken us out to Sweden, to a place called Östersund, to train at altitude and really get us putting in the fitness work. He'd made it clear that if we wanted to play the kind of football he was after then we'd have to be fit enough to do it – fitter than we'd ever been. Every drill was with a ball at our feet, and there'd be drills all day. Even at night a few of us would be out running – me, Robbo, a Scouse lad called Ian Craney who we'd signed from Accrington the year before and young Joe Allen, all out putting the extra yards in and doing fat-burning runs. The 'Fat Club', we called it.

Roberto had let a fair few lads go – Bayo, Izzy and Big Willy all gone – but he'd also brought in some quality players. We had Paul Anderson on loan from Liverpool, who was lightning quick, and a couple of Dutch lads – Ferrie Bodde in midfield, who was just a class act, and Dorus de Vries, this giant of a goalkeeper who'd been playing in the SPL with Dunfermline.

Then there were the Spaniards, Angel Rangel and Guillem Bauza, or Bussy as everyone called him. Throw in Jason Scotland from Trinidad, who Roberto had brought in to play up front with me, and we were starting to look like the United Nations.

Some things never change, though. We'd been on about getting a night out from the moment we'd landed in Sweden, but we knew we couldn't push it with Roberto just yet – it was too early to start trying it on. So we'd be onto his No. 2, Graeme Jones, or Bonner as everyone called him.

'C'mon, Bonner lad, we've worked hard, it'll do us good.'

We knew if he asked Roberto, and with Rob being so keen on team-bonding, we'd get our night – that's why we'd all packed gear to wear out before we'd even left Swansea.

Not the Spanish lads, though; all they had was their training kit, which says something about the different cultures. Neither of them spoke great English, so the pair of them were in their hotel room with me and Robbo, giving their thumbs ups and managing a 'Yes' and a 'Thank you' as we kitted them out for a night out.

But Roberto wasn't daft. The message came in to be in by two, but we were in the middle of nowhere with not a lot happening, so we were all back well before the curfew.

By the time we were back in Swansea, the first offer had come in. Bristol had gone up into the Championship at the end of the season before, and they were looking for a striker. August wasn't far away and they'd not brought anyone in, so I think the fans had started to put them under a bit of pressure to make a signing that would get them excited.

But the first few offers were just jokes. It was going back and forth for weeks, and I think Swansea thought they were taking the piss. The first offer was something like £300,000 up front with loads of add-ons – extra money if Bristol stayed up, if they got promoted, if I scored so many goals. The Swans board hated all that, and by the end they were saying it's up front or nothing. All of a sudden it jumped from £600,000-odd with add-ons to a straight £1 million. I knew it was serious.

Plus, I knew how much I'd be getting. I knew a few of the lads at Bristol, so I knew the kind of money they'd be offering – and how much I could ask for. I was looking at doubling me wages. Of course, that's going to get anyone thinking, especially when I was looking at finally getting a chance at the higher level. I'd turned down the chance to go to Sheffield Wednesday and I never regretted that, even when we didn't go up ourselves, but I wasn't sure I could afford to do that kind of thing again.

Me and Sangy arranged to meet Roberto and Huw on the Wednesday afternoon. I don't think Roberto thought for a second I was thinking about going, and although the bid was big, big enough for the club to accept, they would have turned it down if I'd given them the nod. It's what he was expecting, telling one of the local press lads as much in a meeting just before ours, telling him about the plans he had for me that season. He genuinely believed it; he'd been through it all with me as a player, known the way I'd been with the club and how much it all meant to me. He thought this was just another bid.

Only it wasn't. This was £1 million, which might not seem much in the grand scheme of things and nothing in the worlds of Cristiano Ronaldo and whoever, but for me, for the lad who grew up on Ashbury, this was a landmark. To say I was a £1 million player after coming out of non-league was a big deal. And then there was the wages.

Me heart was still telling me to stay at this point, but in me head I knew I couldn't. In an ideal world I'd have both, so I tried to ask for it, asking the club to match what Bristol were preparing to offer me. They said they could increase me money, but it didn't get close to the kind of package I was looking at with Bristol. Looking back, it might have seemed a little like I was holding the club to ransom, that I must have known Swansea wouldn't have been able to go any higher, but I had to ask. It was more hoping that, as well as the club had been run, there might have been a way to make it happen. The thing was, Huw and the board had done brilliantly to keep the club financially sound, and they'd done that by sticking to a budget and a wage structure. They weren't going to rip all that up – as much as they might have liked to.

And that was that. I was given permission to talk and to miss the friendly against Port Talbot that night. With the rest of the squad there, the rumours flew around in no time when I didn't turn up. The phone didn't stop with different mates and different reporters all trying to find out what was going on. I was trying – for once – to keep a low profile and Roberto was playing it down too, not giving too much away after the game but also making sure everyone knew that if I went it was because I had decided to go, that it was me who had made the call.

And he was right. Perhaps I didn't want to admit that to meself, but that was the bottom line.

And the money was behind it all. It sounds cold to say it, but it was the truth. Championship football was still a massive factor, of course it was. I'd waited long enough to go and show I was good enough to play there when others were saying I was too fat, too slow, too much of a showboat, that I was only ever good enough to be a star in the lower leagues, all that crap. Just getting the move was shutting a few people up, everyone who reckoned there was a reason why no one had ever taken a chance on me. Perhaps they didn't think that I'd never tried to engineer a move away, that I was happy at Swansea, that I believed I'd get where I wanted to with the club.

I still believed it, but I knew I couldn't have set meself up for life the way I could do with this move. It was all a long way from Frankie's sports shop. It was all spelled out to me when we had the talks – doubling me money, a signing-on fee now and every year of a three-year contract and a lot of other incentives, including a big bonus for making twenty appearances in a season. They really wanted me, they wanted their big signing, and they knew I'd get their fans going; a 'bums on seats player', Johnson called me.

I started to think of the opportunities – playing at the bigger grounds, stepping up again, being just one step away from the Premier League. I wanted to do all that with Swansea, but I knew there'd be no guarantees. This was a chance I couldn't turn down. Not for me, not for me career, not for Brooke. All those years I'd wasted in non-league, fucking around when I could have been setting meself up – and here was the chance to make up for it all. It was the right time.

I knew I couldn't come out and say money had such a big part in the move. It's not just the fact you sound like a greedy prick, especially when you realise as a footballer you earn more money than most of the fans watching you ever would. But it's all relative; you have to be able to look yourself or your children in the eye and say, I did the best I could when I had the chance.

And also, saying you're going somewhere for the money doesn't exactly get you off to the best start at a new club. Not that I had a chance to say anything on what was supposed to be my big unveiling.

Pretty much everything had been agreed by the Friday, and a press conference was set up for the afternoon at Ashton Gate. The cameras were all there, Sky Sports ready to screen it live, and fans had all gathered in the car park – but there wouldn't be any interviews. Huw was in Holland with the rest of the Swans for a week of games out there, and he was refusing to let it all go through until I'd officially handed in a transfer request. It all seemed a bit petty at the time, like they were deliberately trying to spoil me big moment of being paraded as a Bristol City player, as a Championship player. But he was right – and I probably knew it at the time. I wanted it all. I wanted the move, wanted the money, but didn't want to be the bad guy leaving Swansea in the lurch. If Huw could say I had requested the transfer then he knew that the club wouldn't have any backlash, that no one could start questioning their ambition because they'd just sold their top scorer. It still made me feel as if I was doing the dirty, but that was the choice I'd made.

A few cameras and a few reporters were still there when we finally decided to call it a day without the transfer going through. The paperwork needed to be with the Football League, and by the time Swansea had sent theirs back the offices had closed for the weekend. Nothing was stopping the move, though, and the club were working on getting me special dispensation to play in a friendly against Yeovil on the Saturday, even though I wouldn't technically be a Bristol City player until the Monday. We didn't think I'd get the go-ahead to play at the time, though, so I went out with Gary Johnson for a big Chinese meal to celebrate, talking about our plans for the season. I'd already spoken to Daz Way about him and he only had good things to say about him. And, as we sat and ate, Johnson only had good things to say about me –that I was the final piece in the jigsaw because he wanted someone who could take the ball into feet, to link things up. It was what I wanted to hear, and although managers are always going to be a bit like that when you just sign, the £1 million he'd just spent made me think that there'd be no reason to bullshit. It was a lot of money, I was his big signing of the summer, and we both needed this to come off.

I was buzzing – up for the challenge and everything that was to come – but I'd not really taken it all in at this point. I hadn't spoken publicly since the talk of the move, so the Welsh press were desperate to get hold of me, especially now everything had gone through. I wanted to try and explain things and make sure everything ended on a good note. I took the call on the Friday night, and the idea was put to me to do an open letter to the Swansea supporters in the *Wales on Sunday* newspaper. It sounded like the perfect way to say what I wanted to say. I did the interview over the phone as I sat in the hotel room in Bristol with Liz, talking about the pull of Championship football being too much and how hard a decision it had been for me – all of which was true. I'd just had a call to say I'd been given the go-ahead to play that afternoon – despite the Chinese sitting on me belly – so I went off to get ready when the call came back and the finished letter was read back to me. And only then did it hit me. I listened quietly, gave me OKs for them to print it and went into the toilet. Everything had happened so fast I hadn't stopped to think what I'd actually done until that moment. I'd been so caught up with becoming a £1 million player, becoming a Championship player, driving to Bristol, all the excitement of the talks and the photo shoots with me new shirt – the fact I'd left Swansea had only really become clear when me own words were read back to me. I was crying at the realisation of it all, the size of the step I'd taken, the enormity of the decision I'd made. I'm not sure Liz knew what to do. It wasn't regret, because this was something I wanted to do, that I felt I just had to do. So why was I so sad and hurting so much when I'd just got the money, got Championship football? It was leaving Swansea behind to do it that was killing me. I'd not made many sacrifices in me career, but this definitely felt like one.

It wasn't just the fact I wouldn't be playing for Swansea, it was the mates I'd made there, the connection I felt with the fans and everyone in the city. From the start, I don't think I was sure it would ever be the same at Bristol. But, to be fair, their fans took to me from the off. On that first Saturday there were already kids wanting to know what number I was getting so they could put it on their shirts – a No. 23 like Beckham, although that wasn't me choice.

And I gave them something in that first game, scoring the first and setting the other up. The buzz was back, and I knew I just had to look ahead now – I'd done what I'd done and it was about getting on with it and enjoying it.

So I did. I settled in right away with the Bristol lads, especially Bradley Orr – another Scouse lad. We'd already met each other a fair few times back in Liverpool, although our last meeting wasn't the best. Swansea had played at Ashton Gate towards the end of the previous season and it kicked off a bit, Izzy going eye to eye with Gary Johnson and me and Bradley having a row. We'd proper fallen out over it and not bumping into each other over the summer meant I was still mad about it when I signed. Of course, who should be the first person I saw when I got out of me car at Ashton Gate but Bradley. I looked over and straight away we both started laughing at how things had worked out.

There were quite a few characters in the squad, lads like Scott Murray, who'd been at the club for years and was funny as anything. Then there was Ivan Sproule, a Northern Irish lad who reminded me a lot of Robbo – a fiery character who would be messing around one minute and then snapping the next, wanting to fight the world. He was great with me, though, and him and his wife Janet looked after me when I first arrived, inviting me around for tea if I was on me own. I got close to David Noble too, probably because he didn't mind a night out. But they were all good lads and all up for a joke – and I knew I was going to be on the end of them as the new boy.

I still didn't see the first one coming. At Swansea we'd always made the new lads sing a song on their first away trip, as a way of getting them involved in things quickly. Daz Way must have mentioned it to the old Yeovil lads in the squad, the gaffer's son Lee and Phil Jevons, so I wasn't surprised when they asked me to do the same before the first game of the season. I stood up in the middle of the dressing-room and belted out 'Shout' by Lulu, really giving it some. I thought I must have impressed with the way all the other lads were cheering and laughing – before I realised this wasn't a tradition and I'd been the first one daft enough to start singing solos stood on a chair.

We were at home to QPR first game of the season, and Ashton Gate was bouncing – when it was close to full there was always a good noise in the place and it was the kind of environment I was used to. The supporters seemed keen to get behind me, to give me a bit of time – after all, this wasn't just my first time at this level, the club hadn't played in the Championship in eight years. As players we'd all sat down and written down where we thought we could finish and given the pieces of paper to the manager. I think the lowest anyone had put down was sixth or play-offs, so we thought we could do well – but the key was, no one was expecting us to. It meant we would have patience from supporters and the press – but I wanted to make me mark quickly, I wanted to show I could cut it at this level. Why? Because I wanted this to be a stepping stone. If I'd broken away from the club where I wanted to be, I wanted to get to the top. If I was going to put ambition first, then I wanted to do it properly. Plus, I was back thinking about Ireland again, that surely they couldn't overlook me if I was scoring goals in the Championship – they'd capped players for a lot less.

The goals didn't come in the opener, a 2–2 draw, nor the League Cup win over Brentford or the 1–1 draw with Blackpool. I was happy enough with what I was doing, though, and after Andy Morrell – again – had scored for Blackpool, I got us back into things with a nice bit of skill and a shot that Scott Murray scored from. I knew I'd been signed to score goals – I'd had twenty-plus a season at Swansea for four seasons – but me game was much more than that; it was about being different, doing something a bit different. I had two sides – the goalscorer and the spark – and I managed to show them both in the next game.

I'd always done well against Scunthorpe, and about ten minutes from half-time I got the goal I was after, smashing it into the top corner. They pulled one back, but I wasn't done and not long after we restarted I chipped one in from the angle. The place went nuts, and I knew I'd given the fans what they wanted, what I wanted – and what the manager wanted. He'd have a funny way of showing it, though. Like after that game he was on about how he remembered who I was now; he was full of sarky comments like that, but it can be so easy not to take them the right way and it can get very tiring very quickly.

I was on too much of a high to care too much at that point anyway, especially when we were drawn to play Man City in the Carling Cup. There was loads of press about them going into the game, Sven Göran-Eriksson having been appointed their manager and the new owners giving him a fair bit of cash to spend. It was a big game, live on telly, but it had a different feel from the cup games I'd been involved in before. Yeah, it would've been a shock if we'd beaten them, but it wasn't the David and Goliath stuff I'd been used to in the lower leagues. People were expecting us to give them a go – it kind of underlined the step up in class I'd made, the fact I was fancying our chances. Saying that, being the way I was, I'd always fancied me chances of holding me own against the top players – and I was doing just that. Emile Mpenza had given them the lead, but I was getting plenty of the ball and I worked a bit of space from me markers where they thought I couldn't do anything and dipped a shot that Joe Hart only just managed to tip over. Then I had a shot from the corner, but it flashed just wide. It was strange – I was frustrated because I'd been unlucky not to score, but inside I had a smile because I knew I'd shown a bit of class. New team, new division, new challenge – same old me.

But I was having to change, whether I liked it or not. At Swansea, I'd been left to me own devices, not told to mark, not told to come back and pick up at throw-ins or take the back-post – here it was being barked at me every game. It was a learning curve, but I was being asked to play in a way I'd not experienced before – not at Swansea, not at Wrexham and definitely not in non-league. It was a bit of a necessity I guess; we had stepped up a level as a team, and the teams we were up against had that much more quality, you couldn't leave things to chance, you couldn't leave yourselves open. I didn't mind doing it, but the more it went on the more I found meself doing more work outside the areas I was dangerous in. I was getting dragged out of the positions where I could hurt sides more and more. I'd made a habit of letting play develop and making sure I was in the right place at the right time to make things happen; now I was having to get behind the ball and finding meself further and further away from the goal, where me ability on the ball could do something. The opportunities weren't coming my way because I wasn't playing the way I needed to if I wanted to create them. It wasn't just the way we were setting up; it was how the Championship was as a whole too. But it wasn't being made any easier for me, which I found strange. They'd known what type of player I was and this wasn't it. I was all for adapting and I was prepared to do what was necessary, but was it right if it was coming at a cost?

I was still in the side and doing OK – we'd gone top of the League early on – but I'd only had those two goals and it didn't take long for it all to come out. We played Barnsley away in the October and got a bit of a kicking. We sat in the dressing-room after the final whistle while Johnson went on at us all. I'd not played well, not done meself much justice – and he told me as much.

'I don't care how much I paid for you – you'll be out of this team.'

Now every manager has their own way of doing things, but hammering me like that wasn't something I agreed with. And it definitely wasn't something I was going to respond to on the field. I don't think our relationship was ever the same after that match. I bit me tongue, knowing I couldn't answer back, but I felt he'd disrespected me in front of me teammates and, because of that, I lost respect for him.

Sure enough, as if to make his point, I was dropped the next week.

I wasn't the only one; he'd be changing things all the time. You'd be in for a couple, then out for the next – no matter how you'd done. Like when I came off the bench to score against Norwich one week and then didn't get a sniff the next. It was the same for a few of us, and it wasn't doing much for me confidence.

I wasn't enjoying things as much as I should have been. I'd got a place just outside the city – by the sea in Portishead – but every chance I'd get I'd be back in Liverpool. I just didn't get involved with the city like I had done at Swansea and – as good as the fans were to me – didn't build the same relationship with them as I had done at Swansea. I don't think many players could be lucky enough to have what I had there, so I don't know if I should have expected to have it happen twice. But perhaps that was down to me, that I wasn't fussed about making it happen. It was one thing playing for another club, but I wasn't going to start kissing the badge. Don't get me wrong, when I pulled on the Bristol shirt I gave everything – I wanted to please the supporters and entertain them as much as I had done at every club I'd ever played for. But deep down I hadn't really wanted to leave Swansea, and I guess it showed with how reluctant I was to really give Bristol a chance.

I'd go back to Liverpool for me nights out, and in the end that took its toll on me and Liz. I kind of knew it wasn't going anywhere when we first got to Bristol – I made sure I bought the house on me own, which kind of says it all. I told her it was because we weren't going to stay there long-term, but in truth I probably saw the end coming.

Some people tried to make out we were engaged but that never happened. We'd sort of talked about it, like most couples do if you get serious, but I hadn't proposed and I never gave her a ring. It was more of a press thing; I think someone picked up on her saying I might be 'the one' and the papers and the magazines all loved it. It never bothered me, but it wasn't the truth. Of course I loved her – we were together for more than a year – but, like anyone, you have good times and you have bad times. Then, when the bad times outweigh the good, you have to make a decision. So I did – and decided it wasn't for me.

I was pretty brutal about it too. I'd come back from Manchester where I'd been out with the lads for me birthday and she wanted to cuddle up on the couch, but I just couldn't deal with it all any more and I couldn't hide it. I wasn't going to start pretending, and when she asked what was wrong I couldn't help but just come straight out with it, with no warning.

'I don't want to be with you.'

That was that, tears and a 'ta-ra' and it was over. I'd missed being single anyway. I wanted to be going out with me mates more or having trips away with the lads. I got the impression that she felt that wasn't what I should be doing if I was thinking of settling down – but I just didn't see it that way, so it was probably for the best. It never got nasty, but I've not stayed in touch – once I'm done with someone I don't see the point in trying to be all matey. We were through and that was that – and it was just another example of things not really going to plan since the move to Bristol.

Then again, as a side we were doing OK. We weren't setting the world alight, but we were picking up the points and staying near the top without anyone really taking much notice. We were slipping under the radar, if you want. We went on a few unbeaten runs, but I wasn't getting the kind of regular starts I wanted, that I needed for me to be at me best. And it showed in me performances. When we went top after beating Hull at home with just two months of the season left, I didn't even make it off the bench.

We dropped a fair few points from then on, but we were neck and neck with Stoke at the top for a good while and, although I wasn't getting the starts I needed, it was difficult not to get carried away dreaming of the Premier League.

We were second by the time we had the small matter of Cardiff City at Ninian Park. I'd already had a taste of it in the home game in the December. Back then, there had been a lot of talk in the week about me facing Cardiff for the first time since what had happened at the Millennium, and I was happy to play up me Swansea connection, saying I never got the chance to play in a South Wales derby but this was the next best thing. To be fair, Bristol–Cardiff – the Severnside derby as they call it – had a good rivalry of its own, with an intense atmosphere. Our fans were right up for it in that home game, and I think they could tell I was too, giving me plenty of backing when I was getting booed by the Cardiff lot as me name was read out as one of the starting side. It wasn't just booing, of course, but I was a bit surprised how tame it was.

'She's shagging someone else . . .'

It hadn't long come out about me and Liz splitting up. But, really? Was that the best they could manage? Hardly intimidating, was it? It actually made me laugh that they thought I'd get upset by it. There were a few fat chants from the away end, a few anti-Scouse ones but mainly ones of 'You Jack Bastard' – which I loved anyway. It's something Cardiff fans have sung at Swans fans or players for years – basically because someone from Swansea is known as a Jack – but the Swans fans had turned it on its head and claimed it for themselves. I had to be told when I first heard it at the Vetch, but if the Swans fans sang it at you, it was because they'd taken you as one of their own. The Cardiff fans singing it sort of underlined how well I'd done for Swansea. You could even call it a mark of respect – although I doubt they'd see it that way.

I was desperate to score against them anyway; me phone had been going off all week with lads back in Swansea telling me to put one over on them, and I knew I'd make meself a hero with the Bristol fans to boot. I thought I'd done it too. It'd been a scrappy game and they'd been on top early on – I even had to clear one off the line in the first couple of minutes. But we started to control things after they had a man sent off, and I went close with a shot – and even closer just after half-time. Lee Johnson put a corner in and when Marvin Elliott got a touch, it hit me shoulder and went into the net. I ran off one way trying to claim it and Marv went off the other. They gave it to him in the end, but when we looked at the slowed-down replays you can clearly see it hits me last. Marv was still having none of it though.

I came off towards the end, with the Cardiff fans chanting, 'What a waste of money' – which I think the Bristol fans laughed at more seeing as I'd just helped us get three points.

Three months on and I'd been given a start in the return game at Ninian. It was after weeks of being on the bench too, but to be fair to Johnson, he must have sensed it was a game I'd want to rise to. I was buzzing and looking forward to seeing what kind of abuse I'd get. It might sound strange, especially with there being all sorts of horror stories of what was going to get chucked at me, who was going to do what to me – but who wants to be a nobody? If you want to be a somebody, you have to take the good with the bad. But this wasn't really that bad; not the kind of 'Welcome to Hell' I'd been told I was going to get from the moment I ran onto the pitch. Ninian's no walk in the park, with its stands so close to the pitch, but I'd rather have been there than have been a Cardiff boy at the old Vetch.

Just to be sure, the police felt the need to have a word with me, reminding me that if I scored not to do anything stupid – but I didn't get close to scoring. It wasn't surprising to me after so long without a good run of games, but I couldn't get going in the match and I wasn't sharp enough to really make a mark – especially in a tight derby game. We didn't get the points either, although Steve Brooker's goal should never have been disallowed just before they went up the other end and got the penalty that won the game. I would have loved to have beaten them on their own patch – and they clearly enjoyed beating me – but I was probably more gutted just to be losing at this point bearing in mind what we had at stake. I didn't do meself justice in that game, but I knew the biggest laugh would come if we got promotion – no one could say anything about me not being good enough then.

I don't know whether that spurred me on a little or what, but I came back into me own in those last few weeks. We'd brought in Dele Adebola, the lad who I'd met on trial at Crewe, and we clicked when we were given a go together up front. It was back to me playing off the big target man again – and it worked for both of us.

We'd thrown away too many points at the end to get automatic promotion, but we knew we had a place in the play-offs, just needing to beat Preston at Ashton Gate on the final day to get the home advantage in the semi. The confidence was already creeping back because I'd broken back into the side, but I was also thriving on the occasion again like I hadn't done in so long, feeding off the importance of the games. I knew I hadn't really delivered since signing, for whatever reason, but be a hero in the play-offs and that's all forgotten; come good at the right time and that's all that matters.

And if the confidence was coming back because of that, it went through the roof when I scored early on against Preston. It was a horrible goal, a scrappy poke-in, but being on just four for the season before that point, I couldn't argue. Besides, it loosened me up. I'd felt a lot of pressure on me to score all year, which had kept me in me shell a little bit. It wasn't from the fans, who were brilliant with me, but when you're constantly being dropped after one bad game you feel that the only thing that matters is that you score – and if you don't score, you're out.

This time I'd got me goal in the first ten minutes and the tension just vanished. I was back alive again, setting up Michael McIndoe for the second with a lovely one-two and then, after Noble made it 3–0, I hit the bar from outside the box and had one cleared off the line. The smile was back, the tricks were all back and the way the supporters were lapping it up I felt me old self again – I felt untouchable. It was the last game of the season, but it had been me best game since I'd joined. That was the player that had got the fans excited, and I was desperate to carry it on into the play-offs.

I got me chance in the semi at Palace. I was given the nod to start with Dele, but there weren't many openings for us up front. We'd got the lead through a set-piece routine we'd worked on called 'The Weasel'. It was named after Daz Way who, despite now being a coach at Yeovil, is still called that to this day. The idea was for the free-kick to be put wide then pulled back across the box for me and Dele to come on to and try and get a finish. But the ball was put behind us by mistake, and it was by chance that Louis Carey followed in and smashed it into the top corner. We tensed up a little being in front, but they got back into it with a penalty right at the end – before Noble hit a beauty from 30 yards on 90 minutes.

That goal lifted us all going into the home game, because we just didn't think we could get beat at our place – especially with the kind of noise that there was going to be at Ashton Gate. It was the biggest game for the club in God knows how long, and I was just praying Johnson wouldn't mess around with the team and would stick with me and Dele.

To be fair, he must have seen how well we'd been playing together and how I was buzzing again, and didn't risk changing it. Still, none of us had the best starts and we gave them a soft goal early on to make it 2–2 on aggregate. There were about 20 minutes to go when they won a penalty, and I can remember standing on the halfway line thinking it was all over if Basso, our keeper who'd been our player of the year, didn't keep it out. He didn't have to. The ball pinged off the post – and you could hear the ping because of how quiet the ground had gone – and it gave us all the boost we needed. Me especially, and I thought I'd won it in the last minute when I ran at the defence, took a chance from the edge of the box and curled one – only for it to clip the crossbar and go out.

Some players might get frustrated by that, but hitting the bar or the post used to drive me on, make me feel I was on a roll and that the next one would be a couple of inches lower, a couple of inches the right side.

It was.

It had all got a bit cagey, but I felt dangerous and I sensed the Palace defenders were getting scared of getting too tight to me in case I went past them. It was the space I needed. Dele knocked it down. I took a touch, opened up me body, wrapped me foot around the ball. It flew in.

I raced off to the corner flag, the place exploding with noise. I could see the faces of the Bristol fans – the ones who'd backed me – and knew I'd delivered what they'd wanted when I first signed. That's why I excited people – it was something out of nothing.

Later that summer I bumped into Graeme Jones on a trip back to Swansea and he told me he and Roberto had both been at the game, Bonner laughing as he admitted he'd turned to Roberto about five minutes before me goal saying I should have been brought off at the start of extra time.

'You never take Trunds off at a time like this,' Roberto had replied. I'm glad I proved him right.

It was one of the biggest moments of me career and I knew it. I'd done what I'd promised to do and, for the first time, I was going to Wembley – and I was going as a player. Just as I'd said I would.

I came off a few minutes later, getting a standing ovation on the way, just before I was going to have a go from a free-kick. Normally I'd moan at coming off at any point, but seeing as McIndoe scored when he had a go instead of me, I'll give Johnson the credit for that one.

There were about ten days before the final against Hull, and the build-up was massive. It was too much for some of the lads, who just wanted to shut it all out, but I was in me element. I couldn't wait to get out there, but I was savouring the countdown just as much, enjoying being in the moment. We had a media day on the Wednesday before the final, with what seemed like every newspaper in the country there, every radio station, and speaking to them sort of brought home what I was close to achieving. I hadn't taken much of a step back from it all to take it all in and appreciate I was one game from getting to where I always said I'd be – that I was ninety minutes from the top flight, one goal from the very top. From the Eagle to the Doms, then Burscough to Chorley, to Stalybridge, to Southport, to Bamber Bridge, to Rhyl, to Wrexham, to Swansea, to Bristol City, to the Premier League – it had been a long journey, but I was in touching distance of where I'd always aimed for, no matter what anyone had tried to tell me. From watching Liverpool on the Kop, from turning Blue and going to Goodison.

'I think I'd cry if I ran out to *Z Cars*,' I said to one of the reporters. I wasn't lying.

The only downside to it all was sorting the tickets out. Half of Huyton wanted to come, and there was a bus of about 50 lads on the way down come the final. Me cousin Jamie had got a load of Trundle shirts made up for them all to wear as they caught the coach at six in the morning, straight on the ale. I hadn't worked out where they were sitting when it came to getting out on the pitch, but I didn't have to worry; when it came to the national anthems the camera picked them out – 50 lads all in Trundle T-shirts singing their hearts out on the big screen. Every single one of them bladdered.

I looked around and tried to take it in – 86,000 people at the new Wembley, millions watching on telly, the Premier League waiting to see who was joining them.

'This is what it's about.'

I hadn't felt the same build-up of energy like I had in that game at the Millennium, I just felt relaxed and at ease with the whole thing. The game was tense – which you'd expect for a game where winning is worth £60 million to the club – and it meant there wasn't a lot of space to enjoy. Then Bradley got caught in a challenge with Nick Barmby and smashed his eye socket open. Bradley didn't go off, but a few minutes later Dean Windass smashed a volley just over his head and into the back of the net. I felt sick for Bradley because he was a mess but didn't want to come off – and I could understand why. In the end, he just couldn't carry on and had to be stretchered off with an oxygen mask clamped around his face. The poor lad couldn't even go on the holiday he'd booked with his missus to cheer himself up because he needed an operation the next day.

A goal down going into the second half, the tension started taking over. Every half chance felt like the most important in your life and the defenders were going into the tackles thinking it was their most important challenge. I managed to turn meself into a position for a shot with about 20 minutes to go, but it was on me right. Normally I'd try and work it again to give meself a better chance with me left, but not here. It was an easy save in the end.

As time went on, the tension came down from the stands and started really freezing some of the lads. But then, with about five minutes to go their keeper, Boaz Myhill, made his move too early, not judging the cross well enough and only managing to get a fist to it. If it dropped quickly enough I knew this was mine. I angled me body, hit the shot just right – but Michael Turner threw himself at it. The ball could have deflected anywhere, but it flew over the bar.

There's nothing worse than when the realisation sinks in that it's not going to happen. For me, even with time left, it sank in there and then. There were 95 minutes on the clock when the whistle finally went and that pain I'd felt against Barnsley was back – I was going through it again whether I wanted to or not, whether I was ready for it or not.

The empty feeling was back, sat in the dressing-room wallowing in it because there's nothing you can do to change it. Not until next season at least, but all that does is make you worse because you know how hard it is to get to this point.

And for what? All to have a dream ripped away from you.

CHAPTER SEVENTEEN
April

I GET UP FROM the dug-out and head down the touchline. Again.

It must be the tenth time this half, but I can't sit and watch, so off I go. Side to side, some quick shuttles, a stretch and a quick look back to the dug-out, to the touchline where Paulo's standing. Nothing.

I keep going, waiting to catch the eye and for me chance. Surely he's got to give me a go, surely in this game of all games. I look back. Nothing. The abuse comes down from the stands; it's the usual stuff, nothing I wouldn't have expected, but me chance to shut them up is slipping away.

Come on, Paulo, let me out there.

I'd not played in the home game against Cardiff either, but we'd got the points, which was all that mattered. It's all that matters now, perhaps more so at this stage of the season, but this game's a lot tighter and I know I can do something.

The excitement has been building all week with it all over the papers, on every radio station, every local news slot. Outside South Wales, I don't think people realise the intensity of it all. Everyone has their derbies, but this seems different. I don't know why, what makes it so special. Perhaps it's the pride of Wales thing, like it being a Welsh cup final. Perhaps it's because the sides have not played each other that much in recent years, I don't know. All I know is what it means to every person who stops you in the street, who pulls up to you in the car at the traffic lights, every person who packs your bags at the supermarket. All of them, all of them want us to beat Cardiff.

Some people try to play it down, and I can understand when managers try and take the pressure off players by saying 'it's just another game' – but it's not. You've got to be aware of the pressure because you've got to realise just how much it means to the people you play for, the people you're representing in the shirt you're wearing. You won't win every time, but you've got to do the shirt justice when it comes to games like this.

But I'm not going to get me chance.

I'd been buzzing just in the warm-up, thinking there was a good chance I'd get involved even though I'd only been named sub. I ran out of the tunnel and couldn't help but smile when the boos started from the few Cardiff fans in there – before the roar came from the Swans fans up in the corner. They'd been in there a while, all bussed in together from Swansea with a police escort – a bubble trip, they call it. Tatey had already been out there, first out on the pitch like he always is. He'd done the same at Ninian the year before when I was still at Bristol – going out, taking all the stick and just brushing it off. I think he enjoys it all. He summed it up for himself when he gave an interview after the first game: 'They don't like me and I don't like them. That's how it goes in football derbies.'

I'd said in the press before this one I'd be happy to score off me arse and call it me best ever goal, that's how much a win meant right now. But I knew I'd have to wait.

I'd felt good in the warm-up, even if all the Cardiff fans had a good cheer when I missed a shot in one of the drills. Normally it's more about just putting your foot through and getting the blood pumping around the legs than hitting the target. Not the second time – I made sure I didn't miss, heard the Swansea fans roar and grabbed me badge on me trackie top. Every time I did it I could see the Cardiff fans getting angrier and angrier, getting more and more wound up by someone scoring in the warm-up. You can see hatred in the eyes of some of them, real venom. There are dads with their kids, straining to scream at you – but it's all part of the pantomime I guess. My favourite response is to just do a few tricks, juggle the ball and give a bit of a show and a wink.

I made sure they saw me smiling when we scored too. We'd had a bit of a dodgy start, really out of our rhythm, but we'd settled well and Andrea Orlandi swung one in straight from the corner that their keeper, David Marshall, just didn't judge. But we switched off just before half-time and Michael Chopra made it 1–1 from close range.

It looks like it's staying that way; it looks like we've settled for it. We're on top, but we're not really going for it, not taking risks. We could win – and we've had the chances to – but we can take a point.

I look over and the call comes – only it's not for me. There's six minutes to go, and Mark Gower's going to be the last sub – a midfielder. I sit back down in the dug-out and just wait. The emotions are already starting to take over, the pent-up energy trying to let itself out. The cross comes in for Shefki and I'm out of me seat, trying to head the ball as he does. Only his header hits Marshall's legs.

And then Cardiff hit the back of the net. Chopra – 2–1 Cardiff in injury time. I bury me head as the screams come down from the stands, feeling helpless about it all, the stadium floor shaking. The final whistle goes and I finally get onto the pitch again, straight over to our fans to give them their applause and to apologise for not giving them their win.

In the dressing-room, it feels like we've been relegated, sat there with tears in me eyes, not wanting to get changed. When you understand what the derby means to the people you play for, it lifts you more when you win – but it kills you when you lose.

But we know it's more than just the bragging rights this time. Cardiff are almost safe in the play-offs now – we're not. We're still fifth, but we're only two points above seventh and the whispers have started about us dropping out, losing our heads and losing our play-off spot. We've been the underdogs all year, happy to prove people wrong and having people think we wouldn't be up there very long after our bad start. But then we showed how good we were, had people talking about how good our football was, that we were the new team to be wary of and, all of a sudden, expectations changed. Instead of a point away from home being a decent point, now it's two points dropped and people are talking about how we've slipped up. We're not taking notice of what's being said, but we can't ignore what Blackpool are doing. With every game they win, they're putting us under more and more scrutiny, more and more pressure. We're trying to scrape results, trying not to lose – they've got nothing to lose.

The dressing-room is silent apart from the noise of the Cardiff fans singing in the background, still in the stands soaking up every last second.

Five games left and it's all on us. It's not about dreaming now, it's about reality.

CHAPTER EIGHTEEN

Dead in Red

BEING HONEST WITH meself, I knew the chance had gone the moment the whistle went at Wembley.

I knew then how difficult it was going to be to try and better what we'd done in that first year, to get that close to the top. We'd been the new boys, the ones no one takes that seriously until it's too late and you're up there challenging, full of momentum. When you get to the play-off final, you then become a team people want to beat, a scalp to take – and they're all ready for you. There's no surprises in the second season – I only had to look back to how we did at Swansea after losing to Barnsley to know that.

I had to pick meself up straight away because I was due to be Robbo's best man for his wedding out in Vegas and I couldn't be moping around. But it was hard not to think about what could've been – financially and career-wise. Not only would it have meant me getting to the top, a stage I'd always dreamed of reaching, but I would have doubled me wages in an instant thanks to a clause in me contract. I would have probably played in the Prem for nothing, but it's difficult not to think of the money side of things when you get so close.

I knew it would be a big ask to get that close again, but at least I felt I'd proved a point getting into the side and playing well in that last month. I didn't have any reason to think I wouldn't be given the chance to pick up where I'd left off.

But I didn't see it coming – the first weekend I was out of the squad. There'd not been much of a warning in pre-season, where everyone had got their fair share of minutes. And I'd come with me weight bang on – the only thing anyone could have a go at me about was me hair, which I'd decided to grow long and it looked awful.

But Nicky Maynard had come in for big money, £2.25 million I think, and he and Dele got the nod with Steve Brooker, who hadn't got a sniff the year before, as the cover on the bench.

Me? I had to wait to get a couple of minutes off the bench in Carling Cup games against teams from League One.

I already wanted out. I'd seen it happen to other lads there and knew this was it – Johnson wasn't going to change his mind. When I'd signed, Phil Jevons had been the No. 1 striker – and bang in form too. He'd done brilliantly for Johnson before, helping him to win promotion with Yeovil and then with Bristol the year before I arrived. But he was gone before you knew it and there seemed no good reason to me. I couldn't help thinking that if a lad who'd won two promotions for two teams under Johnson was out of the picture then there were no guarantees for me. I feared the worst.

It didn't take long before I was linked with a move back to Swansea. They'd had a brilliant year under Roberto and won League One, playing some brilliant stuff too, and I was dead chuffed for them. I'd always kept in touch with the lads there and kept an eye on how they were doing – not without stick from the Bristol lot either. When I'd joined, I'd told them Everton were me team, but every week in the dressing-room after our game I'd ask for the Swansea score. Eventually someone twigged.

'You can't have two teams – pick one,' Louis Carey, our captain, shouted. Carey was a Bristol lad, had been a Bristol City fan all his life and was now a Bristol City player. 'No problem,' I said. 'How did Swansea get on?'

People were probably putting two and two together in the press, suggesting Roberto would come in for me seeing as I wasn't involved at Bristol. But as soon as the rumours hit the papers, Roberto put a stop to it. In some ways I should have been chuffed as he did his interview, calling me a legend in the club's history, that I'd done more than most to help get the club to where they were now, but at the same time he spelled it out pretty clearly he wasn't about to come in with an offer. He told the papers that I'd left for financial reasons – which I had – and that things hadn't changed at the club; that they weren't about to rip up their wage structure for me. Privately, I think he was still pissed off that I'd left in the first place and made sure he mentioned that 'the team has moved on' to draw a line under the speculation. Robbo had joined Leeds on a free that summer, and I think that had added to his frustration, especially as we both shared Sangy as an agent. He talked about us not making football decisions and how important it was to enjoy your football first and foremost.

He was right too. I'd gone for the wages, but it was getting to a point where I couldn't give a shit about the money – I had to start enjoying life again. I'd gritted me teeth a bit through that first year at Bristol, but playing in the reserves every week, where the matches just don't mean anything, was crushing me. It was taking away me spirit, what made me get up in the mornings.

I'd been so used to how I'd had it at Swansea – having a smile on me face every day, feeling special, feeling like I meant something. I'd been spoilt and I'd taken what I'd had there for granted. People assumed I wanted to go back because the team were doing well, but I'd never left because the team weren't doing well. I wanted to go back because I wanted to enjoy football again. The confidence I'd built up at the end of the previous season had been wiped out and there definitely wasn't the arm around the shoulder that I needed.

Not even when I scored off the bench against Birmingham. I'd been drafted into the squad because Steve Brooker was ill and came on with about twenty minutes to go when we were two down. Nine minutes later, I'd scored from about forty yards when their keeper had come off his line and the defence hadn't cleared it properly. Alex McLeish, the Birmingham manager, talked afterwards about how I was capable of those kinds of things and he'd warned his players about me. So if that was the case, why wasn't I getting a chance at me own club?

At least I was back in the squad, though, getting a few more minutes off the bench, before I finally got me first start of the season against Norwich. I did OK. I forced the keeper into a few good saves, we got the win, and I started against Charlton on the following Tuesday. I knew I had to make an impression and I thought I did, a nice curler in the first half to put us in the lead – a goal out of nothing after we'd been up against it. Gav Williams got the other to put us fourth in the table, and I honestly thought I'd get the run I needed after that. The run lasted two games – two 0–0 draws where none of us played particularly well. Then I was back on the bench again and back to square one, left wondering how long it would be before I got me next chance. The problem was it always seemed to be the strikers' fault as far as Johnson was concerned, it always felt as if the forwards were the ones getting the blame. In my time under him, there were at least a dozen different strikers who had come into the side within the space of two years and at least half a dozen who were shown the door. Were all of us as bad as each other? Were we all not up to it?

I kept plugging away, though, and things had improved, inasmuch as I was in the squad on matchdays, coming off the bench and making things happen – feeling part of things a little bit more. By the time Swansea were due at Ashton Gate in December, I'd done more than enough to suggest I should be getting more than an impact role. In the week leading up to the game, it looked as though I'd got what I was after when Johnson came up to me in training and told me I was starting. Only the start never came.

I walked out at Ashton Gate for the warm-up, knowing I would be on the bench but unsure of the reaction I was going to get and a little bit scared by it all. Being so down in the dumps about life at Bristol and still clinging on to how happy I'd been at Swansea, I don't think I could have coped if there'd been boos. It had happened with Wrexham – it had only taken a small number of fans to start having a go and it took the gloss off the time I'd spent there, made me question me love for the club. I couldn't handle that happening with Swansea, and I remember wanting to close me ears when I came on the pitch. I needn't have worried. The chant started from the away end.

'Lee Trundle, My Lord, Lee Trundle . . .'

The Bristol fans could have taken it the wrong way, but they didn't, singing me name at the same time, which can't be something you hear every game. I think they understood the connection I had with Swansea, but they knew I was in their shirt that afternoon and that was all that mattered to them. Besides, I always felt they were behind me and supporting me even when I'd been dumped out of the side, always coming over to me in the car park or the stands asking why I wasn't in the side and telling me they wanted to see more of me. I'd always see kids with 'Trundle' on the back of their shirts, something that was guaranteed to pick me up if I was feeling low. The thrill of seeing that never went away after seeing that first shirt at the Racecourse. Wherever I was it was an instant reminder of who I was doing this for and a quick flashback to those dreams I'd had on Ashbury. If the manager had problems with me, it was always good to know that the fans still had faith.

I got me cheers as I warmed up during the first half, and even when I came on – although they definitely stopped from the Swansea end when I had a sight of goal about ten minutes from time. The shot was on, but it took a deflection and in the end it was an easy save. It stayed 0–0.

I clapped both sets of fans at the final whistle, but Roberto was clearly not happy with it all. I read the next day that he'd had a pop at the Swans fans, saying they shouldn't have sung me name and that it was disrespectful to the current Swansea players that they had cheered for a Bristol player. I couldn't work out what he was on about, and I got quite angry about it – it felt as if he was trying to turn them against me. They'd stopped singing me name by the time I'd run onto the pitch, and I knew it hadn't bothered any of the Swansea lads because I'd spoken with them straight after the game. The thing was, I know the same would have happened with him had Swansea ended up playing Chester after he'd left. Someone suggested it was because he was still annoyed I'd left when I did, but he'd won promotion after that and everything was going right for them in the Championship. It wasn't as though they'd gone down after I'd moved or that I'd left them in the lurch. I put it down to frustration about the result in the end – although a 0–0 at Ashton Gate was a decent result in my book – and we left it at that.

Roberto wasn't the only manager to have his say after the game. I'd done an interview a few days before the match saying how much I still loved Swansea as a city, that the club still meant a lot to me and if I'd scored I wouldn't have celebrated. It was nothing you wouldn't have expected, nothing sensational and nothing people didn't really know already – in Bristol and in Swansea. It wasn't until after the game – the following week in fact – when I'd gone to see Johnson for an explanation as to why I hadn't started. It's not something I make a habit of, because every manager picks a side the way he sees fit, but he'd told me I was playing and I wanted to know why he'd changed his mind. Without batting an eyelid he told me it was because of what I'd said in the build-up – that he wasn't sure that I wanted to do well against a club I obviously cared so much for.

I couldn't believe what he was saying. Although I loved Swansea, I was out there in a Bristol shirt with ten other professionals, ten mates, and to me this was saying I was ready to cheat them by not playing well. How could anyone think I'd want to cost me own side three points? How could any footballer do that? We're all winners, and you can forget clubs or colours on your shirt, you want to do well for yourself. You can't switch that instinct off – you wouldn't want to. The only thing I would have done differently in that match compared to any other was to not celebrate if I'd scored – hardly the same as not wanting to win.

I made it clear I wanted to get out and get some games on loan when an offer came up to go to Leeds. I didn't spend much time thinking about it. It meant dropping back into League One, the division I'd spent so long trying to get out of, but by this point I knew I needed to get away from Bristol. Not for good – not at that stage anyway – but just to get me focus back, and the only way of doing that was by playing games. Besides, Leeds United is such a massive club it wasn't exactly stepping down. Yes, they'd suffered on the pitch after messing up their finances, but they were still ambitious as a club, still drawing huge crowds and still Leeds United. They might not have been in the Premier League as a club, but you were still in a Premier League environment when you were there. The fan base aside, the training ground was just incredible, with this massive area all of their own with huge grass pitches, indoor and outdoor artificial pitches, a jacuzzi, a sauna and steam room, a swimming pool on-site and their own fully equipped canteen and relaxation area. At Swansea, when the university students came back to take over Fairwood, we went to Jersey Marine where we got changed in Portakabins or drove back to the gym in our cars, still covered in mud.

I'd arrived on the Friday afternoon after getting the go-ahead that morning, just about managing to grab some stuff together in time and heading for the hotel where I was staying. By the Saturday, I was making me debut for Leeds at Elland Road.

When you walk out at a ground like that, it's difficult not to think of all the great players who have done the same over the years – and now I was one of them. It was a proper football stadium and I felt a proper footballer again, with the same kind of excitement I'd felt when I was just starting out. All that, and I was still only on the bench, but that was to be expected after the deal happening so late in the week. I came on for Malcolm Christie with a good half-hour left and got a good reception from the home end. That was a big boost for me, seeing as the Leeds fans expect a lot from their players. I thought, 'If they're backing me it's because they think I can help them.' The side were tenth in the table at the time, but nothing other than promotion would do – that's why Gary McAllister had been sacked a few weeks earlier and replaced with Simon Grayson. He, and whoever pulled on that white shirt, was under pressure to deliver – but I didn't feel a drop of it. This was about me and playing again, playing when it meant something. And when you play for Leeds, every game means something. I felt alive again after weeks of dead reserve football where there's no atmosphere, no expectation – it's just a run around for fitness, or experience for kids coming through.

I was involved in the game as soon as I came on, going close with a couple of shots, but I could feel I wasn't quite sharp enough. I didn't worry about it because the manager would have known that; he knew I'd need a little bit of time to get fully going and, even though we ended up losing that first game, I was named to start against Brighton the following Saturday. It was only something like the fourth game for the manager, and we all knew there wouldn't be much of a honeymoon period for him – or anyone he brought into the side. But when I looked at some of the players Leeds had, there was no way we were going to struggle to get wins. Robbo was there after getting a big offer at the end of his contract at Swansea, and he was playing well. There was Jermaine Beckford, who, although he was injured at the time, had shown everyone what a good goalscorer he was, and then there was a young lad called Fabian Delph, who ended up going to Aston Villa for something like £6 million. Fabian was in a different class, with all the attributes to go to the top, and he scored a wonder goal in that game at Brighton – but not before I'd got one to get me started at Leeds and get me confidence flowing again. Nothing too spectacular, in fact it was one of me trademarks – a good ball into feet, a quick turn onto me left and a shot from close range.

I was happy. I didn't have much time for Bristol as a city, but here at Leeds I was closer to home, closer to Brooke and me family. Most importantly, though, I felt wanted again – and it showed. I started against Peterborough the following week – a side above us in the table – and had a big hand in setting up Beckford to give us the win. I'd shown I could score, I'd shown I could be an asset, and the Leeds fans gave me a standing ovation when I came off because of that. Not many players can say they've got one of those at a place like Elland Road.

I was happy they'd taken to me, but I knew in meself I wasn't really at me best. As the games went on, the lack of games over the previous six months started to catch up with me and, although I wasn't playing badly, I wasn't standing out like people had expected me to at that level – like I expected myself to.

I began to feel the pressure. Not the pressure of playing for Leeds, which in itself was an eye-opener. And when I've watched them play since, especially when they were still trying to get out of League One, you know whoever they're playing have upped their game. Wherever you go, the opposition don't think about playing the 11 players in front of them, they're playing against Leeds United; the former players, the history.

Over the years, I've heard a lot of people talk about being the 'Manchester United' of a certain division, the side everyone wants to beat. I can even remember one of the lads saying it about Swansea once. But being at Leeds is something else. Every game is huge, a massive deal for the town or city you're travelling to to play in. It doesn't matter if it's a Tuesday night in the middle of winter, it's the other side's cup final. It's great to have that pressure, and I enjoyed that if anything, but it can definitely be draining when the reality is that it's a League One game.

But it wasn't that that was getting to me. No, the pressure I felt was different – it was the one I was putting on meself. I wasn't living up to expectations – I wasn't the nobody who had nothing to lose like I had been when I started out at Wrexham, when I was first at Swansea, even. I was someone who had to do better – and I wasn't.

They extended the loan for a further month, but during the second spell me head went – I wanted to get back to Bristol. I wanted to be back in that Championship because I'd realised that it was a step up, even compared with a club like Leeds. There were the massive crowds at home and a stadium like Elland Road – and even away from home you knew you were playing for a big club with sell-outs everywhere just because it was Leeds, the travelling fans filling up two sides of the ground at places like Walsall and Hereford.

But these were still small stadiums, ones I'd already experienced and thought I'd left behind. I'd look at the fixture list, see who Bristol were playing and immediately wish I was running out there rather than the ground I was about to play in. I'd enjoyed it at Leeds at the start and initially it did me the world of good, but me heart wasn't in it any more. It started to show in me performances for them, and it was clear – as much as we'd helped each other out – this wasn't for the long term. I knew I was getting older, and after taking that long to get to the Championship I knew I didn't want to let it go so easily. I had a slightly better perspective on things; I realised this was the first knock to me career I'd really taken since turning pro and I couldn't just give up. Besides, I had 18 months left on me Bristol contract, and I knew I could start afresh. I knew Johnson had sent people to watch me and he'd talked about how well I'd done for Leeds. He'd kept an eye on things – which, to be fair to him, is more than a lot of managers do – and he wanted me back.

I was happy to go back – and I had someone to go back for. I'd met Charlotte pretty randomly. I'd been invited to a fashion show for the opening of House of Fraser in the new Cabot Circus shopping centre in Bristol. Charlotte was there modelling, looking stunning, and afterwards I managed to get talking to her for a few minutes. It was all we needed to click and things pretty much developed from there. It had been a while since Liz and I had finished, and although I'd enjoyed being single again, I guess I'd had me fill. It's strange, I could have had a girl back at mine every night, but I'd still feel lonely. They'd be over for a couple of hours, but I could never wait for them to go, to be saying me goodbyes at the door. I never wanted to sit and chat about personal things to a girl I wasn't really into and while at one point it might have been a dream come true, by then it was just boring. I hadn't gone out to meet Charlotte; I hadn't gone out looking for a relationship or looking for a girlfriend – I just think I was probably more open for it when it did happen, more prepared to accept it if it happened rather than push it away like I used to. We actually met before I went to Leeds, and she'd come up to Yorkshire with me, but

I thought going back to Bristol would be good for everyone, and I was full of optimism.

But if I was right about me and Charlotte, I was wrong about me and Bristol. It took a month until I was involved in the squad again after coming back, almost another month before I actually got out on the pitch – 13 minutes at Sheffield Wednesday the week before the end of the season.

Every week I'd hope. Whenever I was asked, I'd play in the ressies, even though the lack of atmosphere and intensity was probably doing me more harm than good. And I'd do well, score a couple – and then see the lad I'd played up front with get on the bench or come on ahead of me on the Saturday.

It may sound like I'm crying about it all, that I was moaning and bitter just because I wasn't playing. But that was never me issue. I wasn't foolish enough to think I was going to play every week – I didn't think that when I first signed, let alone at this stage. I'd been dropped enough times at Wrexham and Swansea – not to mention in non-league – to accept that every manager has their opinions and you're not always going to like it. That's fine, I can handle that – I can respect that.

What I couldn't respect was the way I felt Johnson was making his opinions clear. To me, it seemed as if he couldn't give a shit about me and my feelings. Perhaps it's not a manager's place to be worried about upsetting players, but I could never work that one out. How are you going to get players to get behind you, pull out the stops for you, if you don't treat them with at least respect?

It was getting beyond a joke. We'd signed a Slovakian lad called Peter Styvar from MSK Zilna for something like three-quarters of a million. He'd scored against Villa in the UEFA Cup earlier in the season, so there was all this excitement about him coming, but I remember speaking to him one night and he told me he'd spent most of his career at right-back and it was only recently he moved up front. It looked like it too from where I was standing. Going into the Championship, the step up in class looked too much for the lad – but he was still ahead of me. It didn't say a lot about me and me future at the club if he was ahead of me in the pecking order, but I honestly knew it shouldn't have been the case.

It came to a point I had to ask the manager something that had been bugging me ever since I'd noticed how many games I'd played that season.

I was due for a bonus if I hit 20 League games. I was on 17.

I went in to see him and asked if it was about the money – because if it wasn't we had a problem. In training, in reserve games, I honestly believed I was doing better than the lads getting picked instead of me, but we were both clearly thinking different things. If it was about the money, I told him, I'd willingly scrap the bonus just to get that chance. He was honest, he told me it was and that he didn't think my performances warranted another bonus. Fair enough, I thought, so scrap it. I was told we wouldn't have been able to do that.

So that was that. I didn't come off the bench against Swansea at the Liberty, something that ended up with me and Johnson having words in the dressing-room, and then I had me 13 minutes against Wednesday at Ashton Gate in a game that meant nothing – to me or to the division as we finished mid-table. We had Burnley the last game of the season – I wasn't even in the squad. In the end, I'd made eighteen appearances; only four of those were starts.

I was at me lowest point by now, knowing I had another year left of this unless someone came in for me, and I was just thankful I had Charlotte to pick up the pieces when I got home. She hadn't known me that long but she could see this was killing me. I remember once when I'd had a heart-to-heart with Johnson in the summer about me needing to go and telling him I wanted to put in a transfer request. He was great about it, saying it was probably for the best but it was better if we kept it in-house so I didn't have me hands tied if an offer came in from a club I didn't want to go to. He promised to circulate me name to clubs I'd picked out, and I came home to Charlotte telling her about how I never handed in me request. Straight away she told me off for not doing it, that I needed to do it for meself. She was right – two days later Johnson was in the press saying that I wasn't part of his plans and I could leave. So much for keeping it in-house.

It didn't bother me. I wanted out and one way or another it was going to happen. And I knew I'd get a club. I didn't have to rush a decision and I didn't have to worry about paying the bills – I wasn't one of these lads that are genuinely scared what's going to happen to them at the end of the season because they've no contract but kids in school and a massive great mortgage.

And I definitely didn't think I'd have to pack it all in. What was happening was making me wonder if it was all worth it, but it never got to a stage where I was going to walk away from it all. I was depressed, no question of that, but deep down I knew that confidence was still there. I still believed, down in me gut, that I could go somewhere and start it all off again, be a hero again. I don't know whether it's ego, that arrogance that never left me even when I wasn't playing, but I never sat and worried that it was all over for me. I'd always been aware that I'd have a shorter career than so many others because I'd started so late, that if I wasn't careful I'd blink and I'd miss it. I guess that's why it affected me so much not playing at Bristol.

I wanted to go back to Swansea. I'd probably wanted it from day one. Even when I'd first left and was all positive about things going right, in me mind I was thinking about going back after I'd earned me money – if the club would still have me. That was me dream, because I'd already set me heart on staying in South Wales after it all finished. I wasn't sure, though. Not after Roberto had said what he'd said, not after the chairman and Sangy ended up falling out when Robbo left for Leeds. Neil got blamed for that and had some really bad press afterwards, but agents can be the easy target sometimes. He's the one on the front line in these negotiations, the one that seems to be driving the whole thing, either trying to get more money out of a club or to engineer the move away. They're the bad guys – only they're only doing what the player is telling them to do. They're only saying the things, asking for the things that we're not brave enough to ask for. There's no doubt if I'd sat in one of me contract talks over the years I would have ended up with a worse deal because Huw or whoever would have played on me heartstrings and emotion would've taken over. That's fine, and perhaps a lot of fans would prefer to see it that way. But at the same time, only a fool to himself and his family would not want the best deal they could get. Take Robbo's case – Leeds was a massive offer for him and he just had to take it. He was the head of a big family after his mum and dad had passed away fairly young. Yes, he might have stayed at Swansea and things might have worked out better in the football sense, but who knows if it would? Who knows if he'd be another one who stayed with his club, not following the money, and then just got released with no club on the horizon and wondering what was going to be next for him. Look at Kris O'Leary, a lad who had been at Swansea since he was a boy but when it was his time, it was his time – he had to say goodbye. He was released and that was it. As a lower-league footballer – even as a Championship footballer – if you're not ready for that then it's tough shit. Emotion doesn't help you then.

So did I regret it? Regret leaving Swansea for the money? Perhaps, but then perhaps not. I had the chance to earn the kind of money I'd only dreamed of as a kid, and I took it. It came at a cost and, like I said, perhaps I took the fit I had with Swansea at that time for granted. It had all clicked for me so well there – perhaps it was hoping too much to think I could just pick up where I'd left off, when in reality it was always going to be different. I never once thought it was a question of ability as to why it didn't work out as it should have at Bristol – it was a question of happiness.

It always has been with me. I'm happiest playing football. I play at me best when I'm happy, when I can feel the love and attention from the fans and the rest of the dressing-room. It's what made me tick when I started out, it's what made me stand out, it's what made me into a £1 million player and – as tough a time as I ended up having at Bristol – ultimately, it's also what put me to within one game of the Premier League.

And if we're talking regrets, that's the one true one – not getting to the top. Not achieving what I'd said I'd do growing up in Huyton. I played as a pro, I got me name on the back of me shirt, I had me own montage with music playing over me tricks and goals, I always tried to entertain – I even played at Wembley before ever going there as a fan. All just as I'd said I would.

I just never quite made it to the highest level.

And the worst thing of all is that I can't help wondering if it's all because I never gave meself the right chance. All those times when I could have, should have, done it differently. Whether it was with the different trials or training sessions or nights out, could it have made a difference? Those who know me raise a smile at all those stories, saying 'Typical Trunds', but it embarrasses me now. If now I saw a lad pulling the same kind of stuff I did back then I'm not sure I'd have any time for him, not now I can see how frustrating it is to watch someone with ability willing to throw it all away.

I know how close I came to doing just that, to throwing it all away. And even still I wonder what would have happened if I had come onto the scene when perhaps I should have, if I'd made me debut for Wrexham at 17 instead of 24?

But that's me story, that's how it happened.

And I have to wonder, would I have been the same person if it had happened any other way? Would I have been the same footballer if it had happened any other way? Probably not. It wasn't the textbook way to go about things, but that's why I wasn't a textbook footballer, that's why I was different. It's why I'd brought smiles to so many faces while still having one of me own.

That's why I knew I'd get another chance after Bristol.

It still didn't stop it hurting, though, when I was frozen out. After all, it's always been about those 90 minutes for me – it's when I come alive.

CHAPTER NINETEEN
May

Sunday, 2 May 2010

IT'S THE NINETY-FOURTH minute. This is me chance, this is our chance. Our last chance.

One goal and we're in the play-offs, still in with a chance of the Premier League, still in with a chance of the very top.

I'm unmarked inside the box and I can feel the fans freeze.

The ball comes across, missing the defender – and the silence hits, like the calm before the storm. It's 18,000 people drawing in a breath, the same 18,000 who had roared when I came on.

It's just behind me, but I manage to control it, spinning around to connect with me left. It's in the back of the net. Me blood is on fire, me body feels like it's exploding with the emotion and the adrenalin ripping through every inch of me. I run, run hard to the fans. I turn to look behind me.

We'd known exactly what we needed to do before the game. For the first time since December we'd dropped out of the top six, and what had looked like a sure thing with the play-offs was now in the hands of someone else. Bristol City, believe it or not. They were playing Blackpool, who'd gone above us after we'd lost to Sheffield United the previous weekend. Now it was a case of us needing to win at home to Doncaster and hope that Blackpool dropped points.

No one was backing us and, if we're honest, we'd only ourselves to blame for the way we'd fallen away. We'd got a good result against Scunthorpe after the derby defeat, but we were shocking against Bristol – a game I couldn't play in because of the loan agreement. Even then though, we got a win against Barnsley – but Blackpool just weren't losing and the pressure was on us. They had nothing to lose, we did – and it showed. While they were off beating Peterborough, we were blowing it against Sheffield United. We'd had plenty of the ball, but we'd hardly had any chances in front of goal and we weren't troubling them enough. We had our usual penalty shout when Darren Pratley went down right on the edge of the area, but we'd all long given up on the fact that things are supposed to even themselves out over a season. It just wasn't happening for us.

We were one down by the time I came on in the second half, but almost straight away there was a half-chance – Fede Bessone crossing after I'd played him in, but the ball just wouldn't drop enough. I looked how I felt – rusty. I looked like a player who'd taken six games to play an hour's worth of football. With speculation starting up again about me future, people were talking about how me performances didn't justify starting games let alone a new contract. Yet the stats showed I had the best goal-to-minute ratio in the entire Football League – something around a goal every 100 minutes. And in the last month you had legends like John Hartson coming out in the press saying I should have a run, that I could make something happen.

But I wasn't getting starts, I was getting ten minutes – and when that happens it can sometimes take you almost that long to find your feet, to adjust to the pace. At Bramall Lane, just like in so many games, I just felt ready to try something when the whistle went. They'd scored another one on the counter and that was it – down to seventh and down to relying on Bristol to put us in the play-offs, to give me that one last chance.

I had confidence in the Bristol lads, especially with Nicky Maynard on fire. I'd chatted to a few of them, begging them for a favour at the PFA dinner, and they told me they wouldn't be getting the deckchairs out for the summer just yet – besides, with Steve Coppell only just appointed their new manager for the new season, they couldn't afford to mess around. I fancied them too – at least to get a point. Blackpool were such an attacking team that they were always going to give teams chances, and Bristol had shown they were still a good side by finishing the season strongly. There'd still been tears at Sheffield, though – a lot of the Swans lads almost resigned to the fact it was all over, even if it was before the fat lady had sung. But bizarrely, we'd felt a lot more relaxed and confident about things as the week went on. Almost a case of 'what will be, will be' after a lot of the lads had either accepted or prepared for the worst.

I'd also been prepared to be on the bench again and watch someone else have a go at getting the win we needed. It played out as it had done for weeks – possession, pressure, but no one putting the chances away. The fans still believed, and the way they responded to Maynard scoring at Blackpool had us all believing with them.

But time was going on – Blackpool had equalised, and tension had started to creep into things. I'd already seen Beattie and Pintado go on ahead of me, and I'd wondered if I was going to get me chance, struggling to accept being overlooked when all afternoon fans had kept on saying how this was made for me, how I was going to write the fairytale ending, how this was my stage, my time.

If it was, it came with ten minutes to go. I couldn't believe the roar that went up. If me head had dropped when twice I saw someone else get called over by the gaffer to go on, now I was focused. That roar told me they believed in me, they thought I could get something for them even when all the signs were pointing to the fact we were going out of the play-offs. They were depending on me, and I wanted to deliver for them. I was still among the top scorers for the season, even with the lack of minutes I'd had. I knew if I had a chance I'd put it in the back of the net.

I hammered around the pitch, desperate just to find the ball, but we'd lost our way and the structure had gone. It was all so loose, and rather than staying patient and carving out the chances now we had extra bodies in the box, we were just hitting it hopefully.

And then we did have hope. Pratley put a ball over, Beatts ran through and the defender just took him out. He had his arm around Beatts' shoulder and their legs had tangled – it was a penalty twice over. It was a penalty to anyone in the ground – anyone except the referee and the linesman.

We still went for it, just praying things would fall for us, when Nathan Dyer nicked the ball off his man, headed down the left and put in a cross.

It's the ninety-fourth minute. This is me chance, this is our chance. Our last chance.

One goal and we're in the play-offs, still in with a chance of the Premier League, still in with a chance of the very top.

The ball is slightly behind me, too far behind me. It's only about half a yard away, but it's too far. The ball appears late in me vision, through the bodies of the defenders, and the only way I can control it is by just dropping me hand to the side of me body. I have to try it, I have to do something, I have to make something happen – and I just have to hope the referee doesn't see it.

I spin around to connect with me left. It's in the back of the net. I run, run hard to the fans. I turn to look behind me.

Nothing. I run towards the fans, wanting to share the moment with them, but their faces drop. I turn to look behind me and there it is – the flag. Soon comes the whistle.

It's pretty much the last kick of the game, our last chance gone.

Straight away the realisation sets in – it's not just a game but an entire season. Maybe more for me, who knows?

And just like at Bristol, will this be it for this team? There's already been talk of the team breaking up, of Britts going to the Premier and of lads like Darren Pratley, Ashley Williams and Angel Rangel all going. Even the manager has had a go at the board on a couple of occasions. Right now, though, it's about the moment, about the frustration, disappointment, anger – if Blackpool had won 5–0 it may have been easier to take, but things were back in our hands and we'd dropped it.

I walk around the pitch with the rest of the team, doing a pretty bad job of stopping the tears and the worries about me dreams being over.

But then I stop. I look around at a stadium that wasn't built when I first came to Swansea. I look at fans still singing, still chanting me name – the same fans who have made me who I am. We all wanted the same thing on this day, just like we've always wanted the same thing. Not just to reach the top but to enjoy getting there. After all, it's why you fall in love with football in the first place.

EPILOGUE

July

IT'S SATURDAY. SWANSEA are away to Yeovil. I'm not there.

Instead, I'm trying me best to follow the directions the estate agent has given for me for this house me and Charlotte fancy. It looks perfect, the type of place we could really settle down in. I've always said I wanted to stay in Swansea and now that's going to happen – just not as a Swansea City player.

It's not the first time me and Charlotte have been around house-hunting. It must have been back in April when we'd found a lovely place just to the west of the city, lovely location, nice and quiet, and we'd put the wheels in motion to buy it. After all, when you're told you've got a deal for the following season, you've no reason to think you're not going to be staying.

Me and Paulo had sat down together over food and talked about the future, about his plans, about me. He'd always been decent enough with me, and although I had me frustrations at not playing as much as I'd have liked, it wasn't the same situation as the one I'd been in at Bristol, and I still felt part of things.

He talked about the fact I was seen as an icon at the club, which was all very nice, but there was only one thing I wanted to hear. And then he came out with it, giving me the impression that there'd be a deal on the table for me. We had talked about coaching and that there might be something down that avenue for me too, but this was a playing deal – exactly what I'd been striving for from the moment I came back.

He spoke to me agent, nothing more was said about it and we agreed to talk again at the end of the season, that we'd sort it out after the play-offs. The play-offs never came; neither did the meeting with Paulo.

The other lads out of contract all got things sorted the day after the Doncaster game, whether it was being told they were being let go, like Bussy, Marcos Painter and a few of the younger ones, or if they were getting a new deal. Paulo had told me he wanted to go for a meal later that week, that he wanted to go over a few things. Because the coaching subject had been brought up, I assumed it was something to do with the details in that so didn't read too much into it.

After arranging to meet on the Thursday, the alarm bells started ringing when I couldn't get hold of him to check what time. Answerphone, ringing out, even his wife answering for him and promising to pass a message on. Each time there was nothing back.

I went away on holiday trying not to worry too much, although both me and Charlotte had pulled back on our plans with the house – I guess it was a hope-for-the-best, fear-the-worst kind of situation. Nothing had been made public about the deal we'd agreed, but I'd started to look daft the longer time went on with no answer from Paulo, especially when Bristol confirmed I was officially a free agent after the end of me contract there. As far as I was concerned, I'd been told I was staying at Swansea and I was waiting for the talks to sort it out – to some on the outside they must have been thinking why was I holding on to discuss me future when I wasn't officially Swansea's player in the first place. To some, they saw it as me loan spell finished and that was that – the club didn't have an obligation to offer me a deal.

As I waited, it began to dawn that all me eggs were in one basket – I'd not even asked Sangy to put me name around any other clubs because of what I'd been told. There had been a couple of sniffs – and two interesting offers from America and Australia to go play over there – but me name hadn't been circulated like every other out-of-contract footballer's would be.

The longer it went on waiting for Paulo, the more worried I got, the less hopeful I got, the more frustrated I got. I could take being told I wasn't staying a Swan, but just tell me. I was in the dark.

By the time the answer finally came, I'd already come to terms with the fact me chance at Swansea had gone. There was an offer, but purely a coaching one – and one the club would have known I wouldn't accept at the age of thirty-three.

I never did get to speak to Paulo. I saw him the next day, sat in his car at a red light as I pulled up alongside. He looked across and saw me – and began laughing. I couldn't believe it. He wound the window and asked me where I was heading. 'Liverpool,' I snapped back, and sped away as the lights changed. He sent me a text later, saying he'd seen that day's papers with the news of me release splashed all across them and now understood why I was so mad and that I should ring him to talk about it. I was too angry at the time, but when I tried a few days later, I couldn't get hold of him.

He had other issues to deal with. In fact, within a few weeks he'd left Swansea to take over at Leicester. He'd done brilliantly to begin with, but when things started to slide, he didn't change anything. We'd be too reluctant to go for it in games, and it cost us. I remember the game up at Sheffield where Chris Morgan, their centre-back, asked me if we were going to start putting them under pressure any time soon, seeing as it was a win-or-bust game for us. We didn't. There'd also been talk of a fall-out with the chairman and, while he could end up being a success as a manager, in my opinion Paulo could sometimes come across as too stubborn and appear difficult to deal with because of that.

I kept quiet about what I'd been told about staying on; I hadn't wanted to cause a fuss and look bitter. Plus, I still had hopes of coming back to the club in some form later down the line, so I didn't want to go out kicking and screaming.

But I was out – and not really sure what to do next. I wanted to keep on playing, I knew that much. There were quite a few different teams interested, but the concrete offers weren't coming. With the World Cup on, the Premier League was being slow in doing its business, so the Championship was biding its time as a result, as was League One and so on. There was a deal on the table from Yeovil; I had a chat with Tranmere after I started pre-season training with them, but they couldn't get near the kind of wages I was looking at. It was the same with Rochdale and Leyton Orient, and although there were other enquiries, the excitement just wasn't there. Neil even had a chat with Darren Ferguson, who is now the Preston manager, and there might have been something in the pipeline there, but not even the thought of staying in the Championship was enough to get me blood pumping about the whole situation.

The fact was, I'd been happy at Swansea. Not just at the club but in the city too and, after what had happened at Bristol, I'd come to value how important happiness was in life. I'd set me heart on staying, and the thought of going somewhere else, going through the motions in League One, living out of a suitcase again, it just wasn't turning me on.

Then there was the fact there were only one-year and two-year contracts on offer anywhere. I didn't blame them – not many players over thirty-three get long-term deals – but I knew I could be facing the same problem in less than a year's time if I wasn't careful.

So perhaps that's why the offer from Neath FC got me so intrigued. Neath is a town just outside Swansea and more famous for its rugby than football, but they had an ambitious – and wealthy – chairman who wanted to make the football club a success. It would mean stepping back to the Welsh Premier, stepping back in time if you want after me spell there with Rhyl, but it would also mean staying in Swansea for three years – and on a good wage too.

I talked it over with a few different people and the surprise was clear in their voices, but the more I spoke, the more I was convinced in meself it was the right thing. The security of three years was a big thing, but staying happy was even bigger.

We kept the offer quiet, but it began to leak out – and the papers went crazy. No one could believe it – a £1 million player back in the Welsh Premier. Some were calling me mad to turn down Football League offers – especially after working so hard to get there in the first place – but football had broken me heart a little bit. I'd not really played at Bristol, then seen me hopes raised and dashed at Swansea; this was a chance just to go out and play every week, play with a smile again. Just as I'd started out.

The first chance I got was, funnily enough, against Swansea. A pre-season friendly, pissing down with rain, but still 2,000 there at the Gnoll

– the ground Neath share with the rugby club. I wasn't the only one – Kris O'Leary had turned down a deal with Wrexham to sign for Neath too, and I've no doubt he did it for similar reasons to meself.

It's something different. There's the chance to play in Europe, one of the things I've not done in me career, and hopefully the chance to open a few doors with the coaching side of things. Plus, staying near Swansea means I can keep a good eye on how the club does, because I don't think I'm surprising anyone by saying I'd love to end up in management at the Liberty.

But for now, I'm not going to lie, it does seem strange planning ahead for life in the Welsh Premier League when it wasn't long ago I was hoping to be in the English version. Who knows – if that goal had stood against Doncaster, it could have been us in the top flight instead of Blackpool, the team that took our place in the play-offs and ended up beating Cardiff in the final at Wembley. But I've never been one for the straightforward, to do it the way you're supposed to.

It's stepping away from League football – but it's on me own terms, done in me own way. It's not as if I've a lot left to prove to people, is it? I proved I could play at the top of the game, I proved I could play the way I always believed the game should be played. Now I can stop proving and just play, just enjoy and just be settled in life.

While I know I'm not going to be playing in front of thousands and thousands again, the Welsh Prem gets a good bit of coverage – and me mum and me nan can turn their aerials back towards Wales to watch me games again. Plus there is the opportunity for Swans fans to come over to Neath and watch me as me career winds down. I guess if I couldn't finish at Swansea, this is a good way of bowing out in front of the supporters who made me so happy.

I look at the house, I look at Charlotte, I look at me life – right now, I am happy. And, when it comes down to it, in football and in everything else, isn't that what it's all about?

Swansea City 2009–10

Date	Comp.	Opposition		Result	WDL	Scorers	Pos
AUG							
Sat 8	Ch	Leicester (a)		1–2	L	Williams	23
Tue 11	CC	Brighton (h)		3–0	W	Monk, Dobbie	2
Sat 15	Ch	Boro (h)		0–3	L		24
Tue 18	Ch	Reading (h)		0–0	D		23
Sat 22	Ch	Coventry (a)		0–1	W	Williams	15
Tue 25	CC	S'thorpe (h)		1–2	L	Dobbie	
Sat 29	Ch	Watford (h)	+	1–1	D	Tate	19
SEP							
Sat 12	Ch	Preston (a)	*	0–2	L		20
Tue 15	Ch	Bristol C (h)		0–0	D		19
Sat 19	Ch	Barnsley (h)	U	0–0	D		20
Sat 26	Ch	Sheff Utd (h)	+	2–1	W	Trundle	17
Tue 29	Ch	Doncaster(a)	U	0–0	D		16
OCT							
Sat 3	Ch	QPR (h)	+	2–0	W	Gower, Trundle	14
Sat 17	Ch	Ipswich (a)	U	1–1	D	Beattie	16
Tue 20	Ch	West Brom (a)	U	0–1	W	Beattie	11
Sat 24	Ch	Blackpool (h)	+	0–0	D		12

Sat 31	Ch	S'thorpe (a)	U	0–2	W	Beattie, vd Gun	11
NOV							
Sat 7	Ch	Cardiff City (h)	U	3–2	W	Dyer, Pratley 2	9
Fri 20	Ch	Derby (h)	+	1–0	W	Bessone	3
Sat 28	Ch	Newcastle (a)		0–3	L		6
DEC							
Sat 5	Ch	P'borough (a)	+	2–2	D	Trundle 2	7
Tue 8	Ch	Plymouth (h)	+	1–0	W	Trundle	5
Sat 12	Ch	N Forest (h)	+	0–1	L		6
Sat 19	Ch	Sheff Wed (a)	U	0–2	W	Pratley 2	5
Sat 26	Ch	Reading (a)	+	1–1	D	Pratley	6
Mon 28	Ch	Crystal Palace (h)	U	0–0	D		6
JAN							
Sat 2	FA	Leicester (a)	+	1–2	L	Cotterill	
Sat 16	Ch	Leicester (h)	U	1–0	W	Pintado	4
Sat 23	Ch	'Boro (a)	U	1–1	D	Pintado	4
Tue 26	Ch	Coventry (h)	+	0–0	D		5
FEB							
Sat 6	Ch	Preston (h)	U	2–0	W	Cotterill, Williams	5
Tue 9	Ch	Crystal Palace (a)	U	0–1	W	Kuqi	5
Sat 13	Ch	Newcastle (h)	U	1–1	D	Cotterill	4
Tue 16	Ch	Plymouth (a)	*	1–1	D	Pratley	4
Sat 20	Ch	Derby (a)	U	0–1	W	Kuqi	4
Sat 27	Ch	P'borough (h)	+	1–0	W	Cotterill	4
MAR							
Sat 6	Ch	N Forest (a)	U	1–0	L		4
Tue 9	Ch	Watford (a)	+	0–1	W	Kuqi	4
Sat 13	Ch	Sheff Wed (h)	+	0–0	D		4
Tue 16	Ch	West Brom (h)	U	0–2	L		5
Sat 20	Ch	QPR (a)	U	1–1	D	Dyer	5
Tue 23	Ch	Blackpool (a)	U	5–1	L	vd Gun	5
Sat 27	Ch	Ipswich (h)	+	0–0	D		5
APR							
Sat 3	Ch	Cardiff City (a)	U	2–1	L	Orlandi	5

Mon 5	Ch	S'thorpe (h)	+	3–0	W	Williams, Edgar, Kuqi	5
Sat 10	Ch	Bristol C (a)		0–1	L		6
Sat 17	Ch	Barnsley (h)	+	3–1	W	Williams, Kuqi, Pratley	6
Sat 24	Ch	Sheff Utd (a)	+	0–2	L		7
MAY							
Sun 2	Ch	Doncaster (h)	+	0–0	D		7

* Denotes start
+ Denotes substitute appearance
U Denotes unused substitute
Ch = Championship
CC = Carling Cup
FA = FA Cup

FINAL TABLE

		Played	GD	Pts
1	Newcastle	46	55	102
2	West Brom	46	41	91
3	N Forest	46	25	79
4	Cardiff City	46	19	76
5	Leicester	46	16	76
6	Blackpool	46	16	70
7	Swansea City	46	3	69

Statistics

NAME: Lee Christopher Trundle
BORN: Huyton, Merseyside, 10 October 1976
JUNIOR CLUBS: Eagle & Child, Whiston Juniors, Huyton Labour, Knowsley Borough, Liverpool County FA Youth
AMATEUR CLUBS: The Dovecot, St Dominics, Deysbrook, The Boundary, The Quiet Man

NON-LEAGUE

Stats are for all senior competitions.

Burscough (Free, September 1995–November 1995)

1995–96 (North West Counties)   10 appearances (+ 0 as sub)   5 goals

> I first saw Lee play in an English FA County Youth Cup Final between Liverpool County FA and Essex FA. The match was attended by many bigwigs from the English FA and there was an after-match meal at the Beaufort Hotel in Burscough. Lee was on my table and I had been really impressed by his performance so asked him for his phone number. I went up to his gran's house to try and persuade him to sign for Burscough – it wasn't easy but we

eventually got him to sign on non-contract forms.

The following Tuesday, we were at home to Blackpool Rovers and won 4–2, Trundle scoring all four goals and every one a beauty. I recall saying after the game that we must get him signed up on a contract before he left the ground.

It didn't happen that night and I was furious and came close to resigning. Fortunately we signed Lee on professional forms on the Thursday evening and I have followed his career with great interest ever since – and also with a little pride that I had played a small part in it.

Stan Strickland, former Burscough FC club secretary

Chorley (£7,000, November 1995–May 1997)

1995–96 (Unibond)	31 (0)	8 goals
1996–97 (Unibond)	35 (0)	13 goals
Total	66 (0)	21 goals

People had a go at me because I said he would be the first £1m non-league player. Some people are so cynical and want others to fail and I remember in one game a director from the opposing side walking past our dug-out and saying, 'Trundle will never make it.' But he did – and he was one of the most gifted players I've ever seen.

He was a lovely lad who I had a real soft spot for, but he was often distracted with one or two other things, like looking after his gran. I always felt if he could knuckle down and concentrate on his football he would have a good career, which he did.

But I always felt he could have done better. If he'd had the heart of some players – if he'd had my heart – then he would have been one of the top players because ability-wise he was as natural as any I've come across. It's a shame he couldn't have pushed himself harder because he could have really been one of the best players this country's ever seen.

Dave Sutton, former Chorley FC manager

Stalybridge Celtic (£8,000, September 1997–December 1998)

1997–98 (Conference)	28 (0)	10 goals
1998–99 (Unibond)	24 (0)	15 goals
Total	52 (0)	25 goals

> Lee was the most skilful player I'd seen in semi-pro football at that time – and certainly at Stalybridge Celtic. I remember one evening during a period of bad weather we had to train indoors in this very, very small gym which was only big enough for three-a-side. Lee's control was so good no one could get the ball off him. He got on very well with my son, who used to watch his tricks and try and copy him – Lee loved that.
>
> He was a very laid-back character who was never fazed by anything. He was a smashing lad, a smashing lad.
>
> *David Pover, physio Stalybridge Celtic*

Southport (£16,000, December 1998–May 2000)

1998–1999 (Conference)	27 (2)	6 goals
1999–2000 (Conference)	0 (9)	2 goals
Total	27 (11)	8 goals

> He was a player who well and truly divided the fans . . . and even families. I thought he was brilliant as I loved skilful players with a bit about them and I was often quoted as saying how good he was. Others saw him as lazy and one who would never make it in the game as his workrate was never the best and he seemed to some to just 'trundle along'.
>
> *Rob Urwin, Southport FC programme editor*

Bamber Bridge (Loan, February 2000–May 2003)

1999–2000 (Unibond)	10 (0)	11 goals

Rhyl (Free, July 2000–February 2001)

2000–01 (Welsh Premier)	17(1)	15 goals

> I remember the first time I watched him and I was just amazed – I couldn't believe a player with his talent was so low down in the leagues. People warned me off, saying he was bad news – but he was great news for me.
>
> When you mention his name people automatically think of his tricks because what he could do with the ball was superb – but he was a clever player who would create for others and I don't think he's got as much credit as he should have.
>
> He was someone always up for a laugh but I also found him a very dedicated lad who wanted to make it – he just needed someone to believe in him. When he found that he was a joy to watch.
>
> *Mickey Thomas, former Manchester United, Chelsea & Wrexham legend and ex-Rhyl FC director*

Non-league Career Total	182 (12)	85 goals

FOOTBALL LEAGUE

Wrexham (£50,000, February 2001–May 2003)

2000–01 (League One)	12 (2)	8 goals
2001–02 (League One)	31 (7)	10 goals
2002–03 (League Two)	35 (15)	12 goals
Total	78 (24)	30 goals

> He is your archetypal Scouser, just so full of wit and confidence. I remember seeing him for the reserves when he was on trial and turning to a steward just gobsmacked about what this lad could do on the ball. But the best thing about him was the rapport he had, not just with the fans but with everyone around the club. He was your best mate the moment you walked into a room and always had a minute to chat to anyone who asked. He made people around him feel special, when he was the one who was special.
>
> *Geraint Parry, Wrexham AFC football secretary*

Swansea City (Free, June 2003–July 2009)

2003–04 (League Two)	35 (3)	22 goals
2004–05 (League Two)	49 (1)	23 goals
2005–06 (League One)	38 (8)	21 goals
2006–07 (League One)	34 (5)	20 goals
Total (1st Spell)	156 (17)	86 goals

Not since I witnessed Kevin Keegan launch his first revolution at Newcastle nearly 30 years ago have I seen one player dominate a whole club the way Lee Trundle did at Swansea. He entranced us all. The fans loved his spectacular goals, his mesmeric skills, his sometimes outrageous showboating and his innate ability to identify with the terraces.

Even his fellow players, as a breed notoriously hard to please, were captivated by his Scouse wit, his warmth and the sheer power of his personality.

As for us in the media . . . Lee was manna from heaven. He never refused an interview, never ducked a controversy. Even a hardened old hack like me could not fail to warm to him. A special player and a very special man.

Ken Gorman, football writer Welsh Sunday Mirror

BRISTOL CITY (£1M, JULY 2009–MAY 2010)

2007–08 (Championship)	25 (16)	6 goals
2008–09 (Championship)	4 (16)	2 goals
Total	29 (32)	8 goals

There were big expectations of him when he signed and it was clear he was a player who thrived on confidence. He was well received by the fans even when perhaps he wasn't at his best. When he got himself fit he played some great football but, like a few players, his face didn't seem to fit.

I know he didn't score as many as he would have liked, but that was a problem for the whole team. But when he did score, they were class goals, ones where he would beat defenders. Not opportunist ones, but ones of guile and skill. And if it hadn't have been for that Hull goalkeeper, he would have been the one who took us to the Premier League.

Tony Thorne, Bristol City supporter of more than 50 years

Leeds United (Loan, January 2009–March 2009)

2008–09 (League One)	7 (3)	1 goal

Lee's loan played out at the start of a transitional period for Leeds, and his two months in Yorkshire were not an unqualified success. He was Simon Grayson's first signing as manager and was widely viewed as an excellent addition to the squad at Elland Road – a proven goalscorer with a touch of flair – but a handful of instrumental performances aside, notably against Brighton and Peterborough United, it was a move which fell short of expectations.

Phil Hay, football writer Yorkshire Evening Post

Swansea City (Loan, August 2009–May 2010)

2009–10 (Championship)	2 (19)	5 goals
Total (Overall)	158 (36)	91 goals

To me, Trunds was always someone who was different in every sense. Although he had the media attention, he always remained unassuming and almost grateful for what he had rather than accepting it as the norm. He always had time for the supporters and he would always be the last to leave things like the kids' Christmas party, an hour and a half after the other players, because everyone would be queuing for his autograph.

There were fears when he came back because no one wants to have their memories tainted – and we'd had four years of wonderful memories. But Lee will still get you something, he'll still create and make things happen and just to have him back gave everyone a lift. No one at this football club could have a bad word for him.

Phil Sumbler, chairman Swansea City Supporters Trust

Career Total (Professional only, to May 2010)	272 apps (+ 95 as sub)	130 goals